Understanding Employ
Engagement in Educat

G000126641

This book explores employer engagement in education, how it is delivered and the differentiated impact it has on young people in their progression through schooling and higher education into the labour market. Rather than narrowly focusing on vocational or technical education or work-related learning, it investigates how employer engagement (work experience, internships, careers education, workplace visits, mentoring, enterprise education etc.) influences the experiences and outcomes of the broad range of young people across mainstream academic learning programmes. The chapters explore the different ways in which education can support or constrain social mobility and, in particular, how employer engagement in education can have a significant impact upon social mobility – both positive and negative.

Leading international contributors examine issues surrounding employer engagement and social mobility including:

- conceptualisations of employer engagement;
- trends in social mobility;
- employer engagement and social class;
- access to and management of work experience;
- social capital and aspiration;
- access to employment.

Understanding Employer Engagement in Education makes employer engagement an innovative focus in relation to the well-established fields of social mobility and school-to-work transition. By examining what difference employer engagement makes, this book raises questions about conventional models and shows how research drawing on different fields and disciplines can be brought together to provide a more coherent and convincing account. Building on new theorisations and combining existing and new data, the collection of essays offers a systematic exploration of the influence of socio-economic status on school-to-work transitions, and addresses how educational policy can shape more efficient labour market outcomes. In doing so, it draws on and speaks to existing literature that has considered such questions from the perspectives of gender, ethnicity and social disadvantage.

Anthony Mann is Director of Policy and Research at the Education and Employers Taskforce.

Julian Stanley is Head of Centre, Centre for Education and Industry, University of Warwick, UK.

Louise Archer is Professor of Sociology of Education at King's College London, UK.

Understanding Employer Engagement in Education

Theories and evidence

Edited by Anthony Mann,
Julian Stanley and Louise Archer

Routledge
Taylor & Francis Group

LONDON AND NEW YORK

First published 2014
by Routledge
2 Park Square, Milton Park, Abingdon, Oxon OX14 4RN

and by Routledge
711 Third Avenue, New York, NY 10017

Routledge is an imprint of the Taylor & Francis Group, an informa business

© 2014 Anthony Mann, Julian Stanley and Louise Archer

British Library Cataloguing in Publication Data
A catalogue record for this book is available from the British Library

Library of Congress Cataloging in Publication Data
    Understanding employer engagement in education : theories and evidence / edited by Anthony Mann, Julian Stanley, and Louise Archer.
    ISBN 978-0-415-82345-6 (hardback) – ISBN 978-0-415-82346-3 (paperback) – ISBN 978-1-315-77996-6 (e-book) 1. Business and education. 2. Social mobility. I. Mann, Anthony. II. Stanley, Julian C. III. Archer, Louise.
    LC1085.U523 2014
    370.113–dc23   2013043509

ISBN: 978-0-415-82345-6 (hbk)
ISBN: 978-0-415-82346-3 (pbk)
ISBN: 978-1-315-77996-6 (ebk)

Typeset in Galliard
by Sunrise Setting Ltd, Paignton, UK

Printed and bound in Great Britain by
TJ International Ltd, Padstow, Cornwall

Contents

Figures

Tables

Contributors

Louise Archer is Professor of Sociology of Education at King's College London. Her research focuses on educational identities and inequalities, particularly in relation to 'race', gender and social class. She currently directs two large research projects and a research programme focusing on young people's engagement with science/maths.

James Dawkins is currently studying for a PhD at University College London and was a former Research Analyst at the Education and Employers Taskforce. He holds a Master's degree in Social Science Research Methods and has worked at a number of leading policy institutes, including the Centre for Economic and Social Inclusion, the think tank Reform, and the British Youth Council.

Fiona Devine is a Professor of Sociology at the University of Manchester. Previously Head of the School of Social Sciences, she is now Interim Head of Manchester Business School. Her research lies in the areas of social stratification and mobility, and politics and participation, in which she has published widely.

Becky Francis is Professor of Education and Social Justice at King's College London. Best known for her work on gender and achievement, her research has focused on social identities in education and educational in/equalities. She has recently combined education policy work with her academic career.

Zane Hamm has a doctorate in education from the University of Alberta. Her research interests include youth apprenticeship and the trades, intergenerational learning, and rural youth migration and mobility.

Richard Hatcher is Professor of Education at Birmingham City University. His principal research interest is in the field of policy sociology, in particular the analysis of government education policy and its impact on the school system, with a focus on issues of democracy and social justice.

Kathrin Hoeckel is a policy analyst at the Organisation for Economic Co-operation and Development (OECD) and visiting fellow at Harvard Graduate School of

Education. She coordinated the OECD Skills Strategy and reviewed vocational education and training systems in several countries. Her research interests are in skills development, education-to-work transition and youth unemployment.

Nancy Hoffman is Vice President and Senior Advisor at Jobs for the Future, a national non-profit based in Boston, MA, focused on education and workforce development.

Craig Holmes is Research Fellow of the Economic and Social Research Council's Centre on Skills, Knowledge and Organisational Performance at the University of Oxford and a lecturer in Economics at St Anne's College, University of Oxford. His research interests include labour economics, the economics of education with a particular interest in higher education, inequality and labour market mobility, skills policy and economic growth.

Muir Houston is a lecturer in the School of Education at the University of Glasgow. A sociologist by training, his current research includes widening participation, adult education and learning cities and regions. In addition, he has published on the relative salience of class and sectarianism on Clydeside in Victorian Britain.

Prue Huddleston is Emeritus Professor and formerly Director of the Centre for Education and Industry, University of Warwick. Her research focuses on vocational education, vocational qualifications and work-related learning. She worked previously within the further education sector and on community and outreach programmes. She has published extensively on the sector and has been involved in teacher training for over 20 years.

Steven Jones is a Senior Lecturer in the Manchester Institute of Education at the University of Manchester. He writes about higher education, focusing on how participation, satisfaction and performance are influenced by students' socio-economic backgrounds. He authored the Sutton Trust report, *The Personal Statement: a fair way to assess university applicants?*

Elnaz T. Kashefpakdel is a PhD candidate at University of Bath working in the area of educational policy evaluation. She also collaborates with Education and Employers Taskforce as a research assistant, undertaking quantitative data analysis.

Keith Kintrea is Senior Lecturer in Urban Studies at the University of Glasgow. His research focuses on the impacts of living in disadvantaged neighbourhoods and on housing and urban regeneration policy and practice.

Tricia Le Gallais taught in both the secondary and further education sectors before joining Birmingham City University as Senior Lecturer/Teacher Trainer in post-compulsory education and training. She now works as a researcher within Birmingham City University's Centre for Research in Education. Her particular research interests include vocational education and training.

Yaojun Li is Professor of Sociology at the Institute for Social Change, University of Manchester. His research covers social mobility, social capital, generosity and ethnic integration. He has published widely in these areas and has conducted many research projects funded by academic and government bodies in the United Kingdom, United States, China and Australia.

Anthony Mann is Director of Policy and Research at the Education and Employers Taskforce.

David Massey is a Senior Manager at the UK Commission for Employment and Skills (UKCES), where he works predominantly on youth labour markets. He is the lead author of the *Youth Employment Challenge* and *Scaling the Youth Employment Challenge* reports, both of which can be found on the UKCES website.

Ken Mayhew is Professor of Education and Economic Performance at the University of Oxford and Fellow & Tutor in Economics at Pembroke College, Oxford. He is also Director of Skills, Knowledge and Organisational Performance, an Economic and Social Research Council research centre on skills, knowledge and organisational performance. Ken has published widely on labour economics, skills and education.

Emma Norris is Senior Policy Adviser at the Institute for Government where she works on governance and policy. She was previously an Associate Director at the Royal Society of Arts and has also worked at the Institute for Public Policy Research and was the President of Oxford University Student Union.

Christian Percy is an independent academic and econometrician with research interests in emerging economies, social structures and incentives. He works in strategy consulting with experience across the public, private and third sectors. Previous publications and seminar presentations include work on youth employment, parental mortality and urban renewal in China.

Milosh Raykov is a postdoctoral researcher in the department of Educational Policy Studies at the University of Alberta. He is involved in studies of labour relations, quality of work life, occupational health and safety, and outcomes of lifelong and experiential learning.

Robert Schwartz is Professor of Practice Emeritus at the Harvard Graduate School of Education (HGSE). Hoffman and Schwartz lead the Pathways to Prosperity State Network, a collaboration of nine states focused on ensuring that many more young people complete high school and attain a post-secondary credential with currency in the labour market. Among their recent publications are *Schooling in the workplace: how six of the world's best vocational education systems prepare young people for jobs and life* (Hoffman, Harvard Education Press, 2011) and *Pathways to prosperity: meeting the challenge of preparing young Americans for the 21st century* (Ferguson, Schwartz and Symonds, HGSE, 2011).

Julian Stanley is Head of Centre, Centre for Education and Industry, University of Warwick. Julian has many years' experience as a coordinator of work-related learning and business partnership in schools. Since joining the University of Warwick, he has led research and evaluation projects locally, nationally and internationally in the fields of work-related learning, education–business partnership, vocational education and employer engagement.

Ralf St Clair is Professor and Department Chair of Integrated Studies in Education at McGill University, Montreal, Canada. Before that he worked at the University of Glasgow in areas around access issues in higher and adult education. He has a strong interest in social issues in education, including equity and outcomes.

James R. Stone III is a Distinguished University Scholar, University of Louisville, and is Director of the National Research Center for Career and Technical Education. He is author of more than 150 articles, book chapters, reports of research and books, most recently, *College and career ready for the 21st century: Making high school matter.*

Alison Taylor is Professor of Educational Policy Studies and Director of Community-Service Learning at the University of Alberta. She is the author of several journal articles about school-to-work transitions and youth apprenticeship, and co-edited the book *Challenging transitions in learning and work* (Sense Publishers, 2010).

Preface

Nancy Hoffman and Robert Schwartz

Employer engagement with schools – so easy to say, so urgent, so hard to accomplish – that's the general perspective of educators and policymakers in all but a few countries across the globe. As the demands of the labour market become increasingly complex, requiring skills, technical knowledge and a wide array of interpersonal and critical thinking capacities, schools, colleges and universities hear the imperative to work closely with employers from multiple quarters.

For some countries, the policy focus in the last decades has been elsewhere. Policymakers have directed their education investments to increasing the tertiary degree completion rates of young people – focusing attention not so much on work readiness as on academic performance at high levels. Today, several of these countries face a shortage of young people to take the many 'middle skill' positions that reflect renewed demand in manufacturing, information and communications technology, health care, engineering, technology and the like. And even in the handful of countries with well-entrenched dual systems where high percentages of upper secondary students alternate school and work during their upper secondary years (for example, Austria, Finland, Germany, Norway, the Netherlands and Switzerland), vocational education and training (VET) systems everywhere face status issues and complaints about a gap between what employers need and what schools teach.

The urgency to engage employers in the transition from school to work is not only about the labour market. It's about the welfare of young people. Youth unemployment has risen to historic proportions in many countries as a result of the global fiscal crisis, and youth across the world have articulated their frustrations about the lack of opportunities for their futures. Indeed, such international bodies as the Organisation for Economic Co-operation and Development (OECD), United Nations Educational, Scientific and Cultural Organization (UNESCO), the International Labour Organization, the European Commission, and the World Bank have raised concerns about the scarring of a generation of young people – economists' term for the persistent and long-term effects of sustained unemployment at the normal point of entry into the labour market. Research shows that late entry or poor early integration has a negative impact on lifetime earnings. In addition to these economic concerns, without a structured transition into the labour market, young people have fewer chances for a smooth transition to an adulthood that supports healthy family life, civic engagement and lifelong learning. Their current plight will cost countries in the future in myriad ways.

While not prescribing one form of VET or another, the OECD's *Learning for Jobs* study argues that countries that do well by their young people 'provide well-organized pathways that connect initial education with work and further study and widespread opportunities to combine workplace experience with education'. Given the compelling problem sketched earlier and treated at length in this cutting-edge collection, those positioned to make a difference in young people's transition into the labour market have few proven strategies for creating effective transition systems. By 'those who can make a difference', we mean employers – both public and private – and educators.

For policymakers, the list of solutions to the youth unemployment crisis is limited, costly and generally without systematic evaluation of effectiveness. Among common strategies are:

- a youth guarantee of training, a job or combination of both after a short period of unemployment;
- government-funded public employment;
- stepped-up availability of places in vocational schools and colleges;
- tax incentives or training levies on companies to either train young people or pay for their training.

Each of these solutions requires the engagement of employers. Young people cannot learn *in theory* to be effective in workplaces, to take on increasing responsibility and autonomy, to hone and adapt their skills rapidly according to changes in the market. Even if schools try – and a good number do – they cannot simulate workplaces. How can it be that a critical element of worldwide economic progress – the success of young people in their initial entry into the labour market – can be so fraught with difficulty, so often a subject for the platitudes of politicians who have little systemic strategy for making it happen?

This important book takes the first step in field building – pulling together what researchers know from a variety of cases and databases about the conditions under which employers can be mobilised to create an opportunity structure for young people, and about the barriers to bringing such opportunities to scale. While the cases and studies are heavily tilted toward the UK experience, many of the findings are echoed internationally. It is a credit to the editors and the Education and Employers Taskforce that they have undertaken this work, and that from it a body of knowledge to support employer engagement can emerge. Many of the findings in this collection were first presented at conferences and seminars organised by the Taskforce.

The Taskforce is based on a simple, yet rarely acted-upon, premise: educators and employers need one another in order to accomplish a core element of their respective missions. Employers need a pipeline of skilled, motivated future workers. Educators need young people to understand the relevance of acquiring a solid foundation of academic knowledge and skills if they are to rise to the challenge of meeting more ambitious academic expectations and standards. The Taskforce is rare among such organisations in its commitment to building a much firmer knowledge base through its sponsorship of an ambitious research agenda and its commitment to make the results of its and others' research available to educators, employers and policymakers in an accessible fashion.

The essays in this book highlight both the depth of the challenges in introducing a wide range of young people to the world of work and the contribution of the many social and financial supports that today go in large proportions to young people from prosperous families and to high-achieving schools. The experiences available to such young people should be available to all.

Here are some particular themes that resonate from this collection that are common across nations and are treated in depth in the introduction and essays:

- Young people do not suffer so much from low aspirations as from lack of opportunity and care must be taken when opportunities are provided that they truly broaden the horizons of low-income and working-class young people.
- As the traditional youth labour market dries up, very large numbers of students, especially those without social capital and family connections, are unlikely to get valuable work experience and will enter the labour market unprepared unless schools take responsibility for organising such opportunities.
- The fact that 24 per cent of British employers say they provide some form of work experience for young people and hire from the pool of work experience candidates is a sign that many are interested and might further engage. The obverse, however, is that the majority of employers are reluctant to hire young people without work experience right out of school, and there are far too few places available. Many countries are in a similar situation.

While it is easy to get discouraged about the magnitude of the challenge of engaging employers at scale, numerous countries are working to improve the linkages between education and employers. For example, in the United States we co-lead the Pathways to Prosperity State Network, working with nine states to ensure that many more young people complete high school and attain a post-secondary credential with currency in the labour market. To accomplish this goal, employers and educators in the states are building career pathways systems for 14–19-year-old students. Each state is led by a coalition of stakeholders, including employers. The work initially focuses on two to three regional labour markets within each state, but the long-term goal is to create a statewide system of career pathways.

While lessons from other countries cannot be adopted whole cloth, the strongest of the dual system countries provide proof that the challenge can be met. In March 2013, at the invitation of the Swiss Government, we brought a small delegation of US policymakers, practitioners and employers to Switzerland to spend a week studying the Swiss VET system. In Switzerland, two-thirds of young people participate in the dual system, spending roughly three-and-a-half days a week learning in the workplace and the other day-and-a-half learning aligned academics in a school setting. Roughly one-third of all Swiss employers participate in the system, playing a major role not only in educating and supporting young people but through their industry associations setting the standards for what young people must know and be able to do in order to be qualified for employment in their sector. We observed students and met with supervisors in a variety of work settings: a major bank, a large insurance company, an IT firm and two manufacturing plants. In each workplace, it was apparent that an enormous amount of thought and care had gone into the design of the learning plan for the 'young professionals' (the Swiss term for apprentices) and that the students received an extraordinary amount of formal coaching and informal mentoring and support.

When we asked Swiss employers why they took such an active role in the development of their 'young professionals', we got two answers. First, they said, it is in our economic self-interest to invest in the education and training of our next generation of workers, a response buttressed by cost/benefit research indicating that the gains in productivity generated over three years by apprentices more than offset the wages and associated training costs paid by participating employers. But their second response spoke to the larger sense of responsibility Swiss employers feel for the social and civic well-being of society and for the importance of enabling young people to make a successful transition from adolescence to adulthood. Perhaps the best measure of the success of the Swiss system is that the country has the lowest youth unemployment rate in Europe, and a balanced economy that scores highly on measures of innovation and creativity, qualities that its VET system prizes. Switzerland provides the best evidence we have seen of the role that engaged employers can play in designing and implementing a work-based learning system that effectively serves a broad mainstream of students and supports their integration into working life.

Introduction

Julian Stanley, Anthony Mann and Louise Archer

Employer engagement in the educational experiences of young people is not a new phenomenon. It is, however, one that has changed significantly over time. Notably, in recent decades employer engagement has moved from the margins to the centre of policy and practice in many countries. In the half-century since employer engagement was first tentatively introduced to formal education in Britain, governments of all political persuasions have acted to increase young people's exposure to the workplace through their schools in a variety of ways. It is not only a British trend; policymakers and influential commentators around the world have become increasingly interested in employer engagement. However, this is a policy development with which academic research has arguably failed to keep pace. The aim of this collection of essays – the first on this topic – is to help close that gap. It brings together authors from the United Kingdom and North America to consider how we can best conceptualise this phenomenon and how it should be understood within broader twenty-first century social, economic and political changes. In addition, the collection also has a practical concern: how is employer engagement practised and can it deliver what it promises?

Employer engagement in education: what is it?

The subject of this collection is employer engagement in education. It describes, essentially, the process through which a young person engages with members of the economic community, under the auspices of their school, with the aim of influencing their educational achievement, engagement and/or progression out of education into ultimate employment. Employer engagement in education can be distinguished from work-based learning, which is usually taken to describe learning that takes place through employment, for example through apprenticeships or company training programmes. That is, although work-based learning involves employer engagement, employer engagement denotes a wider domain of employer involvement in education and training.

Using a similar kind of logic, we can distinguish employer engagement in education from enterprise education, careers education and personal finance education. All of these activities can be designed to include a contribution from employers.

Indeed, a case can be made that the employer contribution is of decisive value in such ventures. However, these schemes can be run without the involvement of employers and therefore do not necessarily constitute employer engagement. Moreover, employers can engage in education in a range of other ways.

During the 2000s, the concept of work-related learning came to be understood as a comprehensive framework within which particular interactions between education and work were situated (Huddleston and Stanley 2012). In 2004, the Qualifications and Curriculum Agency (QCA), then the national curriculum authority for England and Wales, introduced a universal entitlement for work-related learning for 14–16-year-olds, which was subsequently endorsed by legislation. Work-related learning was defined as a range of learning experiences that should be offered to young people and which served particular learning objectives: 'learning about work, learning through work and learning for work' (QCA 2003). Work-related learning was defined in terms of curriculum and pedagogy – of what was to be learned and how. When the Coalition Government came into power in 2010, there was a change in thinking about the role and purpose of education and the statutory requirement for work-related learning was abolished.

In contrast to the strong educational focus of work-related learning, 'employer engagement in education' reflects a wider range of foci and interests. For instance, it includes relationships between employers, employees and students in many forms and modes of education and training and is concerned not only with educational outcomes for students but also with understanding how these relationships impact (if at all) on the learning and progression of students, but also the ultimate economic and social well-being of young people, employers and their workforce.

We can distinguish the purposes and the language of employer engagement from that of work-related learning, but there is evidently a considerable overlap. What is entirely distinct is the matter of ownership. Employer engagement is understood as an initiative that is, in some sense, driven or at least authorised by employers as opposed to government or educationalists. It follows that there is a political or political–economic dimension to employer engagement. It is not easy to define exactly what roles and responsibilities are being claimed on behalf of employers under the banner of 'employer engagement'. Indeed, it is one of the purposes of this book to explore some of the competing understandings. However, at the very least we can distinguish four dominant ideas:

1   The educational system cannot, without intervention from employers, fully accomplish its responsibility to educate young people so that they obtain employment, fulfil their potential and contribute fully to society and the economy.
2   Employers and employees have an interest in, and a capability for, contributing to the education, training and progression of young people.

3   Various kinds of collaboration or partnership can be put in place so that these two systems (education and the economic community) will better be able to achieve their own goals.
4   The aims of government will be served by supporting these collaborations and partnerships.

Articulating these ideas immediately raises a number of questions – which this collection aims to pursue. For instance, what services or inputs can employers provide for young people in education? Do these services complement mainstream educational provision or do they, to some degree, attempt to replace certain aspects? Do young people from different social backgrounds have different experiences of employer engagement – and is this fair? Do employers really value, within their recruitment decisions, the episodic and short duration activities which young people often undertake when they are still in school?

Another way of understanding employer engagement in education is to explore the history of public, private and third-sector organisations that have led, or supported, business and employer engagement in education. In the context of the United Kingdom, there are examples such as Business in the Community, Young Enterprise, local Education Business Partnerships and the Education and Employers Taskforce. In addition, there have been, over the years, many organisations dedicated to employer engagement in particular localities, or that served particular business sectors or projects that have come and gone. These organisations have been successful, some for a very long time and on a great scale, at recruiting business involvement in education and attracting educational organisations to take up the business offer. Evidently this demonstrates an appetite for employer engagement in education on both sides; however, it is worth noting that a very large amount of employer engagement is brokered or mediated, which suggests that, without these organisations, employer engagement could not have developed as it has done (Huddleston and Stanley 2012).

Employer engagement in education as a consequence of government policy

In Britain, the beginning of the promotion of employer engagement in formal education, as an element of public policymaking, is marked by the emergence of work experience following the government-commissioned Newsom Report in 1963. This report recommended that 'experiments to enable some pupils over the age of fifteen to participate to a limited extent, under the auspices of the school, in the world of work in industry, commerce, or in other fields, should be carefully studied' (Central Advisory Council for Education 1963: chapter 9). Targeted at 'average or below average ability' pupils, by 1969 the Institute of Careers Officers reported that 2 per cent of young people had undertaken a short period of work experience before leaving compulsory full-time education. In the wake of 1972 legislation that raised the school leaving age to 16, the government acted in 1973 to make it possible for all pupils – regardless of ability – to take up work experience in their last year of schooling (Jamieson and Miller 1991: 5). Over the next 30 years, government increased the expectations on schools and provided dedicated resources to enable growing proportions of young people to gain direct experience of the workplace while still in education. Much of the early growth of work experience was bottom up: schools chose to provide work experience to selected 16-year-olds and local employers chose to offer short periods of work experience. However, largely as a consequence of the Technical and Vocational Education Initiative (TVEI) in the 1980s, work experience placements came to form part of the education of two-thirds of school leavers, a proportion rising to four-fifths by the first decade of the twenty-first century (Jamieson and Miller 1991; Mann 2012). It is important to note that employer engagement was supported by public funding, first through the TVEI pilots and then through dedicated funding to schools and core funding to local Education Business Partnership organisations, which took on the role of meeting the expectation that virtually all 14–16-year-olds should experience a work placement.

It is now some 50 years since the Newsom Report's cautious exploration of the subject. Implementing the recommendations of the recent Wolf Review into vocational education (Wolf 2011), the government has, for the first time, prescribed work experience as a mandatory element in the programmes of study of all young people aged 16–19. Schools and colleges are now 'expected [to] increase their engagement with employers', through such activities as workplace visits, enterprise projects, mentoring, work shadowing and career-focused workshops.[1]

The British interest in seeking to provide young people with school-mediated exposure to the workplace is by no means unique. The Newsom Committee was inspired, in part, by knowledge of practice in Sweden and the United States (Central Advisory Council for Education 1963: chapter 9). Young people in Australia and New Zealand have long undertaken periods of work experience within educational provision, especially Vocational Education and Training tracks (Fullarton 1999; Jamieson and Miller 1991). In Europe, employer engagement has been a long-standing practice within vocational education: 61 per cent of teenage Swiss apprentices, for example, previously undertook a period of work experience with their ultimate employer (OECD 2010: 85). Work experience is not the only pervasive mode of employer engagement: many countries operate entrepreneurial programmes, such as Junior Achievement or Young Enterprise, where school-based businesses are typically mentored, and judged, by volunteers.

While employer engagement in education is not a new phenomenon across the member countries of the Organisation for Economic Co-operation and Development (OECD), the period since the financial crash of 2008 has seen renewed attention given to the area. In 2010, the OECD argued that 'schools and colleges should encourage an understanding of the world of work from the earliest years, backed by visits to workplaces and workplace experience', citing Austria, Germany, Switzerland, Denmark, Norway and the United States as countries containing models of relevant practice (OECD 2010: 85). In the

United States, building on a history of school engagement with employers driven by the 1994 School to Work Transition Act, an influential team based at Harvard Graduate School for Education has since 2011 worked with states to ensure that all students have access to employer involvement, including career counselling, job shadowing, internships and employer-designed learning resources and projects (Symonds *et al.* 2011: 30). In 2011, the European Union initiated dedicated funding for projects specifically designed to encourage and enable employers working in Science, Technology, Engineering and Mathematics to work more systematically with schools across the Union.[2] Growing international interest in the field reflects, moreover, shared thinking on the purposes of such partnerships.

Policy perspective on employer engagement in education

There are many reasons why policymakers promote employer engagement in education but, as discussed next, the four primary objectives are: improving pupils' general preparation for the working world; addressing labour market skills shortages; enhancing social mobility; and improving pupil engagement and attainment. While governments may take different views on the nature, form and role of public-sector education in achieving these goals, something of a consensus has emerged regarding the potential for employer engagement to help to achieve these objectives.

Improving pupils' general preparation for the working world

The interest of the Newsom Committee in recommending formal periods of work experience was to enhance the 'general preparation of school leavers . . . to begin to enlarge their understanding of the world of work' (Central Advisory Council for Education 1963: chapter 9). Driven by the view that the leap from classroom to workplace had become too great, the report looked to Sweden, the United States and isolated models of voluntary practice in Britain for new approaches to enabling pupils in the final year of compulsory schooling (then aged 14) to develop insights and experiences relevant to their transitions into work. The analysis has enjoyed enduring appeal, policymakers and commentators repeatedly seeing employer engagement as a means to improve understanding of career opportunities and to equip young people with a broad range of experiences and skills not otherwise available within education (Davies 2002; CBI 2007; Birdwell *et al.* 2011; NCC 2013; Watts 1991).

At the heart of the 1994 US School to Work Opportunities Act was a desire to 'expose students to a broad array of career opportunities' and to prepare students better for first employment through extensive partnerships between local employers and schools (Symonds *et al.* 2011; Neumark 2007). In the United Kingdom, debates about what it means to leave schooling 'properly prepared' have centred increasingly around the concept of 'employability skills'. The UK Commission for Employment and Skills (UKCES) describes employability skills as the 'lubricant of our increasingly complex and interconnected workplace', being the ability to 'work in a team, communicate clearly, listen well, be interested and keen to learn, take criticism, solve problems, read, write and add' (UKCES 2009: 3). According to the UKCES, employers are central to providing the means by which young people build upon academic achievement and technical skill accumulation to develop employability skills to become successful in the labour market. Championed by employer bodies, most notably the Confederation of British Industry (CBI), the idea of 'employability skills' has captured policymakers' attention (CBI 2007). Addressing a perceived deficit was central to the reform ambitions of the British New Labour Government (1997–2010) which, through the promotion of Enterprise Education and the reform of 14–19-year-olds' education, aimed to equip young people not just with knowledge and skills, but also the 'attributes' demanded by the modern labour market (Davies 2002; Working Group on 14–19 Reform 2004).

New Labour's ambitious approach to curriculum reform centred on the 14–19 Diploma. Promoted as a qualification 'developed with employers for employers', the government called on employers to help 'bring learning to life' by inputting into qualification design and offering extensive engagement activities, including a compulsory period of 10 days' work experience. With a clear emphasis on the development of 'employability skills' and 'functional' numeracy, literacy and ICT use, policymakers determinedly sought to use the Diploma to better prepare young people 'for the world of work whether via college, university or directly into employment' (DCSF 2008). While the Diplomas failed (in any meaningful way) to survive the change of government in 2010, the ambition to improve school-to-work transitions through extensive employer engagement largely, if more loosely, related to courses of study continued, but switched to post-16 provision. From 2013, in order to give students 'a valuable experience of the work environment and develop their employability skills', English schools and colleges have been required to provide work experience opportunities that are 'purposeful, substantial, offer challenge and are relevant to the young persons' study programme and/or career aspirations'.[3]

Behind this policy of employer engagement has been a perception that changes in the labour market demand new skills of young people – to work in teams, communicate effectively, and so on – and that school-to-work transitions have become more difficult. In the United States, this diagnosis has encouraged the use of the metaphor of 'new pathways' as a way to conceptualise young people's navigations from the domain of education to that of work:

> The American system for preparing young people to lead productive and prosperous lives is clearly badly broken . . . Building a better network of pathways to adulthood for our young is one of the paramount challenges of our time . . . Our goal should be that beginning no later than middle school, all students should have access to a system of employer involvement and

assistance. In middle school, this would include career counselling, job shadowing, and opportunities to work on projects or problems designed by industry partners. In high school, it would include programs of study designed in collaboration with industry leaders, as well as opportunities for more intensive work-based learning such as paid internships.

(Symonds et al. 2011: 30)

The OECD has also called for more systematic collaboration between employers and education, calling on government to think not only about vocational pathways but also how young people might enjoy agency when negotiating their school-to-work transitions:

> More complex careers, with more options in both work and learning, are opening up new opportunities for many people. But they are also making decisions harder as young people face a sequence of complex choices over a lifetime of learning and work. Helping young people to make these decisions is the task of career guidance . . . [Career professionals] need to be able to call on a wide range of information and web-based resources. Strong links between schools and local employers are very important means of introducing young people to the world of work.
>
> (OECD 2010: 16)

For the OECD's head of education and skills, Andreas Schleicher, supporting careers decision-making will improve life chances and serve national skills strategies:

> To begin, we need to be able to anticipate the evolution of the labour market: we need to know what skills will be needed to reignite our economies. The coexistence of unemployed graduates on the street, while employers say they cannot find the people with the skills they need, shows clearly that more education alone does not automatically translate into better jobs and better lives. Skills mismatch is a very real phenomenon that is mirrored in people's earnings prospects and in their productivity. Knowing which skills are needed in the labour market and which educational pathways will get young people to where they want to be is essential. High-quality career guidance services, complemented with up-to-date information about labour-market prospects, can help young people make sound career choices.
>
> (Cited in NCC 2013: 16)

Addressing strategic skills shortages

While much employer engagement is valued because it is believed to contribute generally to young people's transitions and/or career decision-making, some forms of employer engagement address particular areas of current and projected skills shortage, notably those identified by the government or employers as being of strategic importance, such as STEM (Science, Technology, Engineering and Mathematics) and modern foreign languages (MFL). For instance, in the United Kingdom, STEMNET has been funded by the Department for Business, Innovation and Skills (BIS) since the 1990s. STEMNET has recruited thousands of ambassadors to work with teachers to help deliver the STEM curriculum in more stimulating learning environments (NAO 2011).[4] Professional bodies like the Royal Academy of Engineering have supported many initiatives and schemes aimed at enhancing the appeal of engineering to students and their teachers. This is also the motivation behind the collaboration between the European Union and the European Round Table of Industrialists (the industry body representing large multinational companies), which connects science professionals with science classrooms to 'reinforce young Europeans' interest in science education and careers and thus address the anticipated future skills gaps within the European Union'. Funded since 2011 by a €8 million EU grant,

> all the actions undertaken in Ingenious aim to improve the image of STEM careers among young people and encourage them to think about the wider range of interesting opportunities that STEM can bring to their lives in the future.[5]

Other areas have also attracted state and private-sector funding. Under New Labour, a publicly funded network of hundreds of Language Champions was recruited to encourage young people to pursue studies in modern languages (Mann *et al.* 2011). Globally, one of the most vigorous forms of employer engagement has been in the promotion of enterprise education and entrepreneurialism (Working Party on SMEs and Entrepreneurship 2007). Programmes run by organisations devoted to the promotion of school-based enterprise such as Junior Achievement/Young Enterprise have, over many decades, recruited business volunteers to work with schools with the purpose of enhancing the entrepreneurial ambitions and capabilities of young people as a means to increase the level of business start-ups. In the United Kingdom, there has been extensive funding from the Department of Trade and Industry and subsequently from the Department of Business Innovation and Skills as well as from the Education department that has made it possible for third-sector bodies to provide free or low-cost volunteer resources, programmes and competitions to schools.

Enhancing social mobility

A third objective behind state and private support for employer engagement in education has been to use it as a tool to improve social mobility. Employer engagement has been seen as a mechanism both to increase individual mobility and also to enable employers to recruit new talent from a wider range of prospective candidates. For the Newsom Committee, it was those school leavers who were 'least well endowed' who had the most to gain from a new culture of employer engagement. UK programmes like Career Academies and WISE (Women into Science and Engineering) have deliberately aimed to provide resources to those groups who are under-represented in STEM careers and to support their progression by providing employer engagement aimed at informing, motivating and enhancing the STEM-related academic achievement of pupils (Morton and Collins 2011).

In 2009, the UK Government-commissioned report of the Panel on Fair Access to the Professions, chaired by New Labour politician Alan Milburn, called for 'new ways of systematically raising the aspirations of . . . youngsters and families who simply do not believe they will ever progress'. The report identified inequalities in cultural capital ('in terms of attitudes, values and aspirations') and social capital ('the values and networks that can be passed down from parents') as important blocks to the meritocratic rise of talent, particularly into the nation's professions. Alongside a renewed focus on enhanced employability skills, the review recommended a national mentoring programme linking young professionals with pupils aged 13–18 in schools with high proportions of disadvantaged pupils. The report recommended reforms to make work experience more career-focused and to introduce a new culture of 'work tasters' or job shadowing. The report also called for more professionals to visit primary and secondary schools to talk about their working lives (Panel on Fair Access to the Professions 2009: 6, 46–59). After the change of government in 2010, the new Coalition Government retained Milburn's involvement with the 2011 Social Mobility Strategy and also developed a new 'Business Compact', which was signed by more than 150 large companies, and set out a commitment to 'raise aspirations in local schools . . . by offering mentoring, talks and other career and skills based activities' and 'fair access to work experience' (Cabinet Office 2011; Deputy Prime Minister, n.d.). Despite shifts in power and policy, employer engagement in education has remained at the heart of approaches to enhancing social mobility.

Increasing engagement and attainment

Since 1973, British governments have sought explicitly to use employer involvement to increase pupil engagement in education and enhance attainment. Among the 'underlying aims' of work-related learning, for example, was to 'raise standards of achievement of students' and to 'increase the commitment to learning, motivation and self-confidence of students' (DCSF 2009: 6). For example, precursors to the 14–19 Diploma programme, a high-profile qualification intended by the New Labour Government to integrate employer engagement within vocationally focused academic courses of study, explicitly targeted pupils 'at most risk of disengagement' (O'Donnell *et al.* 2006). Pilot provision aimed to improve student achievement by providing learning programmes enhanced by employer engagement, including extended periods of work experience (Cowen and Burgess 2009). Such approaches were a defining characteristic of Diploma development.

Government insisted that Diplomas were validated by the employers who had helped both to design and to deliver them through enhanced work-related learning (Lynch *et al.* 2010; Huddleston and Laczik 2012). Business mentoring programmes have also been designed with a core aim of improving academic attainment and improved scholastic outcomes, as illustrated by volunteer reading partners programmes aimed at primary schools (Miller 1998; Miller *et al.* 2011).

Key issues in employer engagement in education

This short review of policy developments in the field of employer engagement in education highlights the breadth and complexity of the subject matter. Employer engagement has been used by policymakers as a vehicle for achieving multiple goals. It has been supported by different government departments in different ways, and delivered through an alliance of state and non-state actors. But employer engagement in education also raises a number of political, economic, educational and sociological questions that need to be addressed. How can we explain, for example, the extent of government interest when, as seen later, reliable research into the effectiveness of the intervention is, to date, so limited? How effective is employer engagement in supporting skills development? How does employer engagement influence pupil attainment and, if so, how can results be optimised? What influence does workplace exposure have on the lived experiences of young people as they move from childhood into adulthood? And how can employer engagement be most efficiently and effectively delivered? Such themes are addressed in the essays presented in this collection.

Employer engagement in education is undoubtedly a popular and pervasive phenomenon. For example, a 2008 survey of 1,034 secondary school classroom teachers for the Edge Foundation found that just 1 per cent felt there was too much employer engagement in education and 59 per cent believed there was not enough (YouGov 2010). Moreover, in the absence of any external requirements, and as illustrated in this collection, many English independent schools have fully embraced employer engagement. Indeed, in the United Kingdom, public debates have focused not on whether employer engagement is 'a good thing' – it is hard to find a dissenting voice across the political spectrum – but around the specifics of implementation. For instance, debating when it should primarily take place (e.g. at ages 14–16 or at 16–19), whether it should be integrated into the mainstream curriculum or set apart, and whether it is the role of government to actively enable the supply of employee volunteers or to devolve responsibility to schools. We believe that it is precisely the popularity and prevalence of employer engagement in education that heightens the need for sustained and critical academic attention and investigation of the area.

There is little sign of the drive for employer engagement abating. For instance, in the United Kingdom, employers are still ready to commit time and resources to employer engagement activities. In 2009/2010, despite the recession, approximately 400,000 different English workplaces provided work experience placements to over half a million teenagers. Many large employers, particularly in the private sector, now employ dedicated staff members to run educational activities or invest in third-sector organisations, such as Business in the Community or Young Enterprise, to do so on their behalf. Employer bodies, like the Confederation of British Industry (CBI), have over the last decade consistently championed greater, more professionally managed employer engagement, notably in terms of work experience (CBI 2007, 2012). The investment by the business community is clear, but does it work? And what does it have to tell us about the culture of current capitalism?

In such circumstances, it is timely to step back and reflect critically on this phenomenon. What has driven governments, schools and employers to place such emphasis and to invest considerable resource in employer engagement? Some researchers have argued that interest in employer engagement has been linked to increases in youth unemployment and economic uncertainty (Huddleston and Laczik 2012: 404; Watts 1991: 51–52). And, certainly, policy documents have commonly located employer engagement initiatives in narratives of rapid labour market change, the pressure of technological change, globalisation and increased uncertainty and instability. The case for employability skills has, for example, been argued for in terms of long structural economic changes from an industrial to a service economy (Davies 2002). The financial crash of 2008 and the global youth unemployment and the public sector austerity that has ensued all raise questions about whether the expansion of publicly funded education and training can, as was believed for a decade or so, deliver both economic prosperity and social justice (Grubb and Lazerson 2004). The OECD, among others, believes that employer engagement may help to keep this politically important win–win on the road (OECD 2010). More than this, the new culture of employer engagement and business volunteering speaks to a conception of what might be deemed 'good capitalism' – that we really are 'all in it together'. In the language of the Clinton and Blair administrations, employer engagement represents a 'third way' approach, being a means of harnessing employer altruism to create new partnerships to deliver more than the state can do alone. Indeed, it might be taken as the mark of 'good capitalists' that employers engage with schools so that the benefits of capitalism and access to professional success might be distributed more fairly. Of course, the extent to which this is achieved – and indeed the extent to which employer engagement is wholly 'altruistic' – remains a moot point. However, what is clear is that the significance and scale of employer engagement in education (and the questions that it raises) demand research attention. In the next section we examine existing research to see what is known about the development of employer education, its practice and its impact.

Employer engagement in education: as a research field

In 2008, the UK Government's Department for Children, Schools and Families (DCSF) commissioned and published a 'rapid evidence assessment' of the available research literature on 'the impact of education links with employers'. Looking specifically for 'high quality studies' using transparent and appropriate social science methodologies to test for attainment and other measurable outcomes for young people, the reviewers' initial literature search generated 42 relevant research outputs, which subsequent assessment narrowed to just 15 studies (relating to a total of 10 different UK and US programmes) that were judged to have been evaluated with sufficient rigour to allow assessments to be made of the findings presented. To the authors, the state of the research base was a disappointment:

> There is no shortage of literature on employers and/or business involvement in education. Much of this literature, however, was excluded from the scope of this review, mainly because it is largely anecdotal . . . or not evaluated to even modest scientific standards. There is a particular shortage of studies of employers' links with education that have used robust research designs . . . that can provide robust evidence of an impact. Many studies are descriptive and/or are based on single group before and after designs without a true comparator. . . . Another weakness of the studies in this area is that they have small sample sizes with low statistical power. This can lead to either inconclusive findings or to erroneous conclusions.
>
> (AIR UK 2008: 28)

Other reviews of the literature have reached similar conclusions (Davies 2002; Athayde 2012).

Although the evidence base is small, the AIR UK review found that there was considerable diversity among the employer engagement programmes that it examined. The two UK programmes reviewed focused on young people aged 14–16. The Increased Flexibilities Programme (Golden *et al.* 2004, 2005, 2006) provided disengaged pupils with employer engagement as part of a curriculum shaped by work-related learning and considered broad outcomes. In contrast, Miller's 1998 and 1999 reviews of business mentoring among 14–16-year-olds focused on the effects of such programmes on the attainment of those pupils at the borderline of achieving five GCSEs A*–C. Three US studies (Linnehan 2001; Donohue *et al.* 2005; Hamilton and Hamilton 1993, 2000) looked at programmes aimed at older students, predominantly aged 17–18, who combined academic study with extended periods of mentored work experience or part-time employment. A third group of programmes combined extensive and wide-ranging employer engagement with project-based learning for students aged between 12 and 18 (Henderson and St John 1997; Coffee and Pestridge 2001; Kemple and Snipes 2000; Shorr and Hon 1999; MacAllum *et al.* 2002), leaving reviewers uncertain whether benefits observed related to the style of learning, the employer engagement undertaken or a combination thereof. Two studies provide further models of delivery: the Center for Children and Technology review (2004) of a programme wherein teachers worked closely with volunteers from computer giant IBM focused around collaborative teaching and access to technology tools within a local school reform programme, and Swail and Kampits (2004) retrospectively questioned 1,613 first-year undergraduate students (by definition, higher achievers) about the extent of their work-based learning while in school and then compared attainment levels on high school completion and at university.

The AIR UK reviewers found reliable evidence of improved attainment in five of the programmes evaluated (Henderson and St John 1997; Miller 1998, 1999; Golden *et al.* 2004; Golden *et al.* 2005; Golden *et al.* 2006; Center for Children and Technology 2004). While no evidence of increased attainment was found in the other studies reviewed, they were not found to have reduced attainment (an important consideration given the opportunity costs involved), and a wide range of positive outcomes were also identified – for example, improving students' preparedness for work, development of job/work skills and work-based competencies, attitudes and behaviours. The programmes were also found to have enhanced students' employability and were linked with higher initial wage rates (AIR UK 2008: 6).

The AIR UK (2008) review arguably raised more questions than it answered and provided little insight into the extent of outcomes observed. For example, what caused different outcomes between programmes? To what extent did they represent efficient investments of public resource? The authors concluded that, while the results discovered were certainly 'encouraging', a deeper understanding of the impact of employer engagement in education 'would require a stronger evidence base' (AIR UK 2008: 30). Further supporting evidence can be found, to an extent, within areas of work that fell outside the review. The work of David Neumark, for example, (e.g. Neumark and Rothstein 2005, 2006) explores US longitudinal databases to test for educational and employment outcomes related to activities promoted through the US School to Work Opportunities Act, including activities that require employer engagement, such as job shadowing and internships, or activities likely to involve employer engagement, such as mentoring and school enterprise. Neumark's work explores whether the consequences of such programmes are disproportionately felt by more disadvantaged young people whereas Neumark and Rothstein find evidence of positive impact related to some engagement activities. Considering the results of an entrepreneurial education programme, Oosterbeek *et al.*'s 2010 study of Dutch enterprise students finds no evidence of increases in entrepreneurial capability when compared to a control group. The work of Carlo Raffo is also instructive. In a series of articles (Raffo and Hall 2000; Raffo and Reeves 2000; Raffo 2006), Raffo and colleagues take a qualitative, ethnographic approach to understand the experiences of young people on British work experience programmes and explore how such programmes influence students' identities and social capital accumulation. His work positions work experience as an often highly meaningful intervention in the lives of young people. Also relevant are a number of quantitative reviews that have drawn on social capital theory to explore how long-term employment impacts relate to teenagers' social networks, including contact with employers, supervisors and work colleagues. That these types of valuable social relations are typically fostered through school-mediated employer engagement also points to the potential value of employer engagement (Flap and Boxman 1999; McDonald *et al.* 2007).

Were a review of the literature surrounding employer engagement in education to take place in 2013, it would have a number of significant new studies to draw upon. From the United Kingdom, a series of detailed evaluations of the delivery of Diploma qualifications are now available (Ofsted 2009, 2010; Lynch *et al.* 2010; Haynes and Richardson 2011); a team from Queen's University, Belfast has undertaken quantitative analysis of an employee volunteer reading partners programme, using random assignment and a control group (Miller *et al.* 2011); the National Audit Office has reported on the effectiveness of STEM volunteering programmes (including those run by STEMNET) on pupil achievement and course selection; and new statistical analysis of the links between volume of school-mediated employer engagement and young adult earnings has appeared in the *Journal of Education and Work* (Mann and Percy 2013). In the United States, the 2008 Career Academies review randomly assigned 1,428 students to intervention and control groups, tracking students' progress for eight years after high school completion. The study had more than 80 per cent retention levels and found that the intervention group enjoyed wage premiums averaging 11 per cent above those of the control group (Kemple and Willner 2008).

This brief review of literature pertaining to employer engagement in education highlights the diversity and immaturity of the field. One ambition of this volume is to advocate for employer engagement in education to be seen as an area that is worthy of critical consideration in its own right. We believe that there is a need to develop a deeper academic understanding of what happens when a young person in an educational setting comes into contact with the economic community. The essays in this collection draw on a range of disciplines and methodological tools to consider this question and the context within which it is asked.

This collection begins with a series of essays considering theoretical perspectives, through which the study of employer engagement in education can be viewed. In Chapter 1, Archer interrogates the concept of aspiration and its use – and misuses – by policymakers seeking to explain and enhance social mobility. Stanley and Mann focus in Chapter 2 on developing theoretical tools to explain and make sense of employer engagement. They propose a general framework that synthesises the concepts of human, social and cultural capital along with the idea of life course. Approaching the subject from the perspective of US career technical education in Chapter 3, Stone considers the breadth of knowledge, skills and competencies demanded by the modern labour market and offers a framework for reform. Part 1 ends with the OECD's Kathrin Hoeckel's review of the current crisis of youth unemployment across OECD countries, exploring its character, causes and the challenge it offers policymakers.

Part 2 of the collection turns to the social and economic contexts within which employer engagement in education takes place. Li and Devine (Chapter 5) and Holmes and Mayhew (Chapter 6) draw on British longitudinal datasets to explore the character of social mobility in the United Kingdom over the last generation to set out the specific challenges that will need to be addressed by employer engagement programmes if they are to generate social mobility. Focusing more qualitatively on the lived experiences of young people, St Clair *et al.* present findings in Chapter 7 from a study of teenagers in three British cities, providing critical analysis of the nature of young people's occupational ambitions and the relationship between place and aspiration. A primary finding of St Clair *et al.* is that the British teenagers they studied rarely possessed good understandings of local labour markets. This insight is shared by Norris and Francis's qualitative study, covered in Chapter 8, which explores the cultural, financial and institutional barriers to the progression of young people attending English further education colleges.

Part 3 turns to questions of equity and access in experience of employer engagement. In Chapter 9, Mann and Kashefpakdel report the findings of a survey of young British adults (aged 19–24) investigating their experiences of employer engagement and perceptions of its utility to school-to-work transitions, segmented by the type of school attended (non-selective state, grammar or independent), the age at which the activity was undertaken and the highest level of qualification at time of the survey. The chapter finds that former pupils of British independent schools commonly undertook employer engagement activities and found them to have been of high value, and these experiences are considered in detail in Chapter 10. Reporting on a qualitative study focused on interviews at six high-performing English independent schools, Huddleston *et al.* explore the character and purpose of employment engagement in this sector. High among respondents' given reasons for participating in employer engagement programmes is a desire to optimise their chances of successful admission to highly selective universities. In Chapter 11, this theme is picked up again by Jones, who uses textual analysis to compare the university applications of young people attending state and private schools, the nature of workplace experiences reported and what they say about differential access to resources of value to university admission. This part ends with Le Gallais and Hatcher's qualitative study that examines the manner in which work experience placements are distributed to students in a small number of schools and explores the implications with respect to social mobility.

The collection draws to a close with three essays that consider the impacts of school-based employer engagement on young people as they progress into the labour market. Percy and Mann in Chapter 13 draw on survey evidence of young British adults to investigate correlations between the extent of teenage school-mediated workplace exposure and later earnings and employment outcomes. In Chapter 14, Taylor *et al.* explore the impact upon employment and achievement for different kinds of student in an apprenticeship scheme in Canada and evaluate whether it could do more for disadvantaged learners. From a British perspective, Massey (Chapter 15) sets out insights from some of the largest employer surveys in the world, exploring employer attitudes towards school-age work experience in the context of structural changes to the youth labour market. The book concludes with a review, by the editors, of what the evidence presented in the collection has to say about the meanings and implications of employer education in education, particularly for young people, and outlines where policymakers, practitioners and researchers should positively focus further attention.

Notes

1 See www.education.gov.uk, 'Work experience and non-qualification activity' [accessed 12 July 2013]. The UK's opposition Labour Party has also signalled strong support for the idea that 'all young people should undertake work experience and community activity' between the ages of 14 and 19 (Skills Taskforce 2013: 4).
2 See www.ingenious-science.eu [accessed 12 July 2013].
3 See www.education.gov.uk, 'Work experience and non-qualification activity' [accessed 12 July 2013].
4 See www.stemnet.org.uk/content/about-us/programmes [accessed 12 June 2013].
5 See www.ingenious-science.eu/web/guest/about [accessed 12 June 2013].

References

AIR UK. (2008). *The involvement of business in education: a rapid evidence assessment of measurable impacts*. London: Department for Children, Schools and Families.

Athayde, R. (2012). The impact of enterprise education on attitudes to enterprise in young people: an evaluation study. *Education and Training*, 54: 709–726.

Birdwell, J., Grist, M. and Margo, J. (2011). *The forgotten half*. London: DEMOS.

Cabinet Office. (2011). *Opening doors, breaking barriers: a strategy for social mobility*. London: HM Government.

Center for Children and Technology (CCT). (2004). *The Reinventing Education Initiative from an evaluation perspective: the role of innovative technology partnerships in addressing significant challenges to education improvement*. CCT Research Summary.

Central Advisory Council for Education. (1963). *Half our future*. London: HMSO.

Coffee, J. N. and Pestridge, S. (2001). *The career academy concept*. OJJDP Fact Sheet.

Confederation of British Industry (CBI). (2007). *Time well spent: embedding employability in work experience*. London: Department for Education and Skills.

Confederation of British Industry (CBI). (2012). *Learning to grow: 2012 education and skills survey*. London: CBI.

Cowen, G. and Burgess, M. (2009) *Key Stage 4 Engagement Programme – Evaluation*. London: DCSF.

Davies, H. (2002). *A review of enterprise and the economy in education*. London: HM Treasury.

Department for Children, Schools and Families (DCSF). (2008). *Improving business by improving the skills of young people: the Diploma – a guide for employers*. London: DCSF.

Department for Children, Schools and Families (DCSF). (2009). *The work-related learning guide*. 2nd ed. London: DCSF.

Deputy Prime Minister. (n.d.). *Social mobility business compact: factsheet*. London: Cabinet Office.

Donohue, B., Conway, D., Beisecker, M., Murphy, H., Farley, A., Waite, M., Gugino, K., Knatz, D., Lopez-Frank, C., Burns, J., Madison, S. and Shorty, C. (2005). Financial management and job social skills training components in a summer business institute. *Behavior Modification*, 29: 653–676.

Flap, H. and Boxman, E. (1999). Getting started: the influence of social capital on the start of career. *In:* N. Lin, ed. *Social capital: theory and research*. New Brunswick, NJ: Transaction, 159–181.

Fullarton, S. (1999). *Work experience and work placements in secondary school education*. Melbourne: Australian Council for Educational Research.

Golden, S., Nelson, J., O'Donnell, L. and Rudd, P. (2004). *Evaluation of increased flexibilities for 14–16 year olds: profile of partnerships and students 2002 and 2003*. London: Department for Education and Skills.

Golden, S., O'Donnell, L., Benton, T. and Rudd, P. (2005). *Evaluation of increased flexibility for 14 to 16 year olds programme: outcomes for the first cohort*. London: Department for Education and Skills.

Golden, S., O'Donnell, L. and Rudd, P. (2006). *Evaluation of increased flexibility for 14 to 16 year olds programme: the second year*. London: Department for Education and Skills.

Grubb, W. N. and Lazerson, M. (2004). *The education gospel and the vocational transformation of schooling*. Boston, MA: Harvard University Press.

Hamilton, M. A. and Hamilton, S. F. (1993). *Toward a youth apprenticeship system: report from the Youth Apprenticeship Demonstration Project in Broome Count*. Ithaca, NY: Cornell University.

Hamilton, S. F. and Hamilton, M. A. (2000). Research, intervention, and social change: Improving adolescents' career opportunities. *In:* L. J. Crockett and R. K. Silbereisen, eds. *Negotiating adolescence in times of social change*. New York, NY: Cambridge University Press, 267–283.

Haynes, G. and Richardson, W. (2011). *Evaluation of the implementation and impact of Diplomas: findings from the 2009/10 survey of higher education institutions*. London: Department for Education.

Henderson, R. W. and St John, L. (1997). *Thematically integrated middle school mathematics: a school-university-business partnership*. Santa Cruz, CA: California University.

Huddleston, P. and Laczik, A. (2012). Successes and challenges of employer engagement: the new Diploma qualification. *Journal of Education and Work*, 25: 403–421.

Huddleston, P. and Stanley. J, eds. (2012). *Work-related learning: a guide for teachers and practitioners*. London: Routledge.

Jamieson, I. and Miller, A. (1991). History and policy context. *In:* A. Miller, A. G. Watts and I. Jamieson, eds. *Rethinking work experience*. London: Falmer Press, 3–15.

Kemple, J. and Snipes, J. (2000). *Career academies: impacts on students' engagement and performance in high school*. New York, NY: MDRC.

Kemple, J. and Willner, C. J. (2008). *Career academies – long-term impacts on labour market outcomes, educational attainment, and transitions to adulthood*. New York, NY: MDRC.

Linnehan, F. (2001). The relation of a work-based mentoring program to the academic performance and behavior of African American students. *Journal of Vocational Behavior*, 59: 310–325.

Lynch, S., McCrone, T., Wade, P., Featherstone, G., Evans, K. and Golden, S. (2010). *National evaluation of Diplomas: the first year of delivery*. London: Department for Children, Schools and Families.

MacAllum, K., Yoder, K., Scott, K. and Bozick, R. (2002). *Moving forward – college and career transitions of LAMP graduates – from the LAMP Longitudinal Study*. Washington, DC: National Institute for Work and Learning.

McDonald, S., Erickson, L. D., Johnson, M. K. and Elder, G. H. (2007). Informal mentoring and young adult employment. *Social Science Research*, 36: 1328–1347.

Mann, A. (2012). *Work experience: impact and delivery – insights from the evidence*. London: Education and Employers Taskforce.

Mann, A. and Percy, C. (2013). Employer engagement in British secondary education: wage earning outcomes experienced by young adults. *Journal of Education and Work*. Available from: http://dx.doi.org/10.1080/13639080.2013.769671.

Mann, A., with Spring, C., Evans, D. and Dawkins, J. (2011). *The importance of experience of the world of work in admissions to Russell Group universities: a desktop review of admissions criteria for six courses*. London: Education and Employers Taskforce.

Miller, A. (1998). *Business and community mentoring in schools*. London: Department for Education and Employment.

Miller, A. (1999). Business mentoring in schools: Does it raise attainment? *Education & Training*, 41: 73–78.

Miller, S., Connolly, P. and Maguire, L. (2011). *A follow-up randomised controlled trial evaluation of the effects of Business in the Community's Time to Read mentoring programme*. Belfast: Centre for Effective Education.

Morton, P. and Collins, J. (2011). *Widening horizons in STEM work experience*. Research Conference, Education and Employer Taskforce, University of Warwick.

National Audit Office (NAO). (2011). *Educating the next generation of scientists*. London: NAO.

National Careers Council (NCC). (2013). *An aspirational nation: creating a culture change in careers provision*. UK: NCC.

Neumark, D. (2007). Improving school-to-work transitions: introduction. *In:* D. Neumark, ed., *Improving school-to-work transitions*. New York, NY: Russell Sage Foundation, 1–23.

Neumark, D. and Rothstein, D. (2005). *Do school-to-work programs help the 'Forgotten Half'?* Bonn: Forschungsinstitut zur Zukunft der Arbeit/Institute for the Study of Labour.

Neumark, D. and Rothstein, D. (2006). School-to-career programs and transitions to employment and higher education. *Economics of Education Review*, 25, 374–393.

O'Donnell, L., Golden, S., McCrone, T., Rudd, P. and Walker, M. (2006). *Evaluation of increased flexibility for 14–16 year olds programme: delivery for Cohorts 3 and 4 and the future*. London: Department for Education and Skills.

Office for Standards in Education, Children's Services and Skills (Ofsted). (2009). *Implementation of 14–19 reforms, including the introduction of Diplomas*. London: Ofsted.

Office for Standards in Education, Children's Services and Skills (Ofsted). (2010). *Diplomas: the second year*. London: Ofsted.

Oosterbeek, H., van Praag, M. and Ijsselstein, A. (2010). The impact of entrepreneurship education on entrepreneurship skills and motivation. *European Economic Review*, 54: 442–454.

Organisation for Economic Co-operation and Development (OECD). (2010). *Learning for jobs*. Paris: OECD.

Panel on Fair Access to the Professions. (2009). *Unleashing aspirations: the final report*. London: HM Government.

Qualifications and Curriculum Agency (QCA). (2003). *Work-related learning for all at key stage 4: guidance for implementing the statutory guidance from 2004*. London: QCA.

Raffo, C. (2006). Disadvantaged young people accessing the new urban economies of the post-industrial city. *Journal of Education Policy*, 21: 75–94.

Raffo, C. and Hall, D. (2000). *Disaffected young people and the work-related curriculum at KS4 – issues of social capital development and learning as a form cultural practice*. Paper presented at the British Educational Research Association Conference, Cardiff University.

Raffo, C. and Reeves, M. (2000). Youth transitions and social exclusion: developments in social capital theory. *Journal of Youth Studies*, 3: 147–166.

Shorr, A. and Hon, J. (1999). They said it couldn't be done: implementing a career academy program for a diverse high school population. *Journal of Education for Students Placed at Risk*, 4: 379–391.

Skills Taskforce. (2013). *Interim report. Talent matters – why England needs a new approach to skills*. London: Labour Party.

Swail, W. S. and Kampits, E. (2004). *Work-based learning and higher education: a research perspective*. American Higher Education Report Series.

Symonds, W. C., Schwartz, R. B. and Ferguson, R. (2011). *Pathways to prosperity: meeting the challenge of preparing Americans for the 21st century*. Cambridge, MA: Harvard Graduate School of Education.

Watts, A. G. (1991). The concept of work experience. *In:* A. Miller, A. G. Watts and I. Jamieson, eds. *Rethinking work experience*. London: Falmer Press, 16–38.

Wolf, A. (2011). *Review of vocational education: the Wolf Report*. London: Department for Education.

Working Group on 14–19 reform. (2004). *14–19 Qualifications and curriculum reform: final report of the Working Group on 14–19 reform*. London: Department for Education and Skills.

Working Party on SMEs and Entrepreneurship. (2007). *Evaluation of programmes concerning education for entrepreneurship*. Paris: OECD.

UKCES. (2009). *The employability challenge: full report*. London: UK Commission for Employment and Skills.

YouGov. (2010). *EDGE annual programme of stakeholder surveys: report*. London: Edge Foundation.

Part 1

Conceptualising employer engagement in education

Chapter 1

Conceptualising aspiration

Louise Archer

Why focus on 'aspiration'?

This chapter introduces one of the core concepts that runs through this edited collection, namely 'aspiration'. The notion of aspiration is often invoked within discussions about young people's educational engagement, choices and future pathways. It also features prominently within education policy and is used within a range of educational interventions, such as a number of those associated with employer engagement.

An aspiration can be defined as 'a hope or ambition'.[1] Aspirations can take many forms – from uncertain, vague hopes for the future, through to 'more concrete and achievable' plans (Brannen and Nilsen 2007: 155). In previous research, my colleagues and I have highlighted the considerable variability found within young people's aspirations:

> From intensely held goals and desires to looser, more nebulous interests; from 'high' or lofty ambitions to more prosaic, mundane or realistic expectations; from 'already known' and concrete expectations to fragile dreams that are constantly mediated and shaped by external constraints.
>
> (Archer *et al.* 2010: 78)

There is, of course, a question as to how far young people's aspirations actually relate to their outcomes in later life. Although there is no simple, direct link, a number of studies do provide evidence that young people's aspirations can give a probabilistic indication of the general type of career that they are likely to pursue in the future (Trice 1991a, 1991b; Trice and McClellan 1993). For instance, Croll's (2008) analysis of UK longitudinal data showed that approximately half of young people expressing particular aspirations at age 15 will end up in a similar type of occupation ten to fifteen years later. Moreover, Tai *et al.*'s (2006) US research also found that a young person who aspires to a career in science at age 14 is almost three-and-a-half times more likely to end up taking a degree in the physical sciences or engineering than a peer without such aspirations.

As a sociologist of education, I am also interested in how aspirations can be used as a 'tool' or device for understanding young people's identities and lives more generally. My theoretical perspective conceptualises aspirations as socially constructed phenomena. That is, aspirations are not merely individual cognitions 'inside' our heads; rather, I see aspirations as cultural and social products that can tell us not only about the young person in question, but also about their social context. Aspirations are formed through a myriad of influences – past and present, individual and collective. The influence of social identities and inequalities on aspirations is revealed by patterns in aspirations that are found within and between particular social groups. Studies of such patterns may focus on gender (e.g. OECD 2012a), ethnicity (e.g. Archer and Francis 2007) or social class (e.g. Archer et al. 2010).

Education policy's focus on aspiration

Aspirations are not merely of academic interest – they also occupy a prominent position within UK education policy. Both the previous New Labour administration (e.g. DfES 2003, 2004, 2005) and the current Coalition Government (e.g. DfE 2010) have developed education policies based on the assumption that differential rates of educational participation and achievement might be due (in part) to a 'poverty of aspiration' among some (working-class and minority ethnic) communities. As noted elsewhere (Archer et al. 2013), this line of rhetoric can be traced, virtually unchanged, from the 2004 White Paper (described in the introduction as 'a White Paper about aspiration', DfES 2005: 7) with its accompanying ministerial references to 'a national scandal of low aspiration and poor performance' (DfES 2004) and the 'problem of low aspirations (DCSF 2007), through to the current Secretary of State for Education, Michael Gove's, calls in the 2010 Schools White Paper for the creation of an 'aspiration nation' (DfE 2010). These sentiments have since been echoed in 2012 by the Prime Minister, David Cameron (Murphy 2012: 6).

This persistent policy belief in the 'problem of aspiration' has been translated into a sizeable deployment of resources and initiatives aimed at 'raising aspirations' among socially disadvantaged young people. In addition to national policies such as *Aiming High* and *Aim Higher*,[2] countless charities and organisations in the United Kingdom organise their activities around the notion that the key to improving educational attainment and post-16 progression lies in raising the aspirations of young people and their families.[3] In other words, 'aspiration' is often a key concept within employer engagement in education.

What do young people aspire to?

There have been a number of highly informative quantitative analyses of large national longitudinal datasets, such as the British Household Panel Survey (BHPS) (e.g. Croll 2008; Croll et al. 2009), the Longitudinal Study of Young People in England (LSYPE) (e.g. Attwood and Croll 2011; Gutman and Schoon 2012), the National Child Development Study (NCDS) (e.g. Schoon 2001), and the Youth Cohort Study (YCS) (e.g. Yates *et al.* 2011). There have also been many smaller, qualitative studies, focused on understanding aspirations among particular groups of young people (e.g. Archer *et al.* 2010; Ball *et al.* 2000).

Contrary to assumptions within education policy, existing research evidence suggests that there is no widespread 'poverty of aspirations'. For instance, studies have found that young people from working-class and/or minority ethnic backgrounds express 'high' aspirations (e.g. Thomas 2001; Archer and Francis 2007; Strand and Winston 2008; Croll 2008; Roberts and Atherton 2011; Kintrea *et al.* 2011). A longitudinal study of 89 urban young people (aged 14–16), who had been identified by their schools as 'at risk' of dropping out of education, found that 30 per cent had at some point during the study expressed 'high' aspirations for professional careers, such as a lawyer, doctor or accountant (Archer *et al.* 2010).

Croll (2008) also notes that young people surveyed by the BHPS in the 1990s (at age 15) were occupationally ambitious; that is, most aspired to professional and technical/managerial careers. More recently, the ASPIRES project (e.g. DeWitt *et al.* 2011; Archer *et al.* 2013; DeWitt *et al.* 2014) conducted a survey of 9,000+ children at age 10/11 and 6,500+ young people from the same cohort at age 12/13, and found that young people in 2011 also seem to be part of the 'Ambitious Generation' (Schneider and Stevenson 1999), with aspirations overwhelmingly for professional, technical and managerial careers.

Similarly to Croll (2008), the ASPIRES study has also found little evidence of a 'poverty of aspiration' because top-line figures seem to indicate that young people from all social class backgrounds express broadly comparable aspirations. Our ASPIRES surveys reveal that very few aspire to skilled manual and even fewer to unskilled manual. Over 90 per cent of 12/13-year-olds aspire to make a lot of money in the future and just over half want to 'become famous' in the future. Students generally report strong parental encouragement and support for their aspirations and future success. For instance, 98 per cent of 12/13-year-olds agree that their parents want them to get a good job in the future, 95 per cent agree that it is important to their parents that their child achieves well in school and 72 per cent say that their parents expect them to go to university. Yet, these widespread 'high' aspirations do not necessarily translate into equally high outcomes for all. For instance, 72 per cent of all young people do not currently end up studying at university – with rates of participation strongly structured by social class (e.g. Archer *et al.* 2003). We also note that while young people in 2011 may be similarly ambitious to those surveyed in 1995, today's young people are less confident that they will achieve their goals, perhaps reflecting the uncertainties engendered by global recession (Archer *et al.* 2013).

Such findings lead us to argue that the key issue for equality and social mobility is not a 'poverty of aspirations', but rather the unequal means available to young people to realise these aspirations. As Croll (2008: 254) argues, 'The availability of jobs in higher socio-economic-status occupations is not going to keep up with the ambitions of the young people.' Referring to Brown and Hesketh's (2004) notion of market 'congestion', Croll shows how ambitious young people from less advantaged backgrounds are 'less likely to be educationally equipped to realise their ambitions' (2008: 255), and that young people's professional ambitions are often not borne out in reality.[4] Comparing ambitions at age 15 with later outcomes among the BHPS sample at age 20–15, Croll found that

> While 14.1% aspired to professional jobs at 15, only 5% of the BHPS sample had such jobs in the late 1990s. In contrast, while only 3.5% of young people aspired to partly or unskilled jobs at age 15, 22% of the adult sample were in these professions ten/15 years later.
>
> (Croll 2008: 255)

Indeed, both Croll (2008) and Yates et al. (2011) (in their analysis of Youth Cohort Study data) draw attention to the potentially negative outcomes for young people from disadvantaged backgrounds who aspire highly (e.g. to professional careers), but who lack the academic attainment and resources to achieve their ambitions.

In terms of the question, 'what do contemporary young people aspire to?', the ASPIRES project surveys indicate that the most popular occupational aspirations between ages 10–13 remain fairly constant, with the favourites being careers in the arts, sports, teaching and medicine (Archer 2012a). Business emerges as a very popular aspiration among students aged 12/13. Indeed, in a closed question asking which jobs (from a list) young people would like to do, business stands out as by far the most popular aspiration, with over 60 per cent of 12/13-year-old students agreeing that they would like to work in business in the future.[5] Yet, as discussed next, beneath these broad-brush trends, aspirations are also profoundly shaped by social class, ethnicity, gender and other social indices.

How are young people's aspirations formed? What influences aspirations?

As discussed in Archer et al. (2010), research indicates that aspirations are complex, multiple and often contradictory – young people may hold several aspirations at any one time, not all of which are complementary. Evidence points to a similarly complex range of influences on aspirations, including the family, schools, personal hobbies and interests, careers education and/or resources, television and the media, to name but a few. Given that ages 10–14 has been identified as a crucial time for the development of aspirations (e.g. Lindahl 2007; Tai et al. 2006), particular attention is given to research conducted with young people during this period.

For instance, Hutchinson et al. (2009) found that among students in early secondary school (key stage 3, KS3), the main sources of careers advice were: family (78 per cent of pupils), careers teachers (50 per cent), subject teachers (48 per cent), form teachers (23 per cent) and careers advisers (20 per cent).

Holman and Finegold (2010) also found that families and friends were the most trusted sources of careers advice among young people. Archer *et al.* (2013) note similar findings among 12/13-year-olds, with family providing the greatest influence on aspirations, followed by school, hobbies/interests and TV. While the exact nature and extent of the influences on aspirations may vary between individual studies, a common picture does emerge in which home and school appear to be major influences. These are discussed next.

How do families influence aspirations?

Archer *et al.* (2012) propose the notion of *family habitus* to explain how families (often unconsciously) shape children's aspirations. Drawing on the work of the sociologist Pierre Bourdieu (1986, 1990, 1992), Archer *et al.* apply his concept of (individual) habitus (e.g. Bourdieu and Passeron 1990) to the collective context of the family. Family habitus is defined as a framework of dispositions, developed through a family's sense of its collective identity, that guides action, shapes perceptions of choice and provides family members with a practical feel for the world (a sense of 'who we are, what we value and what we do'). In particular, we describe family habitus as interacting with capital (economic, social and cultural resources possessed by families), arguing that it is this interaction of family habitus and capital that shapes the sorts of aspiration that children come to see as desirable and possible (conceivable and achievable). In this way, young people develop a feel for particular aspirations as being more, or less, appropriate for 'people like me'. This is underpinned by the extent to which families are able to draw on and deploy capital to help children to gain an understanding of what their career might be and/or to help them to achieve their goals.

Family habitus and the nature and extent of capital that a family is able to draw on are profoundly socially structured (i.e. shaped by social inequalities). As the work of Lareau (2003) explains, family values and parenting practices can vary considerably between differently classed families, and working-class and middle-class families have access to notably different forms of capital. Middle-class families are much more likely to engage in the 'hothousing' of children through practices of 'concerted cultivation' (Lareau 2003), for example engaging in lots of extra-curricular activities and closely monitoring children's educational progress, to ensure 'success'.

Archer *et al.* (2013) found that children from middle-class families were more likely to aspire to become a doctor or a scientist than those from working-class backgrounds.[6] The study also found patterns in aspirations by ethnicity – children from minority ethnic backgrounds were more likely to aspire to work in medicine or in science than White children. For instance, in the survey of 12/13-year-olds, 60 per cent of Asian and 54 per cent of Black pupils aspired to work in medicine, compared to 30 per cent of White pupils.[7]

Gender also plays an important part (e.g. Francis 2000; Fuller 2009), with girls being much more likely to aspire to arts careers than boys. For instance, in the

ASPIRES survey, 64 per cent of 12/13-year-old girls and 27 per cent of 12/13-year-old boys aspire to careers in the arts. In comparison, boys are disproportionately likely to aspire to careers in engineering, with 45 per cent of boys but only 11 per cent of girls aspiring to engineering (Archer 2012b; see also OECD 2012a).

Previous research has found that children's aspirations tend to match parental expectations (Helwig 1998a). Simon *et al.* (2012) show how key adults (usually family members or other significant adults) are important influencers of the routes that young people take post-16. Archer *et al.* (2013) found an increasing use of family narratives over time, with 12/13-year-old students more likely to evoke taken-for-granted notions of particular occupations as 'something that we do in our family' as compared to 10/11-year-old students.

We interpret this process as the effect of the interplay between family habitus (collective dispositions) and capital (resources), through which children increasingly come to 'learn their place' (e.g. Bourdieu and Passeron 1990; Bourdieu 1990; Reay 2001; Archer and Yamashita 2003) seeing particular aspirations as 'right for me' and producing patterns of alignment between children's aspirations and parental class backgrounds. For instance, Archer *et al.* (2013) discuss Tom4 (an upper-middle-class British Pakistani boy), who described how his aspiration to study science at Oxbridge and then pursue a career in either medicine or business 'would be following [in] my family's footsteps' because his father is a medical consultant. Tom4's sense of 'what people like us do' is shaped by his family habitus and is also reinforced and facilitated by his family capital. For example, Tom4 recounts how his family are able to draw on economic, social and cultural resources to help him increase his chances of being successful in his aspirations. His family, for instance, can finance a range of extra-curricular activities, use their knowledge of the education and employment systems to strategise for Tom4's future and seek out additional opportunities to 'add value' to his developing CV, and draw on extensive social contacts in medicine and business to facilitate his progression.

Dorr and Lesser's (1980) review found that although children develop a more extensive and detailed knowledge about occupations as they grow older, earlier gendered and cultural stereotypes tend not to change over time. Subsequent recent research also indicates that boys may remain more gender stereotyped in their career choices than girls (Helwig 1998b; Francis 2000). Findings from the ASPIRES study (e.g. Archer *et al.* 2013; Archer *et al.* 2012) also underline how, by the age of 12/13, children are already sensitive to, and aligning themselves with, quite complex gendered, classed and racialised identities, which shape their aspirations by positioning particular jobs as more possible and/or desirable than others.

How do schools influence aspirations?

Bourdieu argues that the education system plays a key role in social reproduction (e.g. Bourdieu and Passeron 1990), shaping the image that people have of their own destinies (their perceived choices, what is seen as possible and/or desirable) and the resources (capital) available to help them achieve their goals. This influ-ence operates through the interaction of habitus, capital (resources) and the educational field (context). I shall now identify three specific examples of ways in which these processes play out to shape aspirations, in which alignment between home and school habitus can generate more positive outcomes for students from more privileged backgrounds.

First, particular aspirations may be inspired (or depressed) by interest gener-ated through school science classes. Evidence from the Wellcome Trust Monitor report (2013) shows that young people report further investigating particular scientific issues in their own time as a result of science lessons, for instance 60 per cent of young people who had looked for information on medical research said that this was related to something they were studying at school. The ASPIRES project also found that students' experiences of school science are related to science aspirations (DeWitt *et al.* 2014). The extent to which school science cur-rently adequately engages with and represents the issues of all students has been questioned, especially regarding girls and working-class students. Indeed, it is often argued that science needs to do more to increase its relevance and 'fit' with the identities, values, interests and experiences of a wider range of students.

Second, teachers can be positive or negative influences on young people's aspi-rations. Indeed, 'good' or 'bad' teachers are among the most commonly cited reasons given by young people for feeling encouraged or discouraged from learn-ing science (Clemence *et al.* 2012). Teachers can be influential significant adults who encourage particular aspirations by providing encouragement, motivation and information about particular careers (e.g. Simon *et al.* 2012). Teachers can also dissuade young people from seeing particular career routes as possible or realistic, often shaped by the extent to which they perceive particular groups of pupils as conforming or not to dominant constructions of the 'ideal student' (Archer 2008). There are numerous studies documenting teachers' generally lower expectations for particular groups (e.g. working-class and/or minority eth-nic pupils) and in relation to particular subject areas (e.g. lower expectations of girls taking science subjects; Carlone 2004). The following quotes from pupils from two different studies exemplify this:

> I said to Mr W [teacher] . . . And he goes 'oh Marilyn, so what do you want to do when you grow up?' And I said I wanted to be a lawyer and he just laughed and goes 'you?!' and I went 'yes' and he goes 'I don't think so'.
> (Marilyn, Black girl, cited in Archer *et al.* 2004)

> My teacher he goes if you get in there [elite university] he will dance round this hall in a woman's dress.
> (Analisa, Black African girl, cited in Archer *et al.* 2010)

Indeed, research indicates that these low expectations for minority ethnic stu-dents persist irrespective of social class – as noted by research conducted with minority ethnic middle-class professionals (see Archer 2010, 2011, 2012b). This is an issue that appears to still require urgent redress.

The problem of low teacher expectations for particular pupils appears to be an issue not just of individual teacher prejudice, but can be more systemic or cultural. For instance, analysis conducted by the Institute of Physics (2012) shows how the likelihood of girls taking A-level Physics is dramatically affected by whether they attend a mixed or single-sex school. In other words, institutional habitus interacts with pupil habitus to produce particular patterns of aspiration and participation.

Third, careers education can play a part in shaping young people's aspirations. Again, this influence can be positive or negative. For instance, Hutchinson *et al.* (2009) found that 20 per cent of young people reported that careers advisors had positively influenced their aspirations. Equally, young people in studies by Archer *et al.* (2003) and Archer *et al.* (2010) described being dissuaded from particular aspirations and/or generally frustrated by the ineffective or demoralising careers advice that they had received. However, it was notable in the ASPIRES project's research with KS3 students (12/13-year-olds) in 2011 that careers teachers were *not* mentioned by any of the 85 interviewees (indeed, careers resources in general were mentioned by only four pupils, perhaps due to careers education largely only being introduced in Year 9, at age 13/14). Holman and Finegold (2010) also found little evidence of traditional careers advice influencing the aspirations of young people.

There have been substantial changes in careers education provision in the United Kingdom over the last few years, with concerns being expressed by a range of educational and professional bodies and employers regarding the potentially negative impact of these changes (e.g. CaSE 2012; Careers England 2012; Morton 2012; House of Lords 2012). In particular, fears have been expressed about the quality and quantity of careers provision that will be available in schools (House of Lords 2012). For instance, Careers England found in their 2012 survey of 1,500 schools that less that 17 per cent of schools had managed to retain the level of Careers Education, Information, Advice and Guidance (CEIAG) they provided in 2011–2012.

The OECD (2012b) reports how high-performing countries usually have very good Information Advice and Guidance (IAG) provision, which is embedded in the school system. Yet the United Kingdom appears to be moving away from such a model, with its emphasis on a National Careers Service[8] and lack of integrated careers education in schools. This could constitute a particular problem for students with 'low' (or the 'wrong sort' of) capital because it seems to remove possibilities for the acquisition of careers knowledge, information and support. As discussed earlier, middle-class families are much more likely to already possess the cultural and social capital that can facilitate the generation and achievement of ambitions, particularly within the context of science (Archer *et al.* 2012).

Conclusion

The concept of 'aspiration' is integral to many policy and academic discussions about young people's educational engagement, attainment and post-16 futures. It features strongly within government education policy and is often evoked within employer engagement in education – yet it is not always used in a sufficiently critical manner. For instance, there appears to be little evidence to support widespread policy assumptions about a 'poverty of aspiration' causing inequalities in educational and occupational outcomes between different social groups. However, at the same time, there are clear inequalities in terms of the resources and 'capital' available to young people to help support their choices and decision-making. In this respect, employer engagement in education may have an important role to play.

One implication for educationalists and employers who wish to help support young people in their educational and occupational decision-making is to ensure that emphasis is placed on 'supporting and informing' (rather than 'raising') aspirations. The evidence discussed in this chapter also suggests that it would be beneficial to engage with families too, not just young people on their own, given that families are an important influence on young people's aspirations. For instance, employer engagement initiatives might look to work with families to help build social and cultural capital. Work with families might also help embed and reinforce messages being conveyed to young people through school and associated enrichment activities. The evidence discussed in this chapter also signals that there could be a clear benefit to be derived from starting careers awareness activities earlier – from primary through to early secondary years – given that this appears to be a formative time for young people's aspirations and yet is also a period when most receive little or no formal careers education or support. The importance for schools and employers to actively challenge unwitting stereotypical assumptions about particular groups of young people, and their aspirations, is also strongly underlined.

While it is true that young people's aspirations do not accurately predict their future career paths in any detailed way, I have argued in this chapter that aspirations can be useful tools and indicators for researchers, policymakers and practitioners who are interested in issues around employer engagement and progression.

Notes

1 http://oxforddictionaries.com/definition/english/aspiration [accessed 10 December 2012].
2 http://webarchive.nationalarchives.gov.uk/20130401151715/https://www.education.gov.uk/publications/eOrderingDownload/Aiming-High_Young-People.pdf [accessed 31 January 2014].
3 For instance, at the time of writing, the introductory web page of educational charity 'Young Enterprise' states 'We believe that developing strong aspirations is key to boosting

employability and entrepreneurship', www.young-enterprise.org.uk [accessed September 2012].

4 See also Yates *et al.*'s 2011 finding that overambitious adolescents who lack the means to realise their ambitions are more likely to become Not in Education, Training or Employment (NEET).

5 Business was a popular career aspiration across most groups of students – e.g. high proportions of boys and girls aspire to business and the class gap is less noticeable for business than other career areas, such as science (e.g. 56 per cent of students with very low cultural capital and 64 per cent of students with very high cultural capital agree that they would like to work in business). Black students seemed particularly interested, with 80 per cent Black students strongly/agreeing that they would like to work in business (compared to 68 per cent Asian and 59 per cent White students).

6 For example, 22 per cent of children with very low cultural capital strongly/agreed they would like to become a doctor compared to 45 per cent of children with very high cultural capital. Likewise, of those with very low cultural capital, only 8.8 per cent strongly/agreed they would like to become a scientist compared to 23.3 per cent of those with very high cultural capital.

7 These top-level ethnic descriptors are used here in the text for ease in conveying broad-brush patterns. But these top-level descriptors were generated from pupils' self-identifications with far more specific subcategories, e.g. Black included Black British, Black African, Black Caribbean and Black Other; 'Asian' included British Asian and a range of Indian subcontinent ethnic options, such as Indian, Pakistani and Bangladeshi. A range of 'mixed' ethnic identifiers were also used but are not reported here.

8 www.nationalcareersservice.direct.gov.uk/.

References

Archer, L. (2008). The impossibility of minority ethnic educational 'success'? An examination of the discourses of teachers and pupils in British secondary schools. *European Educational Research Journal*, 7 (1): 89–107.

Archer, L. (2010). 'We raised it with the Head': the educational practices of minority ethnic, middle-class families. *British Journal of Sociology of Education*, 31 (4): 449–469.

Archer, L. (2011). Constructing minority ethnic middle-class identity: an exploratory study with parents, pupils and young professionals. *Sociology*, 45 (1): 134–151.

Archer, L. (2012a). What shapes children's science and career aspirations age 10–13? London: King's College London.

Archer, L. (2012b). Between authenticity and pretension: parents', pupils' and young professionals' negotiations of minority ethnic middle-class identity. *Sociological Review*, 60 (1), 129–148.

Archer, L. and Yamashita, H. (2003). Knowing their limits? Identities, inequalities and inner-city school leavers' post-16 aspirations. *Journal of Education Policy*, 18 (1): 53–69.

Archer, L. and Francis, B. (2007). *Understanding minority ethnic achievement: race, gender, class and 'success'*. London: Routledge.

Archer, L., Hutchings, M. and Ross, A. (2003). *Higher education and social class*. London: RoutledgeFalmer.

Archer, L., Hutchings, M., Read, B. and Osgood, J. (2004). *An exploration of the attitudinal, social and cultural factors impacting on Year 10 student progression*. Final report to London West Learning and Skills Council. London: IPSE.

Archer, L., Hollingworth, S. and Mendick, H. (2010). *Urban youth and schooling.* Maidenhead, UK: Open University Press.

Archer, L., DeWitt, J., Osborne, J., Dillon, J., Willis, B. and Wong, B. (2012). Science aspirations and family habitus: how families shape children's engagement and identification with science. *American Educational Research Journal,* 49 (5): 881–908.

Archer, L., DeWitt, J. and Wong. W. (2013). Spheres of influence: what shapes young people's aspirations at age 12/13 and what are the implications for education policy? *Journal of Education Policy,* 29 (1): 1–28.

Attwood, G. and Croll, P. (2011). Attitudes to school and intentions for educational participation: an analysis of data from the Longitudinal Survey of Young People in England. *International Journal of Research and Method in Education,* 34 (3): 269–287.

Ball, S.J., Maguire, M. and Macrae, S. (2000). *Choice, pathways and transitions post-16.* London: RoutledgeFalmer.

Bourdieu, P. (1986). *Distinction: a social critique of the judgement of taste.* London: Routledge and Kegan Paul.

Bourdieu, P. (1990). *The logic of practice.* Stanford, CA: Stanford University Press.

Bourdieu, P. (1992). *Language and symbolic power.* Cambridge, UK: Polity Press.

Bourdieu, P. and Passeron, J. C. (1990). *Reproduction in education, society and culture.* London: Sage Publications.

Brannen, J. and Nilsen, A. (2007). Young people, time horizons and planning: a response to Anderson *et al. Sociology,* 41 (1), 153–160.

Brown, P. and Hesketh, A. (2004). *The mismanagement of talent – employability and jobs in the knowledge economy.* Oxford, UK: Oxford University Press.

Careers England. (2012). *School and careers guidance: a survey of the impact of the Education Act 2011.* London: Careers England. Available from: www.careersengland.org.uk/documents/public/CE%20school%20survey%20REPORT%2020.11.12%20for%20publication%200930%2021.11.12.pdf [accessed 10 December 2012].

Carlone, H. (2004). The cultural production of science in reform-based physics: girls' access, participation, and resistance. *Journal of Research in Science Teaching,* 41 (4): 392–414.

CaSE. (2012). *CaSE response to Lords Inquiry into higher education in STEM subjects.* Available from: http://sciencecampaign.org.uk/?p=10416 [accessed 5 October 2012].

Clemence, M., Gilby, N., Shah, J., Swiecicka, J. and Warren, D. (2012). *Wellcome Trust Monitor,* Wave 2. London: Wellcome Trust.

Croll, P. (2008). Occupational choice, socio-economic status and educational attainment: a study of the occupational choices and destinations of young people in the British Household Panel Survey. *Research Papers in Education,* 23: 243–268.

Croll, P., Attwood, G. and Fuller, C. (2009). *Children's lives, children's futures.* London: Continuum.

Department for Children, Schools and Families (DCSF). (2007). *The children's plan.* London: HMSO.

Department for Education (DfE). (2010). *The importance of teaching – the Schools White Paper 2010.* London: HMSO.

Department for Education and Skills (DfES). (2003). *Using the National Healthy School standard to raise boys' achievement.* Wetherby, UK: Health Development Agency.

Department for Education and Skills (DfES). (2004). *Schools race equality policies: from issues to outcomes.* London: HMSO.

Department for Education and Skills (DfES). (2005). *Higher standards, better schools for all – more choice for parents and pupils.* London: HMSO.

DeWitt, J., Osborne, J., Archer, L., Dillon, J., Willis, B. and Wong, B. (2011). Young children's aspiration in science: the unequivocal, the uncertain and the unthinkable. *International Journal of Science Education,* 35 (6): 1037– 1063.

DeWitt, J., Osborne, J. and Archer, L. (2014). Science-related aspirations across the primary–secondary divide: evidence from two surveys in England. Published online in *International Journal of Science Education,* www.tandfonline.com/doi/abs/10.1080/09500693.2013.871659#.UzltJNNOXTs [accessed 31 March 2014].

Dorr, A. and Lesser, G. S. (1980). Career awareness in young children. *Communication Research and Broadcasting,* 3: 36–75.

Francis, B. (2000). *Boys, girls and achievement: addressing the classroom issues.* Oxford, UK: Routledge.

Fuller, C. (2009). *Sociology, gender and educational aspirations: girls and their ambitions.* London: Continuum.

Gutman, L. M. and Schoon, I. (2012). Correlates and consequences of uncertainty in career aspirations: gender differences among adolescents in England. *Journal of Vocational Behavior,* 80 (3): 608–618.

Helwig, A. A. (1998a). Occupational aspirations of a longitudinal sample from second to sixth grade. *Journal of Career Development,* 24: 247–265.

Helwig, A. A. (1998b). Gender-role stereotyping: testing theory with a longitudinal sample. *Sex Roles, 38* (5–6): 403–423.

Holman, J. and Finegold, P. (2010). *STEM Careers Review.* London: Gatsby Charitable Foundation.

House of Lords. (2012). *Higher education in science, technology, engineering and mathematics (STEM) subjects.* London: HMSO.

Hutchinson, J., Stagg, P. and Bentley, K. (2009). *STEM careers awareness timelines. Attitudes and ambitions towards science, technology, engineering and maths (STEM at Key Stage 3).* Derby, UK: International Centre for Guidance Studies, University of Derby.

Institute of Physics. (2012). *It's different for girls: the influence of schools.* London: Institute of Physics.

Kintrea, K., St Clair R. and Houston, M. (2011). The influence of parents, places and poverty on educational attitudes and aspiration. Joseph Rowntree Foundation.

Lareau, A. (2003). *Unequal childhoods: class, race and family life.* Berkeley, CA: University of California Press.

Lindahl, B. (2007). *A longitudinal study of students' attitudes towards science and choice of career.* Paper presented at the 80th NARST International Conference. New Orleans, LA.

Morton, P. (2012). *Where next for STEM careers education, information, advice and guidance?* Sheffield, UK: Sheffield Hallam University.

Murphy, J. (2012). It's sink or swim, says PM as he promises an 'aspiration nation'. *London Evening Standard,* 10 October 2012.

Organisation for Economic Co-operation and Development (OECD). (2012a). *Education at a glance.* Paris: OECD.

Organisation for Economic Co-operation and Development (OECD). (2012b). *PISA in focus 18: are students more engaged when schools offer extracurricular activities?* Paris: OECD.

Reay, D. (2001). Finding or losing yourself? Working-class relationships to education. *Journal of Education Policy*, 16 (4): 333–346.

Roberts, K. and Atherton, G. (2011). Career development among young people in Britain today: poverty of aspiration or poverty of opportunity? *International Journal of Educational Administration and Policy Studies*, 3 (5): 59–67.

Schneider, B. and Stevenson, D. (1999). *The ambitious generation*. Yale, CT: Yale University Press.

Schoon, I. (2001). Teenage job aspirations and career attainment in adulthood: a 17-year follow-up study of teenagers who aspired to become scientists, health professionals, or engineers. *International Journal of Behavioral Development*, 25 (2): 124–132.

Simon, S., Hoyles, C., Mujtaba, T., Farzad, B. R., Reiss, M., Rodd, M. and Stylianidou, F. (2012). *Understanding Participation rates in post-16 Mathematics and Physics (UPMAP)*. Paper presented at AERA, Vancouver.

Strand, S. and Winston, J. (2008). Educational aspirations in inner-city schools. *Educational Studies*, 34 (4): 249–267.

Tai, R. H., Qi Liu, C., Maltese, A. V. and Fan, X. (2006). Planning early for careers in science. *Science*, 312: 1143–1145.

Thomas, E. (2001). *Widening participation in post-compulsory education*. London: Continuum.

Trice, A. D. (1991a). A retrospective study of career development: relationship among first aspirations, parental occupations, and current occupations. *Psychological Reports*, 68: 287–290.

Trice, A. D. (1991b). Stability of children's career aspirations. *Journal of Genetic Psychology*, 152: 137–139.

Trice, A. D. and McClellan, N. (1993). Do children's career aspirations predict adult occupations? An answer from a secondary analysis of a longitudinal study. *Psychological Reports*, 72: 368–370.

Wellcome Trust Monitor Report, Wave 2. (2013). *Tracking public views on science, research and science education*. London: Wellcome Trust.

Yates, S., Harris, A., Sabates, R. and Staff, J. (2011). Early occupational aspirations and NEETs: a study of the impact of uncertain and misaligned aspirations and social background on young people's entry into NEET status. *Journal of Social Policy*, 40: 513–534.

Chapter 2

A theoretical framework for employer engagement

Julian Stanley and Anthony Mann

This chapter considers the engagement of members of economic communities in the educational experiences of young people and how this engagement can be conceptualised as an influence upon life course. In doing so, it draws on theories of three interrelated concepts – human, social and cultural capital – with a view to developing a theoretical framework that can comprehend accounts of how employer engagement is experienced and how it provides resources that aid progression into the labour market. The chapter examines theories of human, social and cultural capital and explores their applicability to employer engagement. It then offers a case study of work experience to show how the US and UK research can be understood in terms of the proposed framework.

Defining the problem

Employer engagement in formal educational activities takes a variety of forms. For example, there may be contributions to teaching and learning activities in educational institutions, work-based training, staff development, governance and funding. Our focus in this chapter is upon the direct involvement of employers in the education of young people participating in the primary and secondary phases of schooling. This kind of employer engagement has been particularly prominent in England since the 1980s, in particular, work experience for 14–16-year-olds but also employer involvement in enterprise education, careers education, mentoring, reading and numeracy support, curriculum-linked classroom presentations, workplace visits etc.[1] Employer engagement has been promoted by governments and by a succession of educational charities as an intervention that can improve educational and employment outcomes for some, or even all, young people (for example, Education and Employers Taskforce 2010).

Over the last 30 years there have been many separate initiatives in the United Kingdom, including single company initiatives (such as the BP and NatWest education programmes), sectoral initiatives (e.g. coordinated by the Royal Academy of Engineering) and local and national programmes. Initiatives and programmes have come and gone. Broker, advocacy and provider organisations have also come and gone (for example, Trident), although some local and national organisations have survived for many years, for example Business in the Community, Young Enterprise and, until recently, local education–business partnerships. Since the 1970s, a series of government statements, curriculum documents and guidance documents has defined and redefined which kinds of interactions between schools and employers were desirable, what they were intended to achieve and how they should be organised. In the 2000s, for example, employer engagement was formally articulated in terms of the statutory curriculum requirements for work-related learning for 14–16-year-olds (QCA 2003) and in a series of guidance documents culminating in QCA's *Economic Wellbeing 11–19: career, work-related learning and enterprise* (QCA 2008). However, in 2011 Michael Gove, Secretary of State for Education, accepted the recommendation of the 2011 Wolf Review that the statutory entitlement for work-related learning for 14–16-year-olds be withdrawn in place of a more systematic engagement of employers in educational provision for young people aged 16–19.

Research into particular initiatives and activities has generally taken the form of one-by-one evaluations of impact. The scope of such research is, understandably, limited to the particular programme under evaluation. Reviews of such evaluations have been concerned to examine the rigour of the methodologies employed but have also suggested that these evaluations often lack a theoretical understanding of how employer interventions are supposed to lead to educational and labour market outcomes (AIR UK 2008). In this chapter, we seek to address this deficiency. The chapter draws upon theories commonly used to explain how education and social relationships affect educational progression, transition and social mobility, with a view to constructing a theoretical framework that can encompass all employer interventions.

Educational achievement, social mobility and life course analysis

Theoretical and empirical studies routinely conceptualise education as a sequence of experiences, decisions and outcomes that are differentiated in terms of social groups. What young people learn, what they aspire to, what they choose to do and how they behave and achieve are explained by the social groups that they belong to, their current social relationships, the character and quality of their educational experiences and (residual) individual differences. Life course analysis conceptualises this process as a chain of succeeding outcomes, each outcome bearing upon those that succeed (Pallas 2003; Elder 1998). As Evans *et al.* put it: 'Any point in the life span has to be understood as the consequence of past experience and as the launch pad for subsequent experiences and conditions' (2010: 38). Put concretely, the achievement, aspirations and learning behaviour of an English pupil at key stage 3 are, in part, outcomes of their experience at key stage 2, and will become factors that influence educational and social outcomes at key stage 4 (Gorard *et al.* 2006).

In this chapter, we treat employer engagement as a distinctive kind of intervention into a complex, ongoing social process. We want to understand how employer interventions can interfere with or complement existing processes and what kinds of contribution they make.

Theoretical tools

The concepts of human, social and cultural capital are a family of concepts that can be used to understand the effects of employer engagement. In this chapter, we will explore how they are being used singly; however, we also intend to look at how they can be used jointly. Some shared characteristics of the concepts are as follows:

1   All of the concepts provide a theoretical account of how acquired capabilities or relationships work over time to the advantage of groups or individuals. In other words, the capabilities or relationships are analysed as a resource that can have a material impact upon the life chances of young people. This approach is consistent with the life course approach to education, which sees outcomes of earlier phases of education as acting upon later phases.
2   The deployment of each of the concepts is associated with a move towards more complex and less reductive social science, for example, including a social dimension within economics (Granovetter 1973) or resisting over-socialised (Coleman 1988) or over-rationalised (Bourdieu 1994) accounts of human agency.

How then might employer interventions, which are designed to increase capital and distribute it more fairly, impact upon educational processes? We can distinguish three ways: supplementary, complementary and alternative.

Supplementary

Employer interventions are *supplementary* when they are intended to directly support the conventional teaching and learning processes that are deployed to achieve established learning outcomes as recognised by qualifications. For example, reading support programmes, where employer volunteers listen to pupils reading, aim to supplement the conventional processes of classroom learning.[2]

Complementary

Employer interventions are *complementary* when they offer alternative processes that are intended to achieve established learning outcomes as recognised by qualifications. Mentoring programmes can work in this way (Hall 2003). For example, Miller (1998) found that employee mentors helped pupils to improve attainment.

Additional

Employer interventions are *additional* when they are intended to achieve learning outcomes in addition to conventional learning outcomes as recognised by qualifications. Interventions that aim to develop employability skills or entrepreneurial capability are examples of this additionally. Although these kinds of outcomes are not usually recognised by qualifications, they may nevertheless be of value to young people, employers or policymakers.

Human capital

In Gary Becker's seminal account, human capital means the increase in labour productivity that arises through education or training (Becker 1993). Becker's initial analysis focused on work-based training and provided an analysis of training in competitive labour markets; however, economists have followed Becker in conceptualising the economic value of education as an investment that increases labour productivity. Human capital can be denominated in terms of the competences or 'learning outcomes' of those emerging from educational and training processes, i.e. what they are able to contribute to the production of goods and services in employment (Cedefop 2009). Qualifications are usually taken as an index of these competences, although there is recognition that they are an imperfect proxy (OECD 2007). Workplace experience – duration and level of employment – is another indicator of the level of work-relevant skills developed by an individual. For organisations like the Organisation for Economic Co-operation and Development (OECD) or the European Union (EU), one main purpose of education is to increase the stock of human capital in order to add to competitiveness and growth. Another is to distribute human capital fairly – to give all learners the opportunity to maximise their own human capital (European Union 2004).

It is useful to define the limits of what is meant by human capital. In general, human capital refers to outcomes from education and training which have an economic value in work. It is not necessary that these outcomes be recognised by qualifications, though in principle it would be expected that there was some way of recognising them because they are expected to have a market value. Outcomes from education or training that do not have economic value, for example, knowledge resulting from 'liberal arts' programmes, would not contribute to human capital unless they are somehow transferable to work situations. Human capital is usually conceptualised as an attribute of individuals rather than groups, even though human capital could include capabilities to work with others, e.g. team-working or leadership skills.

Social capital

The concept of social capital is more contested than that of human capital. Theories of social capital focus on the way that social relationships can provide a resource to an individual or a group, which will enable them to achieve their goals. According to Bourdieu and Wacquant, for example, social capital represents the 'the sum of the resources, actual or virtual, that accrue to an individual or a group by virtue of possessing a durable network of more or less institutionalized relationships of mutual acquaintance and recognition' (1991: 119). Bourdieu seeks to show that social, financial and cultural capital combine to reproduce social, economic and political inequality. Coleman, Putnam and Halpern are particularly interested in social capital as a property of groups (Halpern 2005; Coleman 1988; Putnam 2000). They are concerned with the way that social relationships influence interactions within groups and between groups. Granovetter (1973) and Portes (1998) focus on the way in which social relationships function as resources that afford or constrain the ability of individuals to achieve their goals. Granovetter's research into the way that different kinds of social network can help individuals to gain employment showed that an extensive but loose network ('weak ties') can be of greater value to an individual than an intensive and exclusive network.

Portes distinguishes between the recipients of social capital (those individuals whose resources are somehow enhanced), the donors (those who provide resources) and the character and usefulness of the resources themselves (what difference the additional resources make) (Portes 1998). Most theorists of social capital draw attention to the way that norms and sanctions, as well as the character of social networks, influence the character and impact of social capital (Halpern 2005).

Social capital theory and research suggests that:

1   economic (e.g. getting a job) and educational outcomes (e.g. completing school) can be partly explained by the operation of social relationships;
2   the character of the social capital (types of networks, norms, sanctions) will shape their effects; and
3   social capital can, at least to some degree, be intentionally influenced by interventions (Halpern 2005).

Theorising about social capital helps us to make analytical distinctions about the way that social and economic factors combine to constrain and afford individual actions. Coleman's important paper, 'Social capital in the creation of human capital', was intended to introduce 'social structure into the rational action paradigm' (Coleman 1988: 95). For Bourdieu, social, cultural and financial capitals are to some degree fungible; that is, they can be converted into one another. However, for Bourdieu, distinctions between different kinds of capital can be made and are significant. Cultural distinctions, for example, may serve to legitimise distributions of advantage and opportunity (Bourdieu and Passeron 1977; Lareau 2003).

Cultural capital

Culture, understood as the shared knowledge, norms and attitudes that influence individual behaviour, is a long-standing sociological concept. Indeed, from the beginnings of sociology, culture was seen as both a key determinant and an outcome of education (Lukes 1972). Bourdieu's concept of cultural capital supercharges the concept of culture by:

1   integrating the analysis of culture within a sophisticated account of social relations, social action and institutions;
2   distinguishing the distinctive role that culture plays, which cannot be reduced to economic, social or intellectual relations; and
3   differentiating three kinds of cultural capital:

    a   embodied or personal culture, e.g. capabilities or 'habitus'
    b   objectified or material culture, e.g. books and tools
    c   institutionalised or symbolic culture, e.g. qualifications.

Bourdieu's innovative concept of habitus has been very influential on the sociology of education. For example, Archer et al. (2010), in considering the educational experiences of disadvantaged young Londoners, use the term habitus to describe 'the taken-for-granted knowledge and ability to understand and navigate the education system that characterises many middle-class families' engagement with education' and as the 'the taken-for-granted knowledge of "how things work" and an instinctive feel for the unspoken "rules of the game"' (Archer et al. 2010: 31, 52).

Bourdieu's sociology has fed into a 'cultural turn' that has moved away from a reliance on the explanatory power of social structures and has sought to do justice to what appears to be a greater diversity of social groups and social outcomes (Reay et al. 2005; Hodkinson and Bloomer 2000). Social scientists, influenced by Bourdieu, emphasise the importance of socially inherited and unconsciously acquired attitudes and dispositions to explain the differential behaviour and outcomes of different social groups. Recently, there has been a greater emphasis on a diverse repertoire of habitus, relating to gender, ethnicity, language, geography and other groupings (for example, Archer and Francis 2007).

If we turn from social research towards policy, we find interventions that seek to change behaviour and affect outcomes by acting upon attitudes, habits and expectations. In the context of this discussion, we can interpret this as an attempt to shape the underlying dispositions of targeted individuals or groups that is their habitus. A well-documented example would be the Aim Higher policy in England, which sought to develop the expectations of young people from disadvantaged backgrounds with respect to higher education. The evaluation showed that, through a programme of experiences, visits and encounters, the expectations of targeted groups were enhanced (NFER 2009). In a similar fashion, the UK

Government's 2011 Social Mobility Strategy places an onus on head teachers to provide young people with access to first-hand information from employers, as well as higher education, to allow effective progression (Cabinet Office 2011). Another example would be Enterprise Insight's campaign around entrepreneurship, which sought to inspire young people to fulfil their ambitions by becoming entrepreneurs (Botham and Sutherland 2009).

How can cultural capital help us to conceptualise employer engagement? Does cultural capital offer any distinctive process over and beyond the contributions of human and social capital? It is not easy to disentangle cultural from social factors; however, research suggests that employer engagement can have a distinctively cultural impact:

- Bourdieu's conceptualisation of habitus suggests that dispositions and attitudes are learned unconsciously, side by side with action in distinctive social situations or 'fields' (Hodkinson *et al.* 2007b). Following this approach, employer engagement, for example work experience, provides an opportunity for young people to participate in practices with employees through whom they can develop new attitudes and dispositions. In other words, the 'field' of work experience supplements other learning 'fields', such as the classroom. Similarly, Stern and Briggs (2001) found that the experience of part-time work can change the attitudes of young people towards their schooling.
- Alternatively, engagement by employees and employers may offer young people an alternative source of cultural norms and judgements rather than an additional field. Some young people may be ready to take on the aspirations and norms of employers or volunteer employees, particularly if they enter into rewarding social relationships with them. Mentoring by employees is one way in which young people might be offered access to norms and expectations that are different from their own. Research suggests that the motivation and aspirations of young people can be raised by this kind of mentoring (Miller *et al.* 2011; Green and Rogers 1997).

Bourdieu's theory of cultural capital continues to provoke debate, and many have not taken on all of what Stephen Ball calls Bourdieu's 'conceptual paraphernalia' (Ball 2003: 8), but have been influenced by his insistence that agents learn from others by living and working alongside them; that is, by participating in social practice. In other words, the development and persistence of dispositions and attitudes can facilitate or constrain social and individual development – the development of social and human capital. We find the same basic insight in the school of sociologists who have been influenced by the work of Lave and Wenger who, using different theoretical terms, placed a similar emphasis on social and cultural factors in work-based learning (Lave and Wenger 1991), which has had considerable influence upon subsequent research, particularly with respect to apprenticeships (Fuller and Unwin 2003).

Towards the development of a framework

Figure 2.1 sets out a schematic model to show how employer interventions can intervene upon a range of other 'environmental' factors to shape the social, cultural and human capital of young people. Human, social and cultural capitals have been decomposed into more specific outcomes for young people, such as qualifications and aspirations. Such outcomes can be defined or 'operationalised' for the purposes of research and, to varying degrees, measured. The following outcomes are indicative rather than definitive. A different research or policy focus would generate a different list of outcomes. It is not proposed that each outcome can be classified as being just one kind of capital, though it is suggested that any one outcome may be more closely associated with one form of capital rather than another.

Reading the diagram from left to right, the model highlights the way that, at any stage of education, the acquisition of human, social and cultural capital will be affected by prior accumulation. For example, whether a young person decides to aim for a high status post-16 education or training programme, and their prospects for getting access to it, will depend upon the levels of human, social and cultural capital they have accumulated during key stage 4 and upon environmental

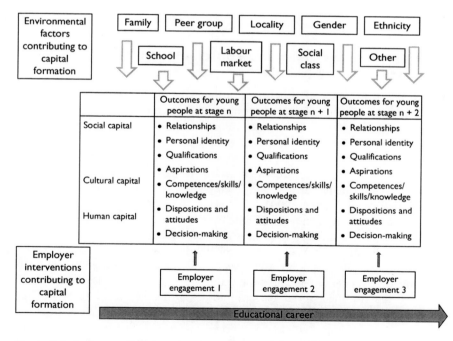

Figure 2.1 A framework for the outcomes from employer interventions over educational career.

factors, such as the character of the careers education and advice they receive and, potentially, upon a succession of employer interventions.

In this model, features of society and the economy that shape the decisions, beliefs and actions of young people as they progress from education into the labour market are conceptualised as environmental factors. These environmental factors may well differ from country to country. The model leaves it open to comparative research to discover whether, as is sometimes argued, there are different 'transition systems', in other words different 'relatively enduring features of a country's institutional and structural arrangements which shape transition processes and outcomes' (Raffe 2008: 278).

The model aims to represent employer engagement as one of a large number of factors that can influence young people as they traverse their life course. In practice, these factors are likely to combine and interact, and therefore, for example, the experience of work experience may be gendered and classed (Hatcher and Le Gallais 2008). These complexes of factors shape the decisions and behaviour of groups and individuals at any point in time but also over time. However, the model would be incomplete without an account of agency; that is, how personality, reflection and decision-making affect outcomes (Archer 2003). Evans *et al.* write of 'actors as having a past and imagined future possibilities, which guide and shape actions in the present, together with subjective perceptions of the structures they have to negotiate, the social landscapes which affect how they act' (2010: 31).

Employer engagement and equity: differential impacts on young people

The conceptual framework proposed in this chapter suggests that the impact of employer engagement will depend on both how much social, cultural and social capital young people have already accumulated and upon environmental factors, for example their families and schools, and institutional features of the labour market. The distribution and exercise of social capital, cultural capital and human capital has been shown to support or retard the goals and interests of various groups and individuals (Strand and Winston 2008; Hodkinson *et al.* 2007a; Reay *et al.* 2005; Ball *et al.* 2000).

It follows that the operation of employer engagement across society could serve to advance the interests of some groups or individuals, leaving other groups or individuals (unintentionally) relatively disadvantaged. This is a matter for empirical investigation. US literature offers evidence to suggest employer interventions are experienced in different ways – children from advantaged backgrounds, due to their social backgrounds, have easier access to school-age workplace exposures and economically relevant social networks, so that social and economically advantaged children are more likely to benefit from such interventions than their disadvantaged peers (Erickson *et al.* 2009; Aschbascher *et al.* 2010). Disadvantaged pupils who do participate in such interventions, however, can expect to secure relatively greater benefit from school-mediated exposures because their pre-existing knowledge and knowledge are comparatively limited (Erickson *et al.* 2009; Packard *et al.* 2009).

This hypothesis has been endorsed by a number of quantitative studies. The 2008 review of the wage premiums of the US Career Academies alumni, for example, found that the quartile with characteristics suggesting highest likelihood of drop-out as teenagers secured premiums of 17 per cent against the control group – significantly higher than the cohort norm at 11 per cent (Kemple and Wilner 2008). Neumark and Rothstein (2005) have also shown that employment and education outcomes from school-to-work transition initiatives were associated with young people whose teenage characteristics suggest that they were unlikely to attend college.

While data is lacking in the United Kingdom, there is some evidence that poor access to social networks, little or low quality careers advice and lack of cultural knowledge of education disadvantages some social groups. Recent analysis of the British Cohort Study by Scott Yates and colleagues has shown that teenagers with low socio-economic status (SES) backgrounds are almost twice as likely as those with high SES backgrounds to be uncertain about career aspirations at 16 (10 per cent versus 6 per cent) or to have career aspirations that are misaligned with qualification expectations (52 per cent versus 28 per cent) (Yates *et al.* 2010). Large surveys of young people who are Not in Education, Employment or Training (NEET) and their parents found decision-making about progression at 16 to be particularly difficult, with youngsters having significantly fewer sources of individual advice (only 51 per cent have three or more compared to 71 per cent of peers who remained in full-time education post-16). Two-thirds of the parents of young people who are NEET feel that they don't know enough about the education system to give good advice (Blenkinsop *et al.* 2006).

Case study: work experience placements

In this section, we seek to apply the general framework proposed earlier to one example of employer engagement: work experience. This will show how the framework helps to organise and comprehend the research on this topic. Since the late 1980s, it has been a feature of the British educational experience for young people, typically at the age of 15, to undertake a short work experience placement of up to two weeks duration. As reported by Mann and Kashefpakdel in this collection (see Chapter 9), survey data suggests some 90 per cent of British teenagers have commonly undertaken placements, with three-quarters being undertaken between the ages of 14 and 16.

Reviewing selected research into work experience allows us to assess:

1   the extent to which researchers found evidence of human, social and cultural capital enhancement resulting from work experience placements; and
2   whether preceding accumulations of these resources influence individual experiences of work experience placements.

Work experience and human capital development

OECD analysts have highlighted research demonstrating enhanced school-to-work transitions being related to teenage experience of paid part-time work or to vocationally focused learning programmes, including significant workplace exposure on the apprenticeship model (OECD 2010). Whereas it would be surprising to expect teenage work experience placements to secure significant technical or vocational skills over a typical two-week placement at age 15, surveys of teenagers on their return from work experience commonly attest to the value of placements in developing general employability skills (CBI 2007; National Support Group for Work Experience 2008). Table 2.1 sets out findings from a 2008 survey of the views of 15,025 British teenagers on their return from work experience.

Social capital

Work experience contributes to the formation of social capital as well as human capital. A survey of 203 UK employers who had taken part in a campaign week focused on closer working with schools (Education and Employers Taskforce, unpublished) found that 82 per cent of respondents who provided both work experience placements and paid employment to teenagers had offered paid work to someone who had previously been on a placement. Asked whether it mattered if the work experience placement had been at their own place of work or not, a majority said that it did and less than 25 per cent said that it was irrelevant. These findings can be explained by postulating that work experience supports transition into employment in two ways: it helps to develop 'employability' skills and it also gives young people a chance to form relationships with potential employers that support recruitment. In other words, employers use work

Table 2.1 Pupil perceptions of work experience following their placement (values in per cent)

As a result of my work experience...	Strongly agree	Agree	Disagree	Strongly disagree
I was able to show my initiative in a workplace	45	48	6	1
I have developed some new skills that employers value (e.g. customer awareness and use of IT)	42	45	10	2
I have developed my spoken communication skills (e.g. talking to adults)	51	42	6	2
I know that I can work well with a team of adults	54	41	4	1

Source: National Support Group for Work Experience (2008).

experience as a probationary process to select potential recruits. Other surveys confirm that work experience is, for at least some participants, connected to entry into employment.

For example, an unpublished 2011 Education and Employers Taskforce survey of 40 learners aged 16–19 in Cumbria found that 23 per cent were offered paid employment after their placement and that a further 20 per cent had discussed the prospect of possible employment at some future date. The same survey found that some young people often stay in touch with the employers who gave them work experience for months or years after their placement, which suggests that its social value may be relatively enduring. This is consistent with findings from a Department for Education and Skills-commissioned survey, which found that 40 per cent of respondents thought that they might get a job in the same place as where they did their placement at some point in the future (Hillage *et al.* 2001).

Cultural capital

A number of studies have explored whether young people return from work experience placements with changed attitudes and dispositions, or in other words with a changed habitus. Research, reported in Table 2.2, found that around 90 per cent of work experience participants reported that work experience had helped them to understand the importance of success at school and that they were, as a consequence, ready to work harder at school (National Support Group for Work Experience 2008).

A 2012 survey (see Mann 2012) of teaching staff undertaken by the National Foundation for Educational Research (NFER) on behalf of the Education and Employers Taskforce approached the same question from the perspective of teaching staff. Based on survey responses from more than 700 teachers with experience of teaching at key stages four and five, nearly two-thirds agreed that young people returned from work experience placements better motivated to do well at school (see Figure 2.2). The results are in keeping with a previous survey,

Table 2.2 Pupil perceptions of education following work experience placements. Survey of 15,025 young people aged 15–16 (values in per cent, rounded)

I understand better why I have to do well at school	Strongly agree	50
	Agree	40
	Disagree	7
	Strongly disagree	2
I am more prepared to work hard in lessons and coursework	Strongly agree	42
	Agree	47
	Disagree	9
	Strongly disagree	2

Source: National Support Group for Work Experience (2008).

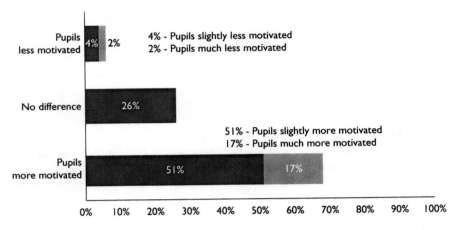

Figure 2.2 Teacher perceptions of the impact of work experience placements on pupil motivation.

Source: National Foundation for Educational Research for Education and Employers Task-force (Mann 2012).

which found that 66 per cent of work experience coordinators agreed that work experience served to motivate students to work hard in school (Mann 2012).

Of course, these are attitudinal surveys rather than objective measures of student behaviour, and it is arguable that work experience coordinators in particular may not be entirely impartial about the benefits of work experience. However, the surveys demonstrate a widespread perception that work experience encourages young people to work harder at school because it makes them appreciate the economic value of school success. This is a causal connection that was difficult to test when almost every student in England undertook work experience; however, in the future it will be easier to test because universal work experience for 14–16-year-olds has been ended.

Do preceding levels of human, cultural and social capital development influence experiences of work experience placements?

Two chapters in this collection explore the ways in which prior accumulation of social capital shape access to work experience placements. Le Gallais and Hatcher (Chapter 12) show that middle-class families use their social networks to access work placements in professionally related organisations. Huddleston, Mann and Dawkins (Chapter 10) show how high-performing fee-paying schools develop and exploit social networks linked to alumni, parents and governors to generate relevant and valuable work placements for their pupils. Francis *et al.*

(2005) have looked at how gender stereotyping has influenced the placements undertaken by young people. They conclude that gender stereotypes do influence selection of placements, with the result that very few young people undertake placements in non-traditional occupational areas in spite of many being open to the idea. Interestingly, they also argue that if non-traditional work placements are experienced, then they can challenge norms associated with gender (Francis *et al.* 2005).

Conclusion

In this chapter, we have sought to provide a theoretical framework that can inform research and evaluation into employer engagement. We have sought to synthesise a variety of well-established theories in order to (1) build a conceptual framework that is broad enough to do justice to the range of employer engagement practised and (2) take account of theoretical approaches which are commonly found in research and evaluation in this domain.

The framework incorporates the concepts of human, social and cultural capital, as well as that of life course, and it factors in the influence of gender, SES and ethnicity. The framework allows for, although it does not imply, the further concept of a transition system, in other words an enduring and coherent set of institutions that structure the route from education into employment. We have reviewed selected recent research into work experience and shown how it fits with the framework that we have described.

We believe that the framework is useful in three main ways:

1 The framework reveals connections between independent research into employer engagement, such as that collected in this volume. The framework helps us to recognise shared strategies for explanation and understanding and to identify gaps. It also suggests ways of synthesising findings to build a bigger picture.

2 The framework can inform future research by offering theoretical tools that in turn suggest particular methods and research questions. For example, our framework highlights the work that individual 'agency' has to perform, which suggests that biographical or narrative studies of young people who experience employer engagements will be of value to understand impact upon decision-making.

3 Last, combining concepts from different research traditions and trying to apply them in the field of employer engagement raises a number of problems. To what extent, for example, can we distinguish between social and cultural capital? How can we measure the accumulation of social or cultural capital as it arises from work experience or careers education? These problems demand the clarification and operationalisation of concepts and their further development in empirical research projects. In this way, theoretical challenges can help to shape future research in the field of employer engagement.

Notes

1 For a recent overview see Huddleston and Stanley 2012.
2 See, for example, the Volunteer Reading Help scheme: www.vrh.org.uk/.

References

AIR UK. (2008). *The involvement of business in education: a rapid evidence assessment of measurable impacts.* London: Department for Children, Families and Schools.

Archer, L. and Francis, B. (2007). *Understanding minority ethnic achievement.* Abingdon, UK: Routledge.

Archer, M. (2003). *Structure, agency and the internal conversation.* Cambridge, UK: Cambridge University Press.

Archer, L., Hollingworth, S. and Mendick, H. (2010). *Urban youth and schooling.* Maidenhead, UK: Open University Press.

Aschbacher, P. R., Li, E. and Roth, E. J. (2010). Is science me? High school participation and aspirations in science, engineering and medicine. *Journal of Research in Science Teaching*, 47: 564–582.

Ball, S. J. (2003). *Class strategies and the education market.* London: RoutledgeFalmer.

Ball, S. J., Maguire, M. and Macrae, S. (2000). *Choice, pathways and transitions post-16. New youth, new economies in the global city.* London: RoutledgeFalmer.

Becker, G. S. (1993). *Human capital: a theoretical and empirical analysis, with special reference to education.* Chicago, IL: University of Chicago Press.

Blenkinsop, S., McCrone, T., Wade, P. and Morris, M. (2006). *How do young people make choices at 14 and 16?* London: Department for Education and Skills.

Botham, R. and Sutherland, V. (2009). *Enterprise Insight impact evaluation: the hubs.* Available from: www.strath.ac.uk/media/departments/huntercentre/research/researchreports/E._I._Impact_Evaluation_Report_-_The_Hubs.pdf [accessed 3 February 2014].

Bourdieu, P. (1994). *Practical reason.* Cambridge, UK: Polity Press.

Bourdieu, P. and Passeron, J. (1977). *Reproduction.* London: Sage Publications.

Bourdieu, P. and Wacquant, L. (1991). *An invitation to reflexive sociology.* Chicago, IL: University of Chicago Press and Polity Press.

Cabinet Office. (2011). *Opening doors, breaking barriers; a strategy for social mobility.* Available from: www.gov.uk/government/publications/opening-doors-breaking-barriers-a-strategy-for-social-mobility [accessed 3 February 2014].

Cedefop. (2009). *The shift to learning outcomes.* Luxembourg: Office for the Official Publications of the European Communities.

Coleman, J. (1988). Social capital in the creation of human capital. *American Journal of Sociology*, 94: 95–120.

Confederation of British Industry (CBI). (2007). *Time well spent.* London: Department for Education and Skills.

Education and Employers Taskforce. Unpublished. *Evaluation: 2010 Visit our schools and colleges week.*

Education and Employers Taskforce. (2010). *What is to be gained through partnership?* Available from: www.educationandemployers.org/ [accessed 3 February 2014].

Elder, G. H. (1998). The life course as developmental theory. *Child Development*, 69: 1–12.

Erickson, L. D., McDonald, S. and Elder, G. H. Jr. (2009). Informal mentors and education: complementary or compensatory resources. *Sociology of Education*, 82: 344–367.

European Union. (2004). *Maastricht communiqué on the future priorities of enhanced European co-operation in vocational education and training: a review of the Copenhagen declaration of 30 November 2002*. Brussels.

Evans, K., Schoon, I. and Weale, M. (2010). *Life chances, learning and the dynamics of risk throughout the life course*. London: LLAKES, Insitute of Education, University of London.

Francis, B., Osgood, J., Dalgety, J. and Archer, L. (2005). *Gender equality in work experience placements for young people*. Report for Equal Opportunities Commission (EOC) in collaboration with JIVE and DfES, Equal Opportunities Commission.

Fuller, A. and Unwin, L. (2003). Learning as apprentices in the contemporary UK workplace: creating and managing expansive and restrictive participation. *Journal of Education and Work*, 16: 407–426.

Gorard, S., Smith, A., May, H., Thomas, L., Adnett, N. and Slack, K. (2006). *Review of widening participation research: addressing the barriers to participation in higher education*. Bristol: HEFCE.

Granovetter, M. (1973). The strength of weak ties. *American Journal of Sociology*, 78: 1360–1380.

Green, J. and Rogers, B. (1997). Roots and wings community mentoring: an evaluation from the Manchester pilot. *Mentoring & Tutoring: Partnership in Learning*, 5: 26–38.

Hall, J. (2003). *Mentoring and young people*. Glasgow: Scottish Council for Research in Education.

Halpern, D. (2005). *Social capital*. Cambridge, UK: Polity Press.

Hatcher, R. and Le Gallais, T. (2008). *The work experience placements of secondary school students: widening horizons or reproducing social inequality?* Birmingham, UK: Birmingham City University.

Hillage, J., Honey, S. and Pike, G. (2001). *Pre-16 work experience practice in England: an evaluation*. London: Department for Education and Employment.

Hodkinson, P. and Bloomer, M. (2000). Stokingham Sixth Form College: institutional culture and dispositions to learning. *British Journal of Sociology of Education*, 21: 187–202.

Hodkinson, P., Anderson, G., Colley, H., Davies, J., Diment, K., Scaife, T., Tedder, M., Whalberg, M. and Wheeler, E. (2007a). Learning cultures in further education. *Educational Review – Special Issue*, 59: 399–413.

Hodkinson, P., Biesta, G. and James, D. (2007b). Understanding learning cultures. *Educational Review – Special Issue*, 59: 415–427.

Huddleston, P. and Stanley, J. (eds) (2012). *Work-related teaching and work-related learning*. Abingdon, UK: Routledge.

Kemple, J. J. and Willner, C. J. (2008). *Career academies: long-term impacts on labour market outcomes*. New York, NY: MDRC.

Lareau, A. (2003). *Unequal childhoods: class, race, and family life*. Berkeley, CA: University of California Press.

Lave, J. and Wenger, E. (1991). *Situated learning: legitimate peripheral participation*. New York, NY: Cambridge University Press.

Lukes, S. (1972). *Emile Durkheim: his life and work*. London: Penguin.

Mann, A. (2012). *Work experience – impact and delivery*. London: Education and Employers Taskforce.

Miller, A. (1998). *Business and community mentoring in schools*. London: Department for Education and Employment.

Miller, S., Connolly, P. and Maguire, L. (2011). *A follow-up randomised controlled trial evaluation of the effects of Business in the Community's Time to Read Mentoring Programme*. Belfast: Centre for Effective Education, University of Belfast.

National Foundation for Educational Research (NFER). (2009). *The longer term impact of Aimhigher: Tracking individuals*. Bristol: HEFCE.

National Support Group for Work Experience. (2008). *Students' perceptions of work experience*. London: Department for Children, Schools and Families & National Education Business Partnerships Network. Available from: www.educationandemployers.org [accessed 3 February 2014].

Neumark, D. and Rothstein, D. (2005). *Do school-to-work programs help the 'forgotten half'?* National Bureau of Economic Research Working Paper 11636.

Organisation for Economic Co-operation and Development (OECD). (2007). *Qualification systems: bridges to lifelong learning*. Paris: OECD.

Organisation for Economic Co-operation and Development (OECD). (2010). *Learning for jobs*. Paris: OECD.

Packard, B. W., Kim, G. J., Sicley, M. and Piontkowski, S. (2009). Composition matters: multi-context informal mentoring networks for low-income urban adolescent girls pursuing healthcare careers. *Mentoring and Tutoring: Partnership in Learning*, 17: 187–200.

Pallas, A. M. (2003). Educational transitions, trajectories, and pathways. *In:* J. T. Mortimer and M. J. Shanahan, eds. *Handbook of the life course*. New York, NY: Kluwer Academic/Plenum Publishers, 165–184.

Portes, A. (1998). Social capital: its origins and applications in modern sociology. *Annual Review of Sociology*, 24: 1–24.

Putnam, R. (2000). *Bowling alone: the collapse and revival of the American community*. New York, NY: Simon and Schuster.

Qualifications and Curriculum Authority (QCA). (2003). *Work-related learning for all at key stage 4: guidance for implementing the statutory guidance from 2004*. London: QCA.

Qualifications and Curriculum Authority (QCA). (2008). *Economic wellbeing 11–19: career, work-related learning and enterprise*. London: QCA.

Raffe, D. (2008). The concept of transition system. *Journal of Education and Work*, 21: 277–296.

Reay, D., David, M. and Ball, S. J. (2005). *Degrees of choice*. London: Trentham Books.

Stern, D. and Briggs, D. (2001). Does paid employment help or hinder performance in secondary school? Insights from US high school students. *Journal of Education and Work*, 14: 355–372.

Strand, S. and Winston, J. (2008). Educational aspirations in inner city schools. *Educational Studies*, 34 (4): 249–267.

Yates, S., Harris, A., Sabates, R. and Staff, J. (2010). Early occupational aspirations and fractured transitions: a study of entry into 'NEET' status in the UK. *Journal of Social Policy*, 40: 513–534.

Chapter 3

A conceptual framework for the American labour market

Engagement, achievement and transition

James R. Stone III

Building an effective vocational education system that responds to the demands of the emergent twenty-first-century workplace will require a close relationship between, and integration of, academic, technical and employability skills and knowledge within what have historically been two separate systems – education and the workplace. Conceptualising a framework for such an integrated system must necessarily begin with the workplace, the ultimate destination for such a system.

The workplace of tomorrow, and indeed of today, is changing in ways that challenge prediction. This, in turn, challenges how educational systems plan and provide occupationally focused education. Government agencies routinely report labour market trends (e.g. the United States Bureau of Labour Statistics). Numerous think tanks that use their own approaches to analysis also project trends (e.g. Georgetown University's Center on Education and the Workforce; see Carnevale *et al.* 2010). Among such analytic groups, general agreement exists that something between one-quarter and one-third of the jobs expected to become available over the next decade in the United States will require a four-year college degree or more for entry. Some dispute exists over the remaining job growth and the education requirements demanded for entry. Two-year college credentials and industry-recognised certifications are estimated to make up perhaps another one-third of the job growth; the balance will require high school or less for entry (Carnevale *et al.* 2010; Sommers and Franklin 2012).

Some have looked at the future through a wider lens and considered how technology is fundamentally reshaping who – or rather what – produces the goods and services needed and desired by our increasingly consumerist society. One inescapable conclusion is that technology – specifically robotics and thinking machines – is displacing humans in the production of goods and services (Brynjolfsson and McAfee 2012).

Considerations like these matter to educators, especially vocational educators, who are obligated to provide the skills needed to facilitate the transition of youth and adults into the workplace. In the United States, a policy framework has emerged for all pre-kindergarten to collegiate education that has come to be called 'college and career readiness' (CCR) (Stone and Lewis 2012). That is, educational policy is increasingly being framed around the idea that all youth must acquire the skills in elementary and secondary education to continue their formal education in tertiary (or post-secondary) education that eventually leads to careers. This diverges greatly from a vision of public education in which some youth prepare for college and others for work. Although various interest groups generally agree on the concept of CCR, robust debate exists regarding how to operationalise the concept. This debate is reviewed in depth by Stone and Lewis (2012).

Regardless of how one defines college and career readiness, general agreement exists that employers ought to be engaged in the discussion of how to frame learning programmes that will prepare youth for an uncertain economic future. One approach involving business has considered the types of fundamental work-ready skills needed for success in the marketplace. An early effort to define such skills was undertaken by the Secretary's Commission on Achieving Necessary Skills (SCANS) (SCANS 1991). This US federal commission identified the skills necessary to 'prepare people to make a living, participate in their communities, to raise families, and to enjoy the leisure that is the fruit of their labor' (SCANS 1991: i). The SCANS commission established a set of foundational skills and qualities – including basic academic skills, thinking skills and personal skills – that they deemed essential. Building on this foundation, the SCANS commission recommended that all workers needed to be competent in five areas:

- The allocation of resources, including time, money, materials, space and staff.
- The use of interpersonal skills, including working with others, negotiating, working in teams, serving customers, and leading and working with others from diverse cultural backgrounds.
- The use of information, including how to acquire and evaluate data, interpret and communicate information and use computers to process information.
- Understanding systems, including social, organisational and technological systems, monitoring and correcting systems performance and design, or improving systems.
- The use of technology, including knowing how to select the right technology and apply it to specific tasks, and to maintain and troubleshoot technology.

These SCANS skills – also called 'soft skills' – have come to shape the CCR response in many states (e.g. Central Pennsylvania Workforce Development Corporation, n.d.) and more broadly, workforce development (ACT Inc).

More recently, a report from the Partnership for 21st Century Skills (2002) identified an approach to education that emphasises core academic subjects, learning skills, the use of modern technology in the classroom, and rigorous, contemporary content taught using more highly tuned assessments. Similar to the SCANS recommendations, the Partnership report (2002) included a focus on critical thinking and problem solving, communication and interpersonal skills. Unlike the SCANS report, the Partnership report aligned more closely with the intent of the primary federal education reform movement of the first decade of the current century – No Child Left Behind (NCLB) – by placing a greater emphasis on more traditional academics (e.g. Algebra II, Geometry) and a test-based approach to assessments. The workforce skills emphasised in the Partnership report include the use of technology tools, defined as information and communication tools like computers, networking, audio, video and other multimedia tools.

What these and similar policy reports (Achieve 2013; ACT 2009) have failed to provide, however, are the kinds of specifics that would help curriculum specialists design courses and programmes that provide a pathway to future employment and educational options for all youth. Asking all students to take more courses in traditional academic subjects will not produce workers with the skills employers want and need. Indeed, a growing body of evidence suggests that non-cognitive skills are more critical to success in any venture – work or education – than scores in tests of academic measures (Duckworth *et al.* 2007; Letzring *et al.* 2005).

An integrative approach to college and career readiness

Programmes that effectively promote college and career readiness are designed to help students achieve mastery of three kinds of knowledge and skills (Stone and Lewis 2012). First and most obviously, academic knowledge is important – especially the occupational expression of academic knowledge. For example, high school graduates should know how to use concepts from mathematics or science to solve real workplace problems. This is supported conceptually in the most recent effort to generate national standards for academic learning, the Common Core State Standards (CCSS) initiative, a joint effort of the Council of Chief State School Officers and the National Governor's Association.[1] A key argument for the CCSS is the idea that academic content knowledge and performance skills are inextricably linked and that it is impossible to have one without the other. College and career readiness includes two further foci not recognised by the CCSS. The first includes employability skills or soft skills. These skills apply across diverse workplaces and include personal qualities such as responsibility, self-management and integrity. Second, college and career readiness requires students to acquire technical skills unique to specific occupational areas. As research by the National Research Center for Career and Technical Education (NRCCTE) has demonstrated, instruction in a specific occupational context offers opportunities to develop academic, employability and technical skills simultaneously (Stone *et al.* 2008).

The challenge for the curriculum or programme designer is how to embed the necessary academic skills, employability skills and specific technical skills into occupational programmes in ways that ensure graduates are truly college and career ready.

Integrating academic, employability and technical knowledge and skills

As previously indicated, many labour market analysts agree that most future employment opportunities will require some education beyond high school – perhaps as many as two-thirds of all jobs. An effective college and career-ready educational programme must not only vertically integrate secondary and post-secondary educational systems in a more purposeful, seamless manner, but also horizontally integrate academic, employability and technical knowledge and skills. Finally, these educational systems must integrate with business and industry as a means of providing students with opportunities to build skills and knowledge not taught in a classroom or lab setting.

Vertical integration

The current focus on more closely aligning secondary and post-secondary education in the United States is the result of the federal legislation governing vocational education (otherwise known as career and technical education or CTE) that calls for the implementation of CTE programmes of study (POS), also referred to as career pathways. POS are the most recent iteration of previous federal policies addressing the alignment of secondary and post-secondary CTE. The legislation mandating POS – the Carl D. Perkins Career and Technical Education Act of 2006, known colloquially as Perkins IV – requires states receiving federal funds for their CTE programs to design POS that:

i   must incorporate secondary education and postsecondary education elements;
ii   must include coherent and rigorous content aligned with challenging academic standards and relevant career and technical content in a coordinated, non-duplicative progression of courses that align secondary education with postsecondary education to adequately prepare students to succeed in postsecondary education;
iii may include the opportunity for secondary education students to participate in dual or concurrent enrolment programs or other ways to acquire postsecondary education credits; and
iv   must lead to an industry-recognised credential or certificate at the postsecondary level, or an associate or baccalaureate degree (Perkins IV, Section 122[c][1][A]).

A key difference between Perkins IV and previous initiatives is the law's requirement that POS lead to an industry-recognised credential or certificate at the post-secondary level, or an associate or baccalaureate degree (Stipanovic *et al.* 2012). A study of exemplary POS sites found that most of the objectives of the legislation were being met (Shumer *et al.* 2011).

Horizontal integration: integrating academics into CTE, integrating CTE into academics

Integrating academics into CTE

Despite the challenges in predicting precisely what the labour market of tomorrow will require, it is widely agreed that today's high school graduates need to be proficient in reading, mathematics and science skills in order to succeed in school, develop lifelong careers, participate in democracy and navigate the information age (Forget and Bottoms 2000; Guthrie *et al.* 1995; Kamil 2003; Meltzer 2001; Snow 2002; Vacca 2002). There is a case to be made that demands on students' academic skills are more intense than at any other time in history (Alvermann 2001; Kamil 2003; Moore *et al.* 1999; National Governors Association 2005; Biancarosa and Snow 2004). More so than for previous generations, the consequences of illiterate, innumerate graduates entering the workforce and society are severe, detrimental and limiting. Individuals lacking literacy skills fail to fully participate in careers and society (Cappella and Weinstein 2001; National Association of Secondary School Principals 2005; National Association of State Boards of Education 2006; Wright 1998).

We know CTE students need to become more proficient in the application of academic knowledge to workplace problems. Knowing this, the next task is to craft appropriate programmes that embed effective pedagogies. There are many perspectives on what makes teaching effective, but for the purpose of this discussion, my focus is on integration: the integration of work or career concepts and traditional academic concepts – the integration of school-based learning and work-based learning.

At the heart of this concept is the notion that integration should involve pedagogic strategies and lessons that allow students to apply academic skills to the solution of authentic workplace problems. It speaks to the importance of addressing CTE's historic purpose of preparing young people to take productive roles in the workplace and society. Stone *et al.* (2008) noted:

> Since its inception as a part of the high school curriculum, CTE has been linked to labour market needs. These links to the workplace are what attract CTE students and provide the engagement that they often find lacking in academic courses. For these reasons, we required that the math to be taught as part of the CTE courses should emerge from the curriculum – not be superimposed into it.
>
> (Stone *et al.* 2008: 70)

The integration of academics into the CTE curriculum has been a focus of school improvement in the United States since at least the mid-1980s. It was a major policy objective of Perkins IV, and was in previous iterations of the Perkins legislation in 1990 and 1998 (see Hoachlander 1999). Beyond the requirement to create rigorous and coherent technical content that aligns with rigorous academic standards, the Perkins legislation requires that (a) opportunities be provided for academic and career and technical education teachers to jointly develop and implement curricula and pedagogical standards, and (b) teachers should receive professional development that is 'high quality, sustained, intensive, and increases academic knowledge' (Carl D. Perkins 2006). This focus on integrating CTE and academics, though desirable, stands in stark contrast to long-established systems and traditions (see Grubb *et al.* 1991).

From its origins in the early twentieth century, US vocational education or CTE has historically focused on preparing youth for specific occupations and creating more efficient social systems (Wirth 1972). As Wirth noted, from the beginning, the United States has favoured the creation of separate schools for vocational students and those who are academically inclined – a parallel educational system that survives today in many or most US states. This practice has led to the dichotomisation – between vocational/CTE and academic foci – of educational institutions, teaching methods, teacher training and students (Grubb *et al.* 1991). One result of this dichotomisation has been that efforts to better meet the needs of all students to prepare for the twenty-first-century workplace have largely fallen on the CTE community. The CTE versus academic dichotomy also serves as a partial explanation of why the concept of an integrated curriculum is most often unidirectional; that is, the effort is largely borne by CTE educators with little effort to integrate occupational learning into traditional academics.

At the heart of effective programmes that link and integrate school-based and work-based learning is the notion that integration should involve strategies and lessons through which students may apply their academic skills to solve authentic workplace problems. It furthermore speaks to the importance of addressing the historical purpose of CTE to prepare young people for a role in the workplace and society by strengthening both CTE and academic skills.

In the NRCCTE's experimentally tested professional development models, CTE teachers introduce and reinforce academic skills that students add to their technical skills – the tools needed in the workplace. Importantly, CTE teachers purposefully bridge the languages of the CTE and academic worlds as they teach. In the NRCCTE's Math-in-CTE study, Stone *et al.* (2008) emphasised the importance of developing lessons that called for the application of maths concepts that are authentic to the workplace:

> Like any other tool, [math] has its place in the toolbox required to solve genuine workplace problems. The mechanic may reach for a wrench or a formula to determine how to improve the performance of an automobile. The marketing CTE teacher will teach advertising, marketing research, statistics, economics, and the like. For all CTE teachers, math is part of their curriculum and it is part of the workplace, and they should share that reality with their students.
>
> (Stone *et al.* 2008: 72)

CTE courses provide a wealth of opportunities for learning mathematics, understanding the importance of science and technology, and enhancing reading skills. These are the technical expression of academics. However, it is important to recognise that CTE teachers, who are not academic educators, often teach without directly linking underlying academic concepts to CTE tasks or concepts. For example, a carpentry teacher may use and demonstrate 'the 3–4–5 rule' to measure a square corner but never specifically refer to the Pythagorean Theorem.[2] CTE teachers often assume students can read and decode text in the technical manuals required for successful CTE course completion. In mathematics and literacy, the opportunities to build students' ability to use academics to address workplace problems are manifold. Unfortunately, most CTE teachers do not use these opportunities to their students' advantage.

Providing students with appropriate technical and academic skills should be the goal of any CTE programme. Accomplishing – or failing to accomplish – that goal has consequences that reach beyond the scope of the individual student:

> The most consistent message of the past two decades of educational reform is that high school students have not acquired the literacy and mathematical skills required for the United States to remain competitive in the world economy, or at a personal level, to qualify for jobs that pay enough to support a family. In an age of instantaneous communication, a nation's most valuable resource is the ability of its workers to access and use information.
>
> (Stone *et al.* 2008: 71)

The NRCCTE's Math-in-CTE study provided quantitative evidence of the positive impact of the integration of CTE and academics on student academic achievement (Stone *et al.* 2008). Incorporating the core principles for effective curriculum integration that emerged from this study, researchers then replicated the research design to evaluate the impact of integrating literacy (Park *et al.* 2010) and science (Pearson and Young 2010).

Integrating CTE into academics

Academic subjects and academic teachers play a vitally important role in the development of a robust approach to college and career readiness. Although CTE teachers can help students learn to apply academic knowledge, it is equally important that academic teachers help students grasp the larger meaning of work and empower them to make career and life choices and understand their role in economic development (Finch and Mooney 1997). Learning about all aspects of an industry is one strategy to this end. All Aspects of Industry (AAI) was initially included in the 1990 iteration of the Perkins Act. Similar language was also included in the 1994 School-to-Work Opportunities Act. Building on the White Paper produced by the Center for Law and Education (n.d.), the 1990 Perkins legislation outlined eight areas for student learning, including planning, management, finance, technical and production skills, underlying principles of technology, labour issues, community issues, and health, safety and environment issues. In a very real sense, this can be a strategy to engage employers in the education of youth by nesting academic learning in a work-related context.

These eight areas find expression in the standard academic curriculum including social studies (e.g. finance, labour and community issues), science (e.g. principles of technology, health and environmental issues) and language arts classes (e.g. reading technical manuals, understanding systems of communication within organisations). Several states and many school districts have adapted the AAI framework, as described by Andrew (1996), who provided four case studies of schools focusing on AAI: a health academy in Oakland, California; a school in Cambridge, Massachusetts, which reshaped its tenth-grade curriculum; a youth apprenticeship programme in Pennsylvania; and a high school in Milwaukee, Wisconsin, which embedded AAI concepts in a hospitality management project. Many states, such as Virginia, implemented AAI as part of their CTE framework and provide resources to teachers in the form of links to lesson plans that draw upon the work of such public agencies as the Environmental Protection Agency, the Internal Revenue Service, the Department of Health, private companies (e.g. Gap, McDonald's, Mitsubishi) and the media (e.g. the *New York Times*, *USA Today*). Although these resources are specifically provided for CTE teachers, these lessons can easily be adapted to core academic classes, especially in the context of the Career Clusters framework that forms the basis of many states' college and career readiness initiatives.[3]

External integration

Work-based learning, particularly the costs and benefits of adolescent employment, has been the subject of much debate, as summarised by Stone (2011), who addressed the many issues attendant to the marked decline of youth working in the United States. In an earlier report, Stone and Aliaga (2003) reported that school supervised work-based learning had also declined.

Despite what has been limited interest or support for work-based learning in US education, recent reports by prominent education researchers indicate a surge in interest in work-based learning. The Harvard Graduate School of Education published a report, *Pathways to Prosperity* (Symonds *et al.* 2011) that argued that in order to prepare youth for a successful adulthood, employers must be actively involved in education. Other recent publications have explored how work-based learning has benefited youth in Europe (Hoffman 2011) and how it could benefit youth in the United States (Stone and Lewis 2012). In *Learning for Jobs*, the Organisation for Economic Co-operation and Development (OECD 2010) concluded that for countries to maintain their economic competitiveness, they need a solid system of vocational education and training (VET) that includes high-quality work-based learning.

The OECD's report also argued that work-based learning is an effective mechanism for both smoothing the transition from school to the workplace and building the transferrable skills deemed necessary for workplace success (OECD 2010). Work-based learning can also improve reading scores (Bottoms *et al.* 2008) and improve academic outcomes (Bishop and Mane 2004). These and other reports validate Grabinger's (1996) argument that 'knowledge learned but not explicitly related to relevant problem-solving situations remains mostly inert, meaning the learner is unable to use it for anything practical when the opportunity arises and thus such knowledge quickly disappears' (Grabinger 1996: 669).

Multiple approaches to increasing employer engagement through work-based learning can support college and career readiness efforts. The least intensive form of work-based learning is *job shadowing*, which can vary from a student simply following an adult worker around for a day to using the experience as a basis for an English or science class assignment (Stone and Madzar 1994). *Internships* are generally considered to be one-time, short-term placements directly related to a student's occupational goal (Hartley 1983). *School-based enterprises* (SBEs) allow students to provide goods or services for sale to or used by people other than the students involved as part of their school programme (see Stern *et al.* 1994). SBEs vary greatly in the intensity of the work experiences they provide; most are unconnected to an external employer but offer a realistic simulation of the workplace as an extension of the CTE classroom. *Cooperative vocational education* is a method of instruction intended to directly link classroom CTE instruction with work experience; it has long been associated with CTE and usually involves a written training and evaluation plan intended to guide the instruction. Students receive course credit for both their work and classroom experiences over the course of an academic term (Stone and Wonser 1990).

The most intensive form of work-based learning is an *apprenticeship*. Alfeld *et al.* (2013) explored the literature on apprenticeships, noting that they are primarily associated with adult occupational education – the average age on starting apprentices in the United States is 27. *Youth apprenticeships*, by contrast, serve adolescents and blossomed during the 1980s youth apprenticeship movement led by Hamilton (1990). Although this movement was short-lived, elements of Hamilton's vision found permanence in programmes around the country. States like Wisconsin have ensconced youth apprenticeship programmes in their departments of workforce development and sought to coordinate adult-style apprenticeships with local high schools.[4] In other states, such programmes are located in and governed by the state department of education.

Contemporary evidence of US industry's interest in work-based learning lies in the growing number of companies starting their own apprenticeship programmes. Many of these companies seek to align their efforts with regional community colleges and high schools. For example, in Tennessee, Volkswagen created a German-style apprenticeship programme with a local community college. Siemens and Blum initiated similar programmes with local North Carolina community colleges. Toyota has created a unique programme linking secondary CTE programmes to redesigned community college advanced manufacturing programmes (DiMattina *et al.* 2013); graduates of this programme have the choice of moving directly into employment as multiskilled technicians or continuing their education at the baccalaureate level (and beyond) in engineering or manufacturing management.

Conclusion

I began this chapter by arguing that US education needs to develop a more purposeful relationship with the workplace. It needs to better bridge the gap between what is learned in school and what is needed in the future workplace. The latter part of the twentieth century, culminating in the 2002 federal policy known as *No Child Left Behind*, was dominated by a college-for-all mindset. And it was a failure (Ravitch 2010). It has been replaced by the college and career-readiness rhetoric recognising the broader goals of public education.

Unfortunately, reality has yet to align with the rhetoric. While there are many efforts to better combine academic and technical learning, engage employers in more meaningful relationships with schools and provide clearer, more transparent pathways to successful integration into the workforce for young people, they are too few in number and meet the needs of far too few youth.

The lessons from the few successful programmes are that they build viable career pathways for youth to follow and they require a three-pronged, integrated approach to developing academic and technical skills. At the secondary level, the academic and technical curriculum needs to be integrated using evidence-based approaches. Secondary CTE programmes must also be well integrated with post-secondary programmes to facilitate a smooth and transparent progression to employment, which includes post-secondary certificates, degrees and industry-recognised credentials. Finally, employers need to be integrated into both levels of the educational system and provide extensive and intensive work-based learning opportunities. This three-way integration model provides the flexibility necessary to adapt to a rapidly changing labour market.

Notes

1 See www.corestandards.org [accessed 11 April 2013].
2 See www.wikihow.com/Use-the-3-4-5-Rule-to-Build-Square-Corners [accessed 18 March 2013].
3 See www.careertech.org/career-clusters/glance/ [accessed 6 March 2014].
4 See http://dwd.wisconsin.gov/youthapprenticeship/program_info.htm [accessed 11 March 2013] and also www.doe.k12.ga.us/Curriculum-Instruction-and-Assessment/ CTAE/Pages/Youth-Apprenticeship-Program.aspx [accessed 8 March 2013].

References

Achieve. (2013). *What does college and career ready mean?* Washington, DC: Achieve Inc.
ACT. (2009). *Ready for college and ready for work: same or different?* Iowa City, IA: ACT Inc.

Alfeld, C., Charner, I., Johnson, L. and Watts, E. (2013). *Work-based learning opportunities for high school students.* Louisville, KY: National Research Center for Career and Technical Education, University of Louisville.

Alvermann, D. E. (2001). Reading adolescents' reading identities: looking back to see ahead. *Journal of Adolescent and Adult Literacy,* 44 (8): 676–690.

Andrew, E. N. (1996). *As teachers tell it: implementing all aspects of the industry. The case studies.* Vol. 1. Berkeley, CA: The National Center for Research in Vocational Education.

Biancarosa, G. and Snow, C. E. (2004). *Reading next: a vision for action and research in middle and high school literacy.* A report to the Carnegie Corporation of New York. Washington, DC: Alliance for Excellent Education.

Bishop, J. and Mane, F. (2004). The impacts of career-technical education on high school labour market success. *Economics of Education Review,* 23: 381–402.

Bottoms, G., Han. L. L. and Murray, R. (2008). *High school experiences that influence reading proficiency: what states and schools can do.* Atlanta, GA: Southern Regional Education Board. Available from: http://publications.sreb.org/2008/08V21_Improving_Reading_Proficiency.pdf [accessed 10 January 2013].

Brynjolfsson, E. and McAfee, A. (2012). *Race against the machine: how the digital revolution is accelerating innovation, driving productivity, and irreversibly transforming employment and the economy.* Lexington, MA: Digital Frontier Press.

Cappella, E. and Weinstein, R. (2001). Turning around reading achievement: Predictors of high school students' academic resilience. *Journal of Educational Psychology,* 93 (4): 758–771.

Carl D. Perkins Career and Technical Education Improvement Act of 2006. Public Law. No. 109–270.

Carnevale, A. P., Smith, N. and Strohl, J. (2010). *Help wanted: projections of jobs and education requirements through 2018.* Washington, DC: Georgetown University Center on Education and the Workforce. Available from: http://cew.georgetown.edu/jobs2018/ [accessed 21 January 2013].

Center for Law and Education. (n.d.). *All aspects of the industry.* City, ST: Author. Available from: www.nrccte.org/sites/default/files/publication-files/as_teachers_tell_it.pdf [accessed 2 April 2014].

Central Pennsylvania Workforce Development Corporation. (n.d.). *PA career education and work standards: lesson planning guide.* Available from: www.pacareerstandards.com/documents/13.3.5a-developing-scans.doc [accessed 22 February 2012].

DiMattina, C., Alagaraja, M. and Stone III, J. R. (2013). *Building regional HRD strategy: a qualitative case study of a community college and industry partnership.* Paper presented at the Academy of Human Resource Development, Conference of the Americas, Washington, DC.

Duckworth, A. L., Peterson, C., Matthews, M. D. and Kelly, D. R. (2007). Grit: perseverance and passion for long-term goals. *Journal of Personality and Social Psychology,* 92 (6): 1087–1101.

Finch, C. and Mooney, M. (1997). Using all aspects of industry in curriculum design. *CenterWork,* 8 (3). Berkeley, CA: National Center for Research in Vocational Education. Available from: http://ncrve.berkeley.edu/CW83/AAI.html [accessed 15 February 2012].

Forget, M. and Bottoms, G. (2000). *Academic and vocational teachers can improve the reading achievement of male career-bound students.* Atlanta, GA: Southern Regional Education Board.

Grabinger, R. S. (1996). Rich environments for active learning. *In:* D. H. Jonassen, ed. *Handbook of research for educational communications and technology.* New York, NY: Macmillan, 665–692.

Grubb, W. N., Davis, G., Lum, J., Plihal, J. and Morgaine, C. (1991). *The cunning hand, the cultured mind: models for integrating vocational and academic education.* Berkeley,

CA: National Center for Research in Vocational Education: University of California at Berkeley.

Guthrie, J. T., Schafer, W. D., Wang, Y. Y. and Afflerbach, P. (1995). Relationships of instruction of reading: an exploration of social, cognitive, and instructional connections. *Reading Research Quarterly*, 30 (1): 8–25.

Hamilton, S. F. (1990). *Apprenticeship for adulthood*. New York, NY: The Free Press.

Hartley, M. P. (1983). Introducing the student to unfamiliar ground: cooperative education and internship programs. *Workplace Education*, 1 (3): 4–7.

Hoachlander, G. (1999). *Integrating academic and vocational curriculum – why is theory so hard to practice?* Available from: http://ncrve.berkeley.edu/CenterPoint/CP7/CP7.html [accessed 13 February 2013].

Hoffman, N. (2011). *Schooling in the workplace: how six of the world's best vocational education systems prepare young people for jobs and life*. Cambridge, MA: Harvard Educational Publishing Group.

Kamil, M. L. (2003). *Adolescents and literacy: reading for the 21st century*. Washington, DC: Alliance for Excellent Education.

Letzring, T. D., Block, J. and Funder, D. C. (2005). Ego-control and ego-resiliency: generalization of self-report scales based on personality descriptions from acquaintances, clinicians, and the self. *Journal of Research in Personality*, 39 (4): 395–422.

Meltzer, J. (2001). *Supporting adolescent literacy across the content areas: perspectives on policy and practice*. Washington, DC: Office of Educational Research and Improvement.

Moore, D. W., Bean, T. W., Birdyshaw, D. and Rycik, J. A. (1999). *Adolescent literacy: a position statement for the Commission on Adolescent Literacy of the International Reading Association*. Newark, DE: International Reading Association.

National Association of Secondary School Principals. (2005). *Creating a culture of literacy: a guide for middle and high school principals*. Available from: www.pdst.ie/sites/default/files/Creatingacultureofliteracy.pdf [accessed 9 March 2013].

National Association of State Boards of Education. (2006). *Reading at risk: the state response to the crisis in adolescent literacy*. Available from: http://carnegie.org/fileadmin/Media/Publications/PDF/reading_at_risk_.pdf [accessed 10 March 2013].

National Governors Association. (2005). *Graduation counts: a report of the National Governors Association task force on state high school graduation data*. Washington, DC: National Governors Association.

Organisation for Economic Co-operation and Development (OECD). (2010). *Learning for jobs: synthesis report of the OECD reviews of vocational education and training*. Paris: OECD.

Park, T. D., Santamaria, L. A., van der Mandele, L., Keene, B. L. and Taylor, M. K. (2010). *Authentic literacy in career and technical education: technical appendices to the Spring 2009 pilot study*. Louisville, KY: National Research Center for Career and Technical Education, University of Louisville.

Partnership for 21st Century Skills. (2002). *Learning for the 21st century*. Washington, DC. Available from: www.p21.org/storage/documents/P21_Report.pdf [accessed 18 January 2013].

Pearson, D. and Young, B. R. (2010). *Science-in-CTE*. Louisville, KY: National Research Center for Career and Technical Education, University of Louisville.

Ravitch, D. (2010). *The death and life of the great American school system: how testing and choice are undermining education*. New York: NY: Basic Books.

Secretary's Commission on Achieving Necessary Skills (SCANS). (1991). *What work requires of schools: a SCANS report for America 2000*. Washington, DC. http://wdr.doleta.gov/SCANS/whatwork/whatwork.pdf [accessed 6 March 2014].

Shumer, R., Stringfield, S., Stipanovic, N. and Murphy, N. (2011). *Programs of study: a cross-study examination of programs in three states*. Louisville, KY: National Research Center for Career and Technical Education, University of Louisville.

Snow, C. (2002). *Reading for understanding: toward an RandD program in reading comprehension*. Santa Monica, CA: The RAND Corporation.

Sommers, D. and Franklin, J. C. (2012). *Overview of projections to 2020. Monthly Labour Review*. Washington, DC: Bureau of Labour of Labour Statistics.

Stern, D., Stone III, J. R., Hopkins, C., McMillion, M. and Crain, R. (1994). *School-based enterprise: productive learning in American high schools*. San Francisco, CA: Jossey-Bass.

Stipanovic, N., Lewis, M. V. and Stringfield, S. (2012). Situating programs of study within current and historical career and technical educational reform efforts. *International Journal of Educational Reform*, 21 (2): 80–97.

Stone III, J. R. (2011). Adolescent employment. *In:* B. B. Brown and M. J. Prinstein, eds. *Encyclopedia of adolescence*. San Diego, CA: Academic Press, 59–67.

Stone III, J. R. and Wonser, R. L. (1990). *Alternative strategies for providing work experience*. St Paul, MN: Minnesota Research and Development Center for Vocational Education, University of Minnesota.

Stone III, J. R. and Madzar, S. (1994). *Improving the US system of school-to-work transition for youth and young adults: a doubly integrated approach*. Presentation to the 12th Annual Entrepreneurship Education Forum, Minneapolis, MN.

Stone III, J. R. and Aliaga, O. A. (2003). *Career and technical education, career pathways and work-based learning: changes in participation 1997–1999*. St Paul, MN: National Research Center for Career and Technical Education.

Stone III, J. R. and Lewis, M. V. (2012). *College and career readiness for the 21st century: making high school matter*. New York, NY: Teacher's College Press.

Stone III, J. R., Alfeld, C. and Pearson, D. (2008). Rigor and relevance: testing a model of enhanced math learning in career and technical education. *American Education Research Journal*, 45 (3): 767–795.

Symonds, W. C., Schwartz, R. B. and Ferguson, R. (2011). *Pathways to prosperity: meeting the challenge of preparing young Americans for the 21st century*. Cambridge, MA: Pathways to Prosperity Project, Harvard Graduate School of Education.

Vacca, R. T. (2002). Making a difference in adolescents' school lives: visible and invisible aspects of content area reading. *In:* A. E. Farstrup and S. J. Samuels, eds. *What research has to say about reading instruction*. Newark, DE: International Reading Association, 184–204.

Wirth, A. G. (1972). *Education in the technological society: the vocational-liberal studies controversy in the early twentieth-century*. Scranton, PA: Intext Educational Publishers.

Wright, E. L. (1998). *The academic language of college-bound at-risk secondary students: self-assessment, proficiency levels, and effects of language development on instruction*. Dissertation Abstracts International, 58 (10), 3909A (UMI No. 9812098).

Chapter 4

Youth labour markets in the early twenty-first century

Kathrin Hoeckel

Record high youth unemployment is one of the tragedies of the early twenty-first century. It affects the majority of Organisation for Economic Co-operation and Development (OECD) countries. Up to half of an age cohort does not manage a successful transition from education to the world of work and adulthood. This has led some commentators to speak of a 'lost generation' (OECD 2010a). Adults, of course, are unemployed too. So what is tragic about youth unemployment? Why should governments care? First, there is the psychological effect of disappointment that young people have to face when they leave the education system with high expectations only to realise that they are nowhere needed and welcome. Some youth just give up after a while and stop searching for a job and become inactive if they have no positive experience to build on. Second, and this is of deep interest to finance ministries, economic research has found that failure to find and keep a first job can have negative long-term consequences on career prospects, future earnings and employment chances way beyond young age. This effect is often referred to as 'scarring' because individuals or even a whole generation can be marked by what they experience at a young adult age (Scarpetta *et al.* 2010; OECD 2010a: 32).

The problem of youth unemployment and its long-term consequences is not limited to those young people leaving education poorly qualified. Even highly educated young people can encounter problems if they fail to enter stable employment. Some individuals, especially in countries with high individual costs of tertiary education, never manage to pay back their study debt during their working lifetime. The sum of US college student debt has doubled over the past ten years, reaching the billion-dollar mark in 2012. On average, an American bachelor graduate leaves higher education with a debt load of US$27,000. And with rising tuition fees, both debt levels and the financial importance of smooth school-to-work transitions are likely to increase in the future.

These negative effects go far beyond the individual. Idleness among youth can come at great costs, not only to them but also to society as a whole. The loss of income among the younger generation translates into a lack of savings as well as a loss of aggregate demand. Governments fail to receive contributions to social security systems and instead are forced to increase spending on unemployment benefits and, in the worst case, on remedial services, including on crime or drug use prevention efforts. Focusing on youth, therefore, makes sense to countries from a simple cost-benefit point of view (International Labour Organisation (ILO) 2010a).

This chapter describes the challenging issue of education-to-work transitions in OECD countries, looking at a variety of indicators as well as factors explaining cross-country differences and changes in the youth labour market over the last generation. It argues that inadequate skills strategies leading to a large gulf between the world of education and the world of work make it difficult for young people to make a successful transition, leaving especially the disadvantaged youth behind and at risk of becoming permanently marginalised.

Evaluation of youth unemployment over the past decades – a mixed picture

The global economic crisis that began in 2008 has hit youth very hard in most parts of the OECD area (Figure 4.1). Starting from the low level of 13 per cent in late 2007, the average OECD youth unemployment rate rose to a postwar high of 19 per cent in 2010. This corresponds to more than four million additional unemployed young persons in only three years. In some countries, the youth unemployment rate reached astronomical heights: in record-holder Spain,

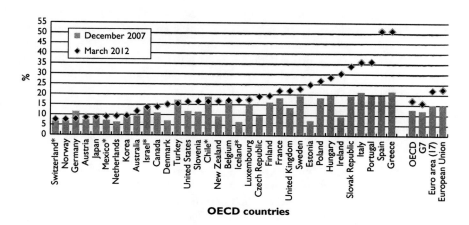

Figure 4.1 Youth unemployment rates in OECD countries (December 2007 and March 2012) as a percentage of the total youth labour force (age 15–24).

Source: OECD calculations based on short-term indicators from Eurostat and various national sources: cut-off date 2 May 2012.

Notes: Countries are shown in ascending order by the youth unemployment rate in March 2012; OECD is the weighted average of 33 countries excluding Mexico.

* Not seasonally adjusted data.

it jumped from 17.4 per cent in March 2007 to 51.1 per cent in March 2012; every other young person in Spain looking for a job could not find one.

In parallel, the OECD youth employment rate – the share of the youth population actually holding a job – declined by three percentage points from the onset of the crisis in 2007 to a low of 40 per cent in 2009. As of 2013, the youth employment rates in Europe, and especially in the United States, had yet to return to their pre-recession peaks, suggesting a 'youth jobless recovery'.

In general, the situation of young people had been relatively benign before the crisis hit. Following improvements in labour market conditions observed in many OECD countries over a decade, as evidenced by lower general unemployment rates, the youth unemployment rate declined slightly from 16 per cent in 1995–1997 to 14.4 per cent in 2005–2007. Just before the onset of the recession, the OECD youth unemployment rate was close to its 1990 level (13 per cent), its lowest level for 25 years.

While on average youth unemployment before the crisis was decreasing, there were, however, significant cross-country differences, both in the level of youth unemployment at the onset of the crisis, as well as in the evolution of unemployment in the preceding decade (Figure 4.2) (Scarpetta *et al.* 2010).

Beyond significant cross-country differences in the development of the youth labour market, young people do not comprise a homogenous group. There are certain subgroups that, in addition to being young, face other disadvantages that make it hard for them to find sustained employment. In most countries, the unemployment rate is higher among young people with lower levels of qualifications. The poorer the parents, the more likely it is that the children will be unemployed. The same holds for ethnic minorities in most countries. The unemployment rate also tends to fall with age: the young (aged 15–19 years) – typically those with the least education and certainly those with the least experience – have the greatest difficulties finding work, preventing the ready acquisition of the experience sought by the employers (ILO 2010a).

Alternative measures to describe the situation of youth in the early twenty-first century

In addition to acknowledging variation across countries and social groups, it is important to recognise that the unemployment rate is a rather blunt measure for the health of the youth labour market. It depicts only part of the reality faced by young people at the beginning of the twenty-first century.

A better indicator used to describe the situation of a young person is NEET, i.e. Not in Education, Employment or Training (Figure 4.3). Unemployment rates look only at the share of those who are active in the labour market, thus disregarding parts of a given youth cohort. In contrast, the number of NEETs is calculated as a proportion of the entire age category, including those who are in education and training as well as those who have given up looking for a job, the inactive (OECD 2010a). In the middle of the crisis in 2008, on average 12 per cent of youth were NEET in the OECD countries.[1]

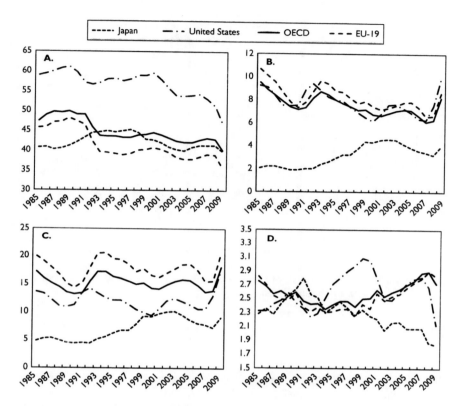

Figure 4.2 Youth labour market indicators for OECD, Europe, United States, Japan, 1985–2009.

Source: National labour force surveys.

Notes: A: Rate of employed youth as a percentage of the population in the age group; B: Rate of unemployed youth as a percentage of the population in the age group; C: Rate of unemployed youth as a percentage of the labour force in the age group; D: Ratio of youth (15/16–24) to adult (25–54) unemployment rates.

Youth aged 16–24 for Iceland, Spain, Sweden, United Kingdom and United States; youth aged 15–24 for all other countries.

To better picture the problems faced by young people, the OECD Jobs for Youth review (OECD 2010a) identified two groups of youth that face particular difficulties in getting a stable job after leaving school: the groups of so-called 'youth left behind' and the 'poorly-integrated new entrants'. The size of these two groups is difficult to approximate. The first group can be approximated by the number of young people who are neither in employment nor in education or training and who lack an upper secondary education. The second group of youth facing difficulties is the group of 'poorly-integrated new entrants'. While these young people often have completed upper secondary qualifications, they find it

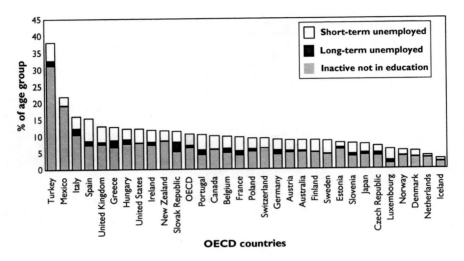

Figure 4.3 NEET youth at risk of losing contact with the labour market as a percentage of the age group, 2008.

Source: OECD Education database.

Note: Data for Mexico refer to 2004; there are no data for Korea; OECD is the weighted average of 31 countries.

difficult to obtain stable employment even during periods of strong economic growth. They frequently go back and forth between temporary jobs, unemployment and/or inactivity. About 30–40 per cent of school leavers in the OECD countries are estimated as being at risk, either because they accumulate multiple disadvantages ('left behind youth') or because they face barriers to find stable employment ('poorly integrated new entrants'). The recent recession has only exacerbated this problem.

Is any job better than no job?

There is a debate on whether suboptimal beginner jobs are desirable or a disaster for young people. Both sides have valid arguments. One situation many young people face is that they are employed in a first job that requires much less technical skill than is possessed by a worker given the qualifications they hold. While the job can serve as a stepping stone to better employment for such young people, it can also put them permanently onto a track of skills mismatch and underemployment, with negative consequences for their earnings prospects and their likelihood of engaging in further learning and progressing in their professional careers (OECD 2011: 191).

Another issue arises when people are able to make use of their skills but have to accept part-time or short-term contracts for several years before they manage to enter a stable job. Again, temporary work should not necessarily be equated with low-quality employment because it may represent a period of 'shopping around' in order to find the appropriate job and thus the pathway to permanent work, particularly for young people with little labour market experience. The risk lies in temporary contracts becoming the norm, thus starting a vicious circle. Firms are less eager to invest in training for those who work on temporary contracts: the investment might not be worthwhile because the young person is expected to leave. Although temporary jobs were already a dominant feature of youth employment in the mid-1990s, the share of youth in temporary jobs increased further over the following decade (Quintini and Martin 2006).

What do we know about the reasons for youth unemployment?

As we have seen, the situation of young people at the transition point between education and work can be very variable. To assess the youth labour market adequately and picture the situation of young people, more variables have to be considered than just rates of youth unemployment. In essence, young people who do not make a smooth transition can either choose to prolong their education in hope of better credentials buying them a job later – as many have chosen to do during the recent recession. Or they can continue looking for a job and build resilience against multiple rejections. Some will eventually give up and become permanently detached from the labour market. Typically, young people fluctuate between these statuses several times before they hold a stable job. And even being off the unemployment register and in employment does not necessarily mean they are carrying out satisfactory, sustained work and earning a living sufficient to support them.

After having zoomed in on these different transition patterns, let us now look at some of the factors that contribute to making it difficult for young people to find their first proper job. Surely, the lack of labour demand prompted by insufficient growth has a significant impact on involuntary unemployment and discouragement, for adults and youth alike. But, putting aside these variables that form part of the large array of factors influencing the health of a labour market in general, even in good economic times young people are almost always more vulnerable in the labour market than adults. There are a number of reasons for this.

A first factor explaining the higher business-cycle sensitivity for youth in the labour market is their disproportionate presence among those holding temporary jobs and their high concentration in certain cyclically sensitive industries such as construction (OECD 2010a). In a recession, employees holding temporary contracts are routinely the first ones to be laid off. And some industries have a particularly high share of people employed on the basis of temporary contracts. This was the case in some countries that experienced extreme rises in youth unemployment during the recent crisis, e.g. Ireland and Spain.

A second set of explanations concerns labour market regulations, which are said to produce a labour market bias against young people (ILO 2010a). For example, employers are usually reluctant to lay off older workers first because the cost to firms or organisations of releasing them is generally perceived as higher than for younger workers because young employees are likely to have less work experience than adults (i.e. less company funds were invested in them for training purposes, young employees have fewer firm-specific skills, and it is more likely that they are on a temporary contract). Also, employment protection legislation usually requires a minimum period of employment before it applies, while compensation for redundancy usually increases with tenure (ILO 2010a).

The rigidity of labour market regulation has been put forward by many commentators as an explanation for the differences between countries' youth labour markets. In particular, studies comparing the United States (as an example of a liberal labour market) and Europe (as an example of regulated labour markets) have pointed out that transition pathways from education to work in the United States are characterised by significantly more dynamism than in Europe: youth in employment tend to change jobs more frequently, while inactive or unemployed youth are more likely to experience several short spells rather than a single long one. School-to-work transition pathways in the United States overall involve less time spent in unemployment than in Europe (Quintini and Manfredi 2009). However, there are significant differences also between European countries. Germany and Switzerland are a case in point: both have low levels of youth unemployment. But Switzerland has a very liberal labour market while in Germany the level of worker protection is very high (Breen 2005). So there must be more to it than the level of rigidity in labour market regulation. Supply-side factors, discussed later, come into play in explaining much of these cross-country differences.

Third, some commentators have argued that higher youth unemployment rates today arise from a historical change in companies' hiring practices. In recent years, human resources departments have been downsized, and their role outsourced to recruiting agencies. The agencies encourage employers to come up with a long wish list of credentials. Then they post the jobs online, which casts a wide, often global, net but might lead to unintended consequences. Many firms rely on software to filter the high volume of applicants. Résumés that do not fill every qualification are shunted aside, even if some of the qualifications or required experiences are non-essential. Careful choosing of young recruits has been replaced by just-in-time hiring of people with exactly the right credentials, training and experience. In a hiring environment in which the currency is experience, the young are at a disadvantage (Cappelli 2012).

A final set of reasons why young people are more vulnerable in the labour market has been subject to less sustained analysis. It has to do with their lack of life skills and experience, which can make them less marketable to employers and less successful in securing employment. The breadth of their social networks, for example, from which job offers often originate is likely to be narrower than that of older persons. Likewise, they may lack knowledge concerning where and how to look for work and may have fewer financial resources to support themselves through the course of the job search process, putting them under pressure to accept poor job offers (ILO 2010b).

The education system: remedy or culprit?

Labour markets, and especially youth labour markets, are highly complex, and this list of explanatory factors is by no means exhaustive. Yet one factor stands out as being crucial for determining the success of education-to-work transitions: the structure of a country's education system or skills strategy and the way in which the world of education and the world of work relate to each other.

Having some form of post-compulsory education is highly desirable in getting access to the labour market today. Young people without any post-compulsory qualification spend on average one year less (namely 2.7 years) in employment during their first five years after leaving education, compared to peers who have obtained at least an upper secondary qualification (OECD 2010a). Having no qualifications is associated with an unemployment rate that is considerably higher compared to peers with at least an upper secondary qualification (Figure 4.4). A lack of qualifications also bears a much higher risk of becoming NEET (OECD 2010a).

Education also makes young people less vulnerable in times of recession. During the 2008–2009 downturn, young people with a lower level of education were hardest hit. The unemployment rate for those aged 15–29 who had not completed high school increased by 5 percentage points in the OECD countries on average. For young people aged 15–29 with tertiary degrees, by contrast, the increase in unemployment rates during the same period was about 2 percentage points (OECD 2010b).

This can in part be explained by a structural element of this crisis: sectors (in particular, construction) where usually low-skilled workers are able to find a job were affected most. In some countries, like Spain for instance, the rapid growth in employment in the construction and tourism areas may have led many young people to drop out of schooling because it was more immediately lucrative to start work as an unskilled worker instead of 'wasting time' by staying in education. As a result of the crisis, many of these same young people subsequently became jobless without any recognised and certified vocational skills (OECD 2010a).

Therefore, continuing education beyond compulsory schooling is crucial to protect young people from unemployment. But some forms of education are more relevant for the labour market than others. Even at the height of the crisis, large numbers of employers were complaining that they could not find workers with the right skills to fill their jobs (OECD 2012). This suggests that there is a substantial mismatch between what the education systems are producing and what labour markets require; there is a lack of a comprehensive skills strategy in

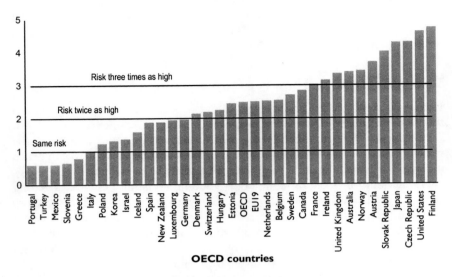

Figure 4.4 Low-skilled to high-skilled youth unemployment ratio for OECD countries in 2008.

Source: OECD Education database.

Note: The data refer to the ratio of unemployment rates of young (15/16–24) high-skilled (ISCED (International Standard Classification of Education) >3) over young low-skilled (ISCED <3) people; data for Japan refer to 2003 instead of 2008.

countries allowing to link skills development to labour markets and skills use (OECD 2012).

Bridging education and work

Analyses have shown that countries with strong dual vocational education and training (VET) programmes have the lowest youth unemployment numbers (OECD 2010c). In some cases, youth unemployment is not even significantly different from general unemployment. Why is this the case? Instead of relying on a 'study first, then work' model, countries with strong dual VET systems manage to smooth the education-to-work transition by building strong links between the two worlds. Young people in the dual system spend half of their time in an education institution (typically a vocational school) to learn the theoretical foundations of the trade, acquire additional general knowledge and, in some cases, practise basic practical skills before applying them in the actual workplace. In the workplace, they are confronted with a real-life situation, with a real boss, customers and co-workers. In addition to becoming familiar with industry-standard technology used in firms, they get the chance to pick up all the soft skills, such as business awareness, effective communication, team-working and problem solving, that employers value highly.

There is also an important recruitment factor involved. Whereas in 'study first, work second' educational systems, young people often come into direct contact with employers for the first time only after they have completed their studies, the dual system obliges young people to connect with an employer while still developing skills and qualifications relevant to the workplace. Both the young person and their sponsoring employer can evaluate whether they would fit together later in an employment relationship. The apprenticeship is in many ways a 'dry run', and the transition between education and work can take place within the protected space of an education programme. Young people in strong dual vocational education systems receive, moreover, career guidance and opportunities to try out a profession and employers. They get to engage with the world of work before they have to face the competition of an entire labour market, and, as a consequence, the transition is much smoother (OECD 2010c).

For a country's overall skills strategy, apprenticeships have a very important regulatory function in the matching of skills supply and demand. In the absence of distorting subsidies, no employer would offer an apprenticeship place if there was not a job behind it. Unlike school-based VET, apprenticeships are therefore automatically, by definition, linked to labour market needs. The 'market' in apprenticeship places becomes a domain where student career objectives have to be balanced with employer interests – a dress rehearsal for the real labour market. In well-functioning VET systems, moreover, employers are involved not only in the provision of the training in their firms, but they also participate in defining the content of curricula taught in schools and in designing exams to test students' performance at the end of the apprenticeship (OECD 2010c). In such arrangements of tight cooperation between the world of work and the world of education, it is much more unlikely that the two systems will grow apart, with a skills mismatch as the result.

During recent decades, many countries have invested heavily in their schools and universities and enrolment in tertiary education has grown. In one respect this was the right strategy given that skills demands of the economy have risen in many sectors and a solid general education makes it easier to continue learning at a later stage in life, which is also increasingly a requirement for keeping pace with the changing needs of the labour market. However, in some countries, a too narrow focus on academic education came at the price of neglecting the vocational education sector responsible for providing middle-level skills to the economy and to foster the links between education and work, especially for those young people who are not particularly academically inclined.

Since the youth unemployment crisis hit, several countries have rediscovered the value of vocational education and training and the importance of engaging employers in education and training to smooth the transition from the world of education to the world of work. Providing some form of valuable workplace experience to young people while they are still in education or as part of their education, be it from a fully fledged apprenticeship or through an internship or traineeship, can be instrumental in facilitating this important transition from education to work and adulthood.

Note

1 But even this more comprehensive measure of the situation of youth can be misleading because it fails to capture the dynamic nature of transitions from school to work, which involve more than just passing from an educational institution to the labour market. Even when the unemployment rate is stable, individuals who are jobless keep changing. Ideally, one would look in great detail at not only the stock of employed, unemployed, inactive and those in education at a given point in time, but also at the flow of young people and the process of transition from school to work, which can include going back and forth between categories and staying in them for different periods of time. Appropriate standardised indicators comparing the process of transition from school to work across countries, however, do not exist today.

References

Breen, R. (2005). Explaining cross-national variation in youth unemployment. Market and institutional factors. *European Sociological Review*, 21: 125–134.

Cappelli, P. (2012). *Why good people can't get jobs: the skills gap and what companies can do about it*. Philadelphia, PA: Wharton Digital Press.

International Labour Organisation (ILO). (2010a). *Global employment trends for youth: special issue on the impact of the global economic crisis on youth*. Geneva: ILO Office.

International Labour Organisation (ILO). (2010b). *Investing in young people: an ILO briefing note on the challenges, urgency and means*. Geneva: ILO Office.

Organisation for Economic Co-operation and Development (OECD). (2010a). *Off to a good start? Jobs for youth*. Paris: OECD.

Organisation for Economic Co-operation and Development (OECD). (2010b). *Education at a glance 2010*. Paris: OECD.

Organisation for Economic Co-operation and Development (OECD). (2010c). *Learning for jobs*. Paris: OECD.

Organisation for Economic Co-operation and Development (OECD). (2011). *OECD employment outlook 2011*. Paris: OECD.

Organisation for Economic Co-operation and Development (OECD). (2012). *Better skills, better jobs, better lives: a strategic approach to skills policies*. Paris: OECD.

Quintini, G. and Manfredi, T. (2009). *Going separate ways? School-to-work transitions in the United States and Europe*. OECD Social, Employment and Migration Working Papers, No. 90. Paris: OECD.

Quintini, G. and Martin, S. (2006). *Starting well or losing their way? The position of youth in the labour market in OECD countries*. OECD Social, Employment and Migration Working Papers, No. 39. Paris: OECD.

Scarpetta, S., Sonnet, A. and Manfredi, T. (2010). *Rising youth unemployment during the crisis: how to prevent negative long-term consequences on a generation?* OECD Social, Employment and Migration Working Papers, No. 106. Paris: OECD.

Part 2

Social and economic contexts

Chapter 5

Social mobility in Britain 1991–2011

Yaojun Li and Fiona Devine

Introduction

There has been increasing private and public anxiety about a possible decline in social mobility and what can be done to reverse this trend (Devine 2009; Payne 2012). In 2011, the UK Coalition Government established a new Social Mobility and Child Poverty Commission, launched by Deputy Prime Minister Nick Clegg and led by Alan Milburn, the Government's Independent Reviewer, who unveiled its Social Mobility Strategy. The strategic document accompanying the launch, *Opening doors, breaking barriers: a strategy for social mobility* (Cabinet Office 2011), focused attention on intergenerational mobility and emphasised the importance of equal opportunities so that everyone can enjoy success, irrespective of class origins. The Commission has to monitor progress towards improving social mobility by way of a set of key indicators and report to Parliament on an annual basis. This reporting process signifies an ongoing concern with social mobility into the foreseeable future.

This chapter outlines the major changes in patterns and trends of intergenerational social mobility in contemporary Britain. It is organised along the following lines. In the first section, we draw on earlier evidence of social mobility for men and women from the 1940s. The key issue is whether upward mobility is flattening out or even declining. We show that economists and sociologists use different analytical approaches and get different results, with the former arguing that there is a decline but the latter contesting that there is no overall decline in upward mobility (although some slight decline in men's upward mobility). In the second section, we discuss new findings from between 1991 and 2011. We draw on the 1991 British Household Panel Survey (BHPS 1991) and the Understanding Society (USoc 2011) and use the National Statistics Socio-economic Classification (NS-SeC) to analyse patterns and trends across the two surveys. In line with our previous analysis (Li and Devine 2011), we find that men's absolute upward mobility is declining while women's upward mobility is increasing. There are modest signs of improved relative mobility chances for men and women alike; that is, when upward and downward mobility rates are taken together.

Patterns and trends in social mobility in Britain since the 1940s

Our discussion of social mobility is based on movements between classes defined in terms of employment relations. It draws on national data from official sources and other survey data used by sociologists and economists. It makes reference to Goldthorpe's class schema, which has been much used in academic research and which was given a new instantiation in official statistics by the NS-SeC (Rose and Pevalin 2003) from around 2000 onwards. The schema is usually operationalised with seven classes defined by people's employment status and occupation. The 'employment aggregate' approach is viewed as appropriate for understanding social mobility (Crompton 2008).

In mobility research, sociologists usually differentiate between absolute and relative mobility. The former refers to the extent to which fathers and sons hold different class positions and can be further differentiated into total (comprising upward, downward and horizontal) mobility and immobility, while the latter refers to the relative chances of people coming from different origin classes ending up in one rather than another destination class.

The main patterns and trends in class mobility in Britain since the Second World War can be divided into two periods: (1) the postwar period 'of the long boom' (1940s–1970s) and (2) the mid-1970s to the present day. Our knowledge of the first period comes from the Social Mobility Inquiry (SMI) conducted in the early 1970s and published in the 1980s (Goldthorpe *et al.* 1980, 1987; Halsey *et al.* 1980; Heath 1981). In terms of absolute (or total) mobility, Goldthorpe *et al.* (1987) found considerable upward mobility, including long-range mobility from manual origins into professional and managerial careers. There was little downward mobility in the opposite direction. Goldthorpe *et al.* (1987) concluded that the changing occupational structure had a profound effect on the shape of the class structure and movement between classes.

Goldthorpe *et al.* (1987) also noted considerable stability in relative mobility, however. Relative rates of mobility had not changed. Middle-class children had a 4:1 chance of securing a professional–managerial 'service-class' occupation compared with working-class children, and they had only a 1:4 chance of falling into a working-class job. The two 'disparity ratios' yield an odds ratio of 16 in favour of the middle-class children and the pattern was fairly constant across the birth cohorts (Goldthorpe *et al.* 1987: 80). The growth of professional–managerial occupations meant that there was 'more room at the top' for men of all class origins but the relative class advantages or disadvantages remained fairly unchanged (the SMI contained information for men only). Thus, changes in the shape of the class structure and patterns of mobility between different classes had not made Britain a more open or meritocratic society. Class origins very much influenced class destinations.

Our knowledge of the second period from the mid-1970s is more limited because we do not have a survey specifically on social mobility in this later era.

Nevertheless, Goldthorpe and Mills (2004) draw on the General Household Survey (GHS) between 1973 and 1992, and Goldthorpe and Mills (2008) extend the time coverage to 2005. On absolute mobility, the trend towards increasing upward mobility among men had been superseded by a slight decline while the trend towards declining downward social mobility had reversed towards a slight rise. In other words, men's mobility chances had become less favourable. For women, they found a steady increase in the rate of upward mobility while downward mobility had decreased or flattened out. Thus, the substantial upward mobility facilitated by the growth of high-level occupations from the 1940s had slowed by the mid-1970s and might now even be reversing for men, although they are improving for women. Owing to the increasing participation of women in the labour market, the growth of service-sector jobs and other factors, gender gaps in occupational attainment were narrowing although men were still more likely to be found in more advantaged jobs. Relative rates had remained the same for men and women.

Whiles sociologists tend to focus on class mobility, economists attach greater importance to family incomes when they study social mobility. A well-known group of economists have suggested that social mobility might now be declining (Blanden et al. 2005; see also Machin and Vignoles 2004). They examined changes in intergenerational income mobility using longitudinal data from the National Child Development Study (NCDS) and the British Cohort Study (BCS), comparing family incomes (in quartiles or quintiles) and sons' and daughters' incomes or educational attainment. They found that income mobility had fallen for those sons born in 1970 compared with those born in 1958. The percentage of sons in the lowest income quartile whose parents were also in the lowest quartile rose from 31 per cent in 1958 to 38 per cent in 1970, while the percentage of sons in the highest income quartile whose parents were also in the highest quartile rose from 35 per cent among the 1958 cohort to 42 per cent among the 1970 cohort (Blanden et al. 2005: 8). Thus they find that income mobility has declined.

Blanden and her colleagues (2005) argued that the decline in intergenerational mobility is the result of a closer relationship between family income and educational attainment between the 1958 and 1970 cohorts. Drawing on data from the British Household Panel Survey (BHPS) to consider a third cohort of children reaching age 16 in the 1990s, they found that more children (sons and daughters) from both rich and poor families stayed on in further education after 16 and then higher education after age 18. However, they found that inequality between the two groups rose between the 1970s and 1980s as the participation rates of the richer children surged ahead, particularly with regard to higher education and the acquisition of degrees (Blanden et al. 2005: 11).

These findings were challenged by Goldthorpe and Jackson (2007), who prefer a class structural approach to class mobility over the economists' focus on income mobility and income relativities on the grounds that class better captures the family and the individual's socio-economic situations and that the NCDS had poor income data. Using the same data sources but adopting the class approach, they found that men's absolute mobility had not fallen while women's absolute mobility had witnessed some changes. For men, the rising rate of upward mobility between the 1940s and the 1960s started to flatten out from the 1970s and downward mobility increased. For women, there has been increasing upward mobility and decreasing downward mobility. Turning to relative rates of mobility, they found no change, indicating that levels of fluidity were unaltered between the two cohorts. Thus, Goldthorpe and Jackson concluded that social mobility may be slackening off for men but it is not actually declining, or not as yet (see also Goldthorpe and Mills 2008). This also shows that using different approaches (class or income) could lead to different results on patterns and trends of social mobility in Britain.

The key substantive difference between the analyses conducted by Goldthorpe and his colleagues on the one hand and Blanden and her colleagues on the other is whether men's mobility (absolute and relative) is constant or declining. This difference is, as shown earlier, related to the methods used. The economist's preferred method is to use income quintiles for mobility tables. In this way, all marginal distributions are made equal by design and, as a result, all upward and downward mobility rates are constrained to be equal (Goldthorpe and Mills 2008: 86). The sociologists' preferred class structural approach to mobility analysis allows for changes in the parents' and children's class distributions and in upward and downward mobility rates. And they use odds ratios (the relative chances of securing advantaged and avoiding disadvantaged class positions) to address relative mobility. Yet, notwithstanding the technical complexities, the messages arising from the research by economists and sociologists are quite clear. The former believe that social mobility is declining and that society is getting more unequal while the latter believe that there are simply trendless fluctuations in relative mobility and that our society is as (un)equal as before.

While the research by Goldthorpe and his colleagues has been highly influential, there are also findings from the sociological perspective that are somewhat different from theirs. In our previous study (Li and Devine 2011), we took note of the shortcomings in the use of cohort data as observed by Goldthorpe and Jackson (2007) by providing population-level estimates. Using the BHPS (1991) and the GHS (2005), we found a significant decline in men's upward mobility and a significant increase in men's downward mobility between 1990 and 2005 (Li and Devine 2011: Table II). We also found that the case was different for women, with a significant increase in upward mobility but no significant change in downward mobility (Li and Devine 2011: Table III). Furthermore, we found a slight but significant improvement in relative mobility for men and women. These findings, especially in the last regard, were in keeping with other research (Heath and Payne 2000; Lambert *et al.* 2007), which also found signs of increasing fluidity. In the present analysis, we wish to update our analysis by drawing on the most recent data (at the time of writing) in the USoc survey (USoc 2011) to be compared with the BHPS (1991). This will allow us to examine patterns and trends of intergenerational social mobility in Britain in the last 20 years.

Data and methods

As noted earlier, we use the BHPS for 1991 and the USoc survey for 2011 in this study (hereafter called 1991 and 2011). Both were funded by the Economic and Social Research Council (ESRC), are national representative sample surveys for respondents resident in private households in Great Britain at the time of interview and both have large sample sizes. (The USoc covers Northern Ireland but as it constitutes only 5.5 per cent of the data used in this chapter, and as further analysis shows no significant difference in social fluidity between it and Great Britain, the Northern Ireland data are used in this analysis.) The BHPS began in 1991 as the premier British panel study and had around 10,000 individuals in that year. The USoc is the largest panel study in the United Kingdom with around 55,000 respondents in 2011. We confine the analysis to men and women aged 25 to 59 in both datasets so that our results can be compared with those in Goldthorpe and Mills (2008) and Li and Devine (2011).[1]

In both datasets, the respondents' origin and destination classes are consistently coded using the NS-SeC schema. The respondent's class is based on his or her current or last main job and the parental class on the father's or mother's jobs (whichever is higher) during the respondent's adolescence using the dominance approach (Erikson 1984). The USoc has a part that is continued from the BHPS and the parental class information of the BHPS part is added in the analysis. We coded the parental and respondent's NS-SeC into the seven-class schema as per Rose and Pevalin (2003: 8–10).

As both male and female respondents' and their parents' NS-SeC codes are available in the long version, we followed the suggestions by Erikson and Goldthorpe (1992: 241) that, where possible, men and women in the lower intermediate class (in sales and personal services jobs) be combined with unskilled manual working class. As women have consistently increased their participation rates in the labour market in the last 40 years (Li and Heath 2010) with a substantial portion being in higher class and earnings positions than their partners (Li and Devine 2011), and as an increasing proportion of families are headed by female single parents, the dominance approach to the classification of origin class is becoming a preferred choice where data are available. After selecting respondents within the age confines and with valid origin and destination classes, we have 5,555 respondents for the 1991 and 19,749 respondents for the 2011 data.

The seven-class NS-SeC schema we use for both origin and destination classes are:

1   higher managerial and professional and large employers (hereafter 'higher salariat');
2   lower managerial and professional (hereafter 'lower salariat');
3   intermediate;

4   small employers and own account workers;
5   lower supervisory and technical;
6   semi-routine; and
7   routine.

(Rose and Pevalin 2003: 13)

In parts the following discussion, we sometimes refer to the first two classes as the salariat, the middle three as the intermediate class, and the last two as the working class. We conduct our analyses for men and women separately, and use standard methods for mobility research, such as cross-tabulations and the so-called 'loglinear models' (explained later).

Patterns and trends in social mobility 1991–2011

As our main interest in this chapter is to compare changes in intergenerational social mobility, we look at absolute and relative rates. In the first respect, we look at the outflow rates (class distributions) and in the second, results from loglinear and log-multiplicative layer effects models (also called uniform difference, or UNIDIFF models – explained later). Tables 5.1 and 5.2 show the outflow rates for men and women, respectively, and Table 5.3, the modelling results.

Absolute mobility

The data in Table 5.1 on men's mobility show some important differences; stability as well as change. First, we see pronounced class differences. Take men from Classes 1 and 7 origins, for example. In 1991, 70 per cent of the men from Class 1 families were found in salariat positions and only 10 per cent were found in working-class positions. This picture was only slightly changed in 2011, at 68 per cent and 12 per cent, respectively (due to space limitations, we do not conduct significant tests for these differences). By contrast, men from Class 7 families had only a weak presence (24 per cent) in the salariat and a salient presence (37 per cent) in the working class in 1991. In 2011, their situation in working-class positions was almost unchanged (at 35 per cent) but they had a larger slice of the salariat (33 per cent). The marked class differences overshadowed the small changes.

If we look at the overall changes in the class structure, we see that there was a continued upgrading of the occupations. Looking at the two rows for 'All', we see that the salariat positions (Classes 1 and 2) had increased by 9 percentage points (from 38 per cent to 47 per cent) and working-class positions had fallen by 3 percentage points (from 27 per cent to 24 per cent). When we compare the distributions to the salariat, we find an increase for men from all non-salariat class origins, although to varying degrees. Salariat intergenerational class stability seems to have reached a saturation point. It is noted, however, that our salariat classes, even those of the higher grade, include fairly broad categories and we are not able to address issues of elite stability here. The contraction of the routine

Table 5.1 Outflow mobility rates for men (% by row): upper figure of each pair 1991 study (N = 2,634), lower figure 2011 study (N = 9,212)[a]

Class of origin	Class of destination[b]							N
	1	2	3	4	5	6	7	
1	36	34	4	7	8	4	6	135
	36	32	5	10	5	5	7	1,183
2	25	33	4	12	11	6	9	510
	24	34	7	10	8	7	9	2,030
3	21	29	4	11	14	8	13	176
	22	29	7	13	11	8	10	1,082
4	17	18	4	26	14	6	15	365
	12	24	4	21	11	12	17	1,315
5	13	20	4	13	18	13	18	552
	15	23	5	15	12	13	16	1,056
6	9	18	3	13	17	18	24	402
	13	22	3	14	13	14	20	1,238
7	8	16	4	15	22	15	22	494
	11	22	4	15	14	13	22	1,308
All	16	22	4	15	16	11	16	
	20	27	5	13	11	10	14	
N	419	597	102	386	415	293	422	2,634
	1,799	2,432	445	1,290	978	951	1,317	9,212

Summary statistics

	1991	2011	2011–1991[c]
Total mobility	77.4	77.7	0.3
Upward mobility	43.6	40.5	−3.1**
Downward mobility	26.0	30.1	4.1***
Horizontal mobility	7.8	7.1	−0.7

Sources: British Household Panel Survey (1991) and Understanding Society (2011).

Notes

a Weighted analyses and unweighted N. For respondents aged 25 to 59 in Great Britain at time of survey.

b Black = immobility; dark grey = upward mobility; light grey = downward mobility; white = horizontal mobility.

c * p<0.05, ** p<0.01, *** p<0.001.

position (Class 7) was shared by men from Classes 5 and 6 origins but not for those from this class background, which was 22 per cent at both time points. The stability in the higher salariat and routine class positions in intergenerational mobility is remarkable. Thus, while the salariat was slowly opening up to men from lower-class origins, the working class, especially those in routine manual positions, were still largely filled by men from working-class origins.

Table 5.2 Outflow mobility rates for women (% by row): upper figure of each pair 1991 study (N = 2,921), lower figure 2011 study (N = 10,537)[a]

| Class of origin | Class of destination[b] | | | | | | | N |
	1	2	3	4	5	6	7	
1	11	51	15	8	1	5	10	182
	19	42	11	6	2	12	8	1,333
2	6	35	20	7	5	14	12	587
	14	42	10	7	3	14	10	2,367
3	6	25	27	7	6	13	16	214
	11	40	12	5	4	17	11	1,287
4	3	20	22	10	5	20	21	371
	9	30	12	9	5	21	14	1,444
5	3	21	19	4	10	20	23	606
	7	32	10	6	5	24	15	1,084
6	2	18	16	4	8	28	25	473
	7	28	11	5	6	26	18	1,471
7	1	19	16	3	8	23	30	488
	6	26	11	5	7	27	19	1,551
All	4	25	19	6	7	19	21	
	11	35	11	6	4	20	13	
N	121	732	579	167	198	561	563	2,921
	1,367	4,380	2,332	753	832	2,884	1,273	10,537

Summary statistics

	1991	2011	2011–1991
Total mobility	77.8	78.5	0.7
Upward mobility	31.0	38.3	7.3***
Downward mobility	37.4	35.4	−2.0
Horizontal mobility	9.1	4.8	−4.3***

Sources: British Household Panel Survey (1991) and Understanding Society (2011).

Notes
a Weighted analyses and unweighted N. For respondents aged 25 to 59 in Great Britain at time of survey.
b Black = immobility; dark grey = upward mobility; light grey = downward mobility; white = horizontal mobility.
c * p<0.05, ** p<0.01, *** p<0.001.

At the bottom of the table, we present some summary statistics of total, upward, downward and horizontal mobility rates, defined by the shades in the table, which capture these findings. Total mobility has barely changed, rising by 0.3 percentage points from 77.4 per cent in 1991 to 77.7 per cent in 2011. There are clear signs of decreasing upward mobility for men over the two decades (by 3.1 percentage points), which is significant at the 0.01 level. Correspondingly, there is an increase

Table 5.3 Results of fitting the conditional independence, constant social fluidity and UNIDIFF models to mobility tables for the 1991 and 2011 studies[a]

Model	G^2	df	p	rG^2	BIC	Δ
Men (N =11,846)						
Conditional independence	1,249.0	72	0	0	573.6	13.8
Constant social fluidity	59.8	36	0.01	95.2	−277.9	2.3
Uniform difference	48.7	35	0.06	96.1	−279.5	1.9
$\beta = 0.981$[b]	11.1	1	0.001			
Women (N =13,458)						
Conditional independence	1,033.2	72	0	0	348.7	11.4
Constant social fluidity	73.6	36	0	92.9	−268.7	2.2
Uniform difference	56.1	35	0.01	94.6	−276.7	1.9
$\beta = 0.977$[b]	17.5	1	0.000			

Notes
a rG^2 = percentage reduction in G^2; Δ = percentage of cases misclassified.
b Constant social fluidity minus UNIDIFF.

in downward mobility (by 4.1 points), which is significant at the 0.001 level. The findings here echo our previous research (Li and Devine 2011: Table II).

Turning to the patterns on women's social mobility as shown in Table 5.2, we see both similarities and differences when compared to men's patterns. First, as with men, we see pronounced class differences. Sixty-two per cent of the women from the higher salariat origins were found in the salariat positions in 1991, three times as high as those from the routine manual families (20 per cent). This difference is similar to men's in magnitude. Only 10 per cent of the women from the higher salariat, but 30 per cent of those from the routine manual families, were found in routine manual positions in 1991, or 15 per cent of the former found in all working-class positions compared to 53 per cent for the latter. In 2011, the overall proportion of women from Class 1 origins found in the salariat positions was similar to that in 1991 and the proportion of women from Class 7 origins found in the salariat increased by 12 percentage points, to 32 per cent. The proportion found in the working-class positions increased to 20 per cent for the former and dropped to 46 per cent for the latter. In this sense, we see some notable changes. There are, therefore, clear class differences for women, as there are for men (discussed earlier).

Second, we also found some differences in women's distributions in the salariat positions when compared to the men's situation. In the case of men, as we have just observed, the expansion of the salariat positions was more likely to benefit those from lower class origins. Yet in the case of women, only the growth of lower salariat positions benefited those from lower classes, but the growth in the higher salariat was more utilised by women from higher rather than lower origins. For the increase of 7 percentage points in the higher salariat positions (from 4 per cent to 11 per cent), those from Classes 1–4 origins took a greater share (by 8, 8, 5 and 6 percentage points, respectively) than those from Classes 5–7 origins (by 4, 5 and 5 points, respectively). The routine manual positions fell from 21 per cent in 1991 to 13 per cent in 2011 as the data in 'All' show. This decline benefited women from lower origins rather than from higher origins by 2 percentage points for women from Class 1 and 11 points for women from Class 7 origins. Here we see both a strengthening of higher salariat advantage and a reduction of routine class disadvantage.

The summary statistics in the lower part of the table show that trends in women's absolute mobility are more favourable than men's. There has been a slight increase in total mobility, increasing by 0.7 percentage points from 77.8 per cent in 1991 to 78.5 per cent in 2011. Behind this picture, however, important changes are afoot. Upward mobility increased significantly by 7.3 percentage points (from 31.0 per cent to 38.3 per cent). Downward mobility declined by 2.0 percentage points from 37.4 per cent to 35.4 per cent. Finally, horizontal mobility declined by 4.3 percentage points (from 9.1 per cent to 4.8 per cent). The growth in upward mobility and decline in downward mobility has facilitated another important change. In 1991, women were more likely to be downwardly rather than upwardly mobile. By 2011, women are more likely to be upwardly mobile than downwardly mobile. The position of women is much improved. These findings confirm our earlier analysis (Li and Devine 2011: Table III).

Relative mobility

Having looked at absolute mobility in some detail, we now turn to relative mobility, which, as noted earlier, refers to the competition of people from different origin classes for one rather than another class destination and is expressed as odds ratios. If there are equal chances of class mobility, there is no association between origin and destination and the odds ratio would be 1. The closer the odds ratio is to 1, the weaker the association and hence the greater equality in social mobility, while the further the odds ratio rises above 1, the stronger the association and the greater the inequality. In a similar vein, the further the odds ratio falls below 1, the weaker the association and the greater the equality. Relative mobility illustrates the net association between origin and destination, independent of the structural changes as reflected in the marginal distributions.

Two statistical models are normally used for relative mobility analysis: the loglinear and the log-multiplicative layer effect (also called 'uniform difference' or UNIDIFF) models (Erikson and Goldthorpe 1992). The loglinear model is subdivided into a baseline (or conditional independence) model and a constant social fluidity (CSF) model. Briefly, the baseline model assumes that the distributions of both origins and destinations varies by the time of survey (year), but there is no association between them. Thus, all the odds ratios or relative chances defining origin and destination classes are equal at a value of one. The CSF model allows for the latter association but does not allow for the three-way association, which would be a saturated model. The UNIDIFF model is a variant of the CSF model, which further allows for a uniform movement for the coefficient of one year to move above or below that of the other. In the present analysis, we use 1991 as the reference point. Thus the further the coefficient for 2011 is above that of 1991, the more unequal society is becoming, and vice versa. For both men and women, we used weighted counts.

Table 5.3 shows the results of fitting the loglinear and the UNIDIFF models to the mobility tables for men and women in 1991 and 2011. For men, the CSF model gives a poor fit to the data. The UNIDIFF model gives a statistically significant improvement in fit over the CSF model. The estimated (β) parameter for 2011 when compared with 1991 was 0.981, indicating a slight but significant increase in fluidity, indicating greater upward as well as downward mobility or a less grip of parental class on children's class positions. This finding is generally in line with that of Goldthorpe and Mills (2008: 92), although they find a somewhat more salient effect (by a factor of 0.86). The patterns are very close to those found by Li and Devine (2011: Table VI). In the case of women, neither CSF nor UNIDIFF model gives an acceptable fit to the data according to the conventional criterion, but the latter does make a highly significant improvement in fit over the former, with the β parameter being 0.977. This shows that there is a somewhat greater (albeit to a small extent) equality in women's than in men's social mobility.

Thus, for both men and women, the evidence suggests some increasing social equality over the period covered, even though the extent of the increase is rather small. The findings here are somewhat at odds with the 'no-change' result on the cohort data as reported by Goldthorpe and Jackson (2007: Table VI), but are in line with the result on the 'complete' tables (conjugal households) as reported by Goldthorpe and Mills (2008: Table 4). They are also in line with studies using the semi-cohort methods (Heath and Payne 2000), and those reported in Lambert et al. (2007a), Li and Devine (2011) and Devine and Li (2013). While there are still pronounced class inequalities, there is a small and significant improvement toward social equality.

Conclusion

In this chapter, we have outlined the main patterns and trends of social mobility in contemporary Britain. Using the best data available containing mobility information on the general population, namely the BHPS (1991) and the USoc (2011), we have extended existing research by Goldthorpe and Jackson (2007), Goldthorpe and Mills (2008), Li and Devine (2011) and Devine and Li (2013) to show the mobility patterns and trends to the most recent time. We focused our attention on class differences in gaining access to the privileged professional and managerial salariat positions and in avoiding the disadvantaged working-class positions, particularly those at the two ends of the class spectrum, on the changing upward and downward mobility rates, and on the relative mobility changes. In all three respects, we conducted analysis for men and women separately.

Given the decline in men's absolute upward mobility and increase in downward mobility, as our results show, it is hardly surprising that these trends are a private problem – for young men and their parents – and a public issue – for employers, policymakers and politicians. Commentators such as Alm (2011) are right to be concerned about the life chances of working-class men and how everyone involved in education and employment can help to reverse these trends by increasing working-class upward mobility. Although women's absolute upward mobility has increased, and downward mobility has decreased, the fate of young working-class women should not be overlooked because they are still only one-third as likely to gain a foothold in the higher salariat as those from Class 1 families. Again, all those involved in education (schools and teachers) and employment (organisations and employers) need to contribute to initiatives to improve their life chances too.

In sum, our current analysis, as well as previous work (Li and Devine 2011; Devine and Li 2013), shows that while there are still pronounced class differences in social as well as in educational mobility, there are also signs for hope. Basically, the middle-class intergenerational stability seems to have reached a saturation point and if employers, educators and government make concerted efforts to increase the educational take-up and occupational upward mobility of working-class children, through apprenticeships, on-job training programmes and strict enforcement of equality laws, we could make our society less unequal. We have seen signs of hope, but we need to make greater efforts. We cannot, in this chapter, give concrete suggestions but we are hopeful that employers and educational scientists/practitioners could design better programmes to help working-class sons and daughters to fulfil their dreams.

Note

1   The datasets are available at www.esds.ac.uk/about/atoz.asp? [accessed 8 March 2011].

References

Alm, S. (2011). *Downward social mobility across generations: the role of parental mobility and equation*. Stockholm: Institute of Futures Studies.

Blanden, J., Gregg, P. and Machin, S. (2005). Educational inequality and intergenerational mobility. *In:* S. Machin and A. Vignoles, eds. *What's the good of education? The economics of education in the UK*. Princeton, NJ: Princeton University Press, 99–114.

British Household Panel Survey (BHPS). 1991. *British Household Panel Survey: Waves 1–18, 1991–2009*. 7th ed. Institute for Social and Economic Research, University of Essex: UK Data Archive, July 2010. SN: 5151.

Cabinet Office. (2011). *Opening doors, breaking barriers: a strategy for social mobility*. London: The Cabinet Office.

Crompton, R. (2008). *Class and stratification: an introduction to current debates*. 3rd ed. Cambridge, UK: Polity Press.

Devine, F. (2009). Class. *In:* M. Flinders, A. Gamble, C. Hay and M. Kenny, eds. *The Oxford handbook of British politics.* Oxford, UK: Oxford University Press, 609–628.

Devine, F. and Li, Y. (2013). The changing relationship between origins, education and destinations in the 1990s and 2000s. *British Journal of Sociology of Education*, 34 (5–6): 766–791.

Erikson, R. (1984). Social class of men, women and families. *Sociology*, 18: 500–514.

Erikson, R. and Goldthorpe, J. H. (1992). *The constant flux.* Oxford, UK: Clarendon Press.

General Household Survey (GHS). (2005). *General Household Survey 2005.* 2nd ed. Office for National Statistics, Social and Vital Statistics Division: UK Data Archive, November 2007, SN: 5640.

Goldthorpe, J. H. (with Llewellyn, C. and Payne, C.). (1980, 1987). *Social mobility and class structure in modern Britain.* Oxford, UK: Clarendon Press.

Goldthorpe, J. H. and Mills, C. (2004). Trends in intergenerational class mobility in Britain in the late twentieth century. *In:* R. Breen, ed. *Social mobility in Europe.* Oxford, UK: Oxford University Press, 195–224.

Goldthorpe, J. H. and Jackson, M. (2007). Intergenerational class mobility in contemporary Britain: political concerns and empirical findings. *British Journal of Sociology*, 58 (4): 526–546.

Goldthorpe, J. H. and Mills, C. (2008). Trends in intergenerational class mobility in modern Britain: evidence from national surveys. *National Institute Economic Review*, 205: 83–100.

Halsey, A., Heath, A. and Ridge, J. (1980). *Origins and destinations: family, class and education in modern Britain.* Oxford, UK: Clarendon Press.

Heath, A. (1981). *Social mobility.* London: Fontana.

Heath, A. and Payne, C. (2000). Social mobility. *In:* A. H. Halsey with J. Webb, eds. *Twentieth-century British social trends.* Basingstoke, UK: Macmillan, 254–278.

Lambert, P., Prandy, K. and Bottero, W. (2007). By slow degrees: two centuries of social reproduction and mobility in Britain. *Sociological Research Online*, 13 (1). doi:10.5153/sro.1493.

Li, Y. and Heath, A. (2010). Struggling onto the ladder, climbing the rungs: employment status and class position by minority ethnic groups in Britain (1972–2005). *In:* J. Stillwell, P. Norman, C. Thomas and P. Surridge, eds. *Population, employment, health and well-being.* London: Springer, 83–97.

Li, Y. and Devine, F. (2011). Is social mobility really declining? Intergenerational class mobility in Britain in the 1990s and the 2000s. *Sociological Research Online*. Available from: www.socresonline.org.uk/16/3/4.html [accessed 26 August 2011].

Machin, S. and Vignoles, A. (2004). Educational inequality: the widening socio-economic gap. *Fiscal Studies*, 25: 107–128.

Payne, G. (2012). Labouring under a misapprehension: politicians' perception and the realities of structural social mobility in Britain, 1995–2010. *In:* R. Connelly, P. Lambert, R. Blackburn and V. Gayle, eds. *Social stratification: trends and processes.* Farnham, UK: Ashgate, 223–242.

Rose, D. and Pevalin, D. (eds). (2003). *A researcher's guide to the national statistics socio-economic classification.* London: Sage Publications.

Understanding Society (USoc). 2011. *Understanding Society: Waves 1–2, 2009–2011.* 5th ed. Institute for Social and Economic Research, University of Essex, and NatCen Social Research: UK Data Archive, November 2013. SN: 6614. Available from: http://dx. doi.org/10.5255/UKDA-SN-6614-5 [accessed 6 March 2014].

Chapter 6

The winners and losers in the 'hourglass' labour market

Craig Holmes and Ken Mayhew

Introduction

The creation of a highly skilled workforce has long been seen as important in order to meet the needs of the twenty-first century labour market. Policymakers argue that there is increasing demand for the skills that make individuals better able to adapt to the changing nature of work, particular those changes driven by technological advances. Moreover, in an increasingly international marketplace, many large employers may move around in order to find the skills they need, so it benefits a country if its workforce can meet these needs (and costs a country if it cannot). As a result, policymakers talk about there being 'room at the top' (HM Government 2011) – high-skilled employment opportunities for expanding numbers of well-qualified workers.

Increasing the number of high-skilled jobs is not just important for economic prosperity at a national level; it is also good for social goals, such as lowering earnings inequality and improving social mobility. In particular, as highly skilled work is typically rewarded with high pay and greater progression opportunities, then increasing the number of highly educated workers in skilled work will spread these benefits to a wider group of people, many of whom may have come from less advantaged backgrounds.

This suggests that over the last few decades, changes in the labour market have largely created a series of 'winners' – those in work with skills who are increasingly valued by employers, those in work without skills who might be encouraged to acquire them in order to benefit from their rising demand, and those soon to enter the labour market who have made significant investments in their education. However, as this chapter will highlight, through both a review of the literature and new empirical analyses, this perspective has some problems. In particular, we argue that the rising demand for skills is not as widespread as it suggests. While some workers appear to have benefited hugely, many have not, despite making investments in their education and even after finding employment in jobs that sound highly skilled. This widening range of outcomes is concealed by focusing on the relative average outcomes of a particular group, such as university graduates. By doing so, however, policymakers have largely focused on getting more people into the highly qualified group, and have tended to assume that high-skilled jobs will emerge in direct proportion to this. The role actually played by employers has been given a second-order importance. However, decisions about what types of jobs to create are the key important determinant on outcomes, and if these decisions do not automatically adjust to increases in the numbers of highly qualified individuals, then policies that do so become a costly and potentially ineffective way of improving on social outcomes. In part, this constraint depends on how employers engage with education and training systems in order to provide the skills and knowledge they actually need. Low engagement could lead to a mismatch between what skills newly qualified workers have and what they need – in this case, the constraint is the result of specific skill supply shortages. On the other hand, low engagement might also be a consequence of employers' wider production strategies – for some, their skill needs might be less than those being supplied by an increasingly well-qualified workforce, giving little motivation to interfere. In this latter case, simply encouraging greater engagement between employers and the education system would be ineffective unless the demand for skills could also be increased.

The second section of this chapter gives a brief overview of social mobility trends in the United Kingdom, focusing on the trends relating to how occupational structure and education have interacted.

The third section presents results from our analysis of the 1958 and 1970 UK birth cohort studies and discusses how occupational structure changes have affected employment, mobility and earning outcomes. This section begins by examining how the occupational structure of the UK labour market has changed since 1980 and how this has affected patterns of occupational mobility. There is increasing evidence that technological change is not biased towards skills, but biased towards particular tasks. Routine tasks are those which, given a certain level of computer technology, could be performed equally well by a machine as by a worker. Typical examples include skilled manual workers in manufacturing and white-collar administrative workers, such as clerks. Non-routine tasks are those where such substitution is not an option. For example, improvements in robotics reduce firms' demand for the process operatives working on a car factory production line. At the same time, however, this raises the demand for the engineers who program and maintain increasingly technical equipment. However, it is unlikely that there are enough engineer jobs to replace all the lost routine jobs, so the question becomes, where else might individuals move to? Part of the answer is that some move to lower-paid non-routine jobs, such as retail assistants, carers or the cleaners employed at the car factory offices. Over the last 30 years, such service occupations have grown at a faster rate than the higher-wage non-routine occupations. Unemployment and inactivity are other possible destinations. Therefore, there might be considerable 'room at the bottom' as the occupations in decline are generally middle-wage (Goos and Manning 2007). This shift in the occupational structure is often referred to as the 'hourglass' labour market. The consequences of this shift potentially apply to those already in increasingly precarious routine jobs and also to those entering the labour market more recently who would have most likely gone to work in a semi-skilled manual job or an administrative position in the absence of these changes.

The third section continues by looking at how the demand side of the labour market may limit the supposed gains to shifting away from middle-skilled routine work. We discuss how many jobs created in growing occupations are not equivalent to those that existed before – they may be classified similarly for statistical purposes, but their pay and skill requirements are becoming increasingly spread out. Put another way, many of the supposed 'winners' are not winning much at all.

The chapter concludes with a brief discussion of how these trends may relate to the social mobility agenda in the future, and considers where employer engagement in education and training matters.

Social mobility in the United Kingdom

Social mobility is typically considered along three dimensions: class, wages and occupations. Policymakers are most concerned with intergenerational mobility; that is, they would like to ensure that individuals have fair opportunities to succeed during the course of their lives, and that these are not impacted by factors out of their control, such as their family background or their local geography.

Describing what has happened to mobility in the United Kingdom depends largely on which of these dimensions is being focused on. Class and occupation are closely related; however, occupational mobility is often considered in terms of how individuals move between different jobs during the course of their working lives and how they form careers. For the moment, we will compare intergenerational mobility measured by either class or earnings, and return to the issue of intragenerational mobility, and its relationship with intergenerational mobility, later in this section.

In terms of class, Goldthorpe (2012) argues that a long tradition of sociological research shows absolute mobility – the chances of entering a professional or managerial level occupation given an individual's parental background – has increased steadily over the last 50 years as the proportion of these jobs in the labour force has increased. He contends that the same research shows that relative mobility – the chances of entering a top occupation compared to those of someone from a more advantaged background – has remained constant, indicating that the increase in the number of such jobs has benefited those from advantaged and less-advantaged backgrounds proportionately. This would indicate that society has become no more or less fluid between different classes once changes in the occupational structure are taken into account.

This contrasts with studies of intergenerational wage mobility, which has been the main measure employed by economists and the one often focused on in policy discussions (see Blanden *et al.* 2005). In this tradition, mobility is seen to have worsened. Specifically, the correlation between parental and child incomes became stronger over time when comparing the members of a cohort born in 1958 with those of a later cohort born in 1970.[1]

It is worth noting (as Goldthorpe and others have) that these correlations largely capture relative mobility – an increasing correlation means that the links between parental and child income strengthen as advantaged children experience less downward mobility and disadvantaged children experience less upward mobility. Policy discussions, despite their repeated use of this finding, tend to be concerned with improving absolute earnings mobility so that children from poorer backgrounds can improve their standing without creating a zero-sum game where those from wealthier backgrounds need to experience greater downward mobility. Given that a growing supply of well-educated workers continues to experience a relatively stable earnings premium over non-graduates on average, this suggests that absolute earnings mobility has increased, even if positions in the earnings distribution have become no less correlated to parental incomes.

This, in turn, has been used to support a belief that labour market outcomes are driven by the supply side. In particular, given increasing demand for skilled work, more children from disadvantaged backgrounds could move towards higher-paid work providing they received greater access to higher levels of education. In this view, relative earnings mobility improves but those from more advantaged backgrounds do not get pushed down the distribution. Rather, the upper part of the occupational structure expands to accommodate all individuals who make the appropriate educational investments – this is the so-called 'room at the top'.

An alternative view is that the occupational structure is driven by demand-side factors, and that while it changes following technological progress or other global trends, the number of good jobs at any moment in time is fixed. Access to these jobs can be seen as a competition for places in a queue, where signals such as educational attainment determine position in the queue (Thurow 1975). In the same spirit, the recent work of Brown *et al.* (2011) describes a growing divide in the increasingly globalised market for skilled labour. On one side, the top jobs are found with the large multinational employers who are competing for a notional pool of 'talent'. Meanwhile, on the other side, the remainder of skilled workers are subject to technology-driven deskilling ('digital Taylorism') and downward wage pressures from new graduates in the developing world.

Clearly, this suggests that the labour market has rather less 'room at the top'. Instead, it implies the stable average graduate premium that supports the 'room at the top' argument is driven instead by rising returns for those in the good jobs, while many new graduates who are unable to find such a job obtain a much smaller premium. It is also worth noting that a demand-side view leads to very different implications for policies to improve social mobility. Improving the educational attainment of less advantaged children may improve relative mobility, but it will necessarily involve increasing the downward mobility of those from more advantaged backgrounds. Consequently, children of wealthier parents will be keen to resist this. They may use their resources to send their children to better schools, move to private education or pay for private tutors to maintain their advantages and place them in a better position to claim the limited supply of good jobs. These investments become increasingly important when they lead to improved chances of accessing the elite higher education institutions where employers looking for 'talent' typically recruit (Brown *et al.* 2011).

However it is measured, intergenerational mobility ultimately depends on two key drivers: the points of entry into the labour market after leaving full-time education and subsequent intragenerational mobility between jobs over the working life. Intra- and intergenerational mobility are not necessarily correlated. For instance, a labour market with limited intragenerational mobility may still exhibit significant intergenerational mobility if the allocation of workers to their first jobs is not influenced by parental background. However, greater intragenerational mobility implies greater competition for all jobs, including high status or high wage jobs, which should mean greater intergenerational mobility overall.

Some studies of occupational mobility have been concerned that labour markets are segmented, meaning there are groups of jobs between which mobility is practically impossible (see Leontaridi 1998 for an overview of the historical development of segmentation theory). However, the UK labour market has traditionally been characterised as having limited mobility, rather than being fully segmented (Mayhew and Rosewell 1979; McNabb 1987). Bukodi and Goldthorpe (2009) and Bukodi (2009) look at occupational entry and mobility across three cohorts in the United Kingdom, born between 1946 and 1970, using two continuous measures of labour market outcome – earnings and social status (using the Hope–Goldthorpe class schema). In terms of initial entry into the labour market, both educational attainment and parental background feature significantly. In terms of occupational status, entering the labour market with a degree had its largest positive effect in the earliest cohort, while other educational levels had larger effects in later cohorts. In terms of earnings, returns to subdegree levels of educational attainment had no obvious tendencies to increase over time, and degree returns were again largest in the earliest cohort. For subsequent mobility, both qualifications (including those gained since entry) and family background continue to exert effects on mobility, but again these effects seem relatively constant across cohorts. There is some evidence that initial employment exerts a long-term effect on future mobility[2] but that the number of transitions also matters – a greater number of transitions are correlated with greater upward mobility, suggesting that some individuals may be able to counteract the effect of entering the labour market through a lower status or wage job.

There is a gap in research, however, on how the underlying mechanisms, through which intergenerational mobility is shaped, have been affected by changes in the occupational structure. Two studies are worth noting at this point. First, Tomkins and Twomey (2000) compare the frequency of occupational transitions in England between 1975 and 1995, finding that mobility increased during the period 1990–1995. They then model transitions between 22 occupational groups at the aggregate level number of transitions made.[3] Mobility was more commonplace for destination occupations that were growing faster, as would be expected; however, there was no evidence of the anticipated negative relationship between slower growing (or declining) origin occupations and higher mobility, which suggests a more complex relationship between occupational mobility and structure. Similarly, Rhein and Trübswetter (2012) argue that occupational mobility may not always support structural changes in occupational employment shares. Comparing Britain and Germany, they find that the relationship between net occupational transitions and employment share change was stronger in Germany, suggesting that increases in employment shares of occupations in the United Kingdom relied more heavily on transitions into employment from non-employment and new labour market entrants, while decreases in employment shares led to transitions into unemployment.

In the following section, we present results from our recent analyses of UK cohort data. We first discuss occupational mobility for those in mid-level routine jobs across the two cohorts, looking at how the decline of mid-level routine jobs has affected the frequency of transitions, and who is most affected by this decline. As mentioned in the introduction, while much of the focus has been on the ability of well-qualified individuals to move upwards, a growing number of low-skilled non-routine jobs increase the prospect of downward moves. Similarly, when we discuss initial entry into the labour market, our interest is in how the decline in the routine jobs has affected where individuals of different educational backgrounds find their first jobs, which includes both access to higher skilled jobs as well as low-skilled work. Our final analysis looks at earnings within these occupational classifications. In particular, we consider evidence that the benefits of occupational structure change may be overemphasised when looking at occupational groups alone, and that increasing heterogeneity in earnings within these groups suggests there is less 'room at the top' than is otherwise accepted.

The implications of an 'hourglass' labour market

Data

The analysis in this section uses data from the National Child Development Study (NCDS) and the British Cohort Study (BCS). The members of the NCDS study were all born in a single week in March 1958. Data have been collected on these members in a series of waves in 1981, 1991, 1999–2000 and 2004–2005. The members of the BCS study were all born in a single week in April 1970. For the purposes of our analysis, we use data collected in 1996, 1999–2000, 2004–2005 and 2008–2009.

Occupations are measured using the most detailed available occupational coding. One problem with doing this over a long period of time is that the system of coding occupations has changed three times since 1980. To make data comparable, a conversion into SOC2000 (4-digit) groups was derived between the various systems using the descriptions of occupations provided for each group (see Holmes 2011 for a discussion). The converted occupational data were then reduced into 3-digit occupational groups and assigned to one of the six occupational categories. 'Professional', 'managerial' and 'intermediate' occupations are three higher-skilled non-routine occupations, while 'manual non-routine' and 'service non-routine' are low-skilled, non-routine occupations. The remainder of occupations are routine, with manual and clerical routine occupations grouped together. Aside from a few obvious cases, a routine occupation is defined as one that experienced a significant decline in employment share over the period 1981–2008. All these occupations have middle-range wages and their descriptions suggest the work involved administrative or manual processes that could be replaced by computer technology. Table 6.1 shows the employment share of these groups between 1981 and 2004.

Across the multiple waves of the NCDS and BCS data used in this chapter, there are numerous systems for recording educational achievement, including detailed data on a wide range of vocational courses that have declined in importance in recent years. As a way to bring all of this data together, the highest National Vocational Qualification (NVQ) equivalent level across time is recorded. At each point in time, the individual has two educational variables – a highest NVQ level in academic courses and a highest NVQ level in vocational courses, which both range from level 0 to level 5.

Mobility

We first look at how mobility patterns have changed as a result of a shift away from routine occupations. Transitions between different occupational groups in the two cohorts are measured at 4–5 year intervals. For the earlier cohort data, we have five periods: 1981–1986, 1986–1991, 1991–1995, 1995–1999 and 1999–2004. For the younger cohort, we use four periods: 1992–1996, 1996–2000, 2000–2004 and 2004–2008. These years were chosen based on when each cohort study collected waves of data, so individuals were mostly responding to questions about current employment rather than recollections about earlier employment and were therefore more likely to give accurate answers.

Table 6.1 Employment shares by occupational group, 1981–2004

	LFS 1981	QLFS 2004
Professional	10.0%	14.4%
Managerial	10.1%	14.8%
Intermediate	5.8%	13.7%
Routine	56.1%	30.8%
Manual non-routine	5.1%	5.8%
Service non-routine	12.9%	20.5%
Total employed	84,471	58,495

Sources: Labour Force Survey 1981, Quarterly Labour Force Survey 2004 Q1, own calculations.

To illustrate typical patterns of mobility, Tables 6.2 and 6.3 show the transitions made between different occupational groups for each of the two cohorts when both were at a similar age (1986–1991 for the NCDS cohort and 1996–2000 for the BCS cohort). These show that the BCS cohort is more occupationally mobile. One reason for this may be that the younger cohort has higher levels of academic attainment, which is associated with greater mobility. Similarly, they have fewer vocational qualifications tying them to particular jobs that employ those skills. Changes in the occupational structure may also have played a role if younger workers were in the labour market during a more turbulent time period.

To investigate the drivers of occupational transitions further, we model the probability of moving from a mid-level routine occupation to each of the possible destination groups.[4] The factors we include in this analysis are gender, educational level, age, cohort, experience in routine occupations and a time-specific measure of the overall decline in routine jobs. This final variable is calculated using the rate of decline in the employment share of routine jobs during a given period across the whole labour market. The regression results are in Tables 6A.1, 6A.2 and 6A.3 in the Appendix. Table 6.4 summarises the results.[5]

The main results can be summarised as follows. For any given educational level and occupational structure, the younger cohort was more mobile towards all possible destinations, including lower-skilled service occupations, unemployment and inactivity. This is to be expected – the ratio of non-routine jobs to routine jobs is higher at each age for the BCS cohort. We observe that downward moves are possible, although relatively infrequent compared to upward moves. Greater academic educational attainment (from level 2 upwards) and vocational attainment (from level 4 upwards) is generally associated with an increased likelihood of moving towards professional, managerial and intermediate occupations. Academic qualifications above compulsory education decrease the chances of less desirable transitions; however, having vocational qualifications does not decrease the chances of moving from a routine job to either a service job or out of work. Finally, a decline in routine jobs has a large and significant effect on mobility, but this was almost entirely found in the older NCDS cohort and was much more muted (particularly for upward transitions) in the younger BCS cohort.

More work needs to be carried out in order to fully understand this last result. One hypothesis is that during the 1980s and early 1990s, the growth in routine jobs created opportunities for both experienced workers and suitably educated labour market entrants to move up. However, as the potential supply to these jobs increased from increasingly well-qualified new entrants, the opportunities to progress for workers already in jobs diminished.

Entry

We shall now look at how the shift away from routine work has affected those entering the labour market. Table 6.5 compares the two cohorts' employment

Table 6.2 NCDS cohort mobility matrix, 1986–1991 (values in per cent)

		Destination							
		Professional	Managerial	Intermediate	Routine	Manual	Service	Unemployed	Inactive
Origin	Professional	79.0	7.2	4.1	2.7	0.4	0.9	1.2	4.5
	Managerial	3.2	76.8	3.9	6.5	0.9	2.9	1.2	4.5
	Intermediate	6.0	7.7	67.0	6.3	0.6	3.2	1.3	8.0
	Routine	3.3	6.4	3.6	69.8	1.6	4.7	2.5	8.2
	Manual	0.4	1.9	1.6	5.4	85.3	1.2	2.7	1.6
	Service	2.3	5.9	4.8	12.5	0.7	60.8	1.9	11.3
	Unemployed	3.2	3.7	4.8	24.3	4.5	9.8	36.2	13.7
	Inactive	3.9	3.3	5.4	14.3	0.4	13.8	1.2	57.8

Table 6.3 BCS cohort mobility matrix, 1996–2000 (values in per cent, rounded)

	Destination							
		Professional	Managerial	Intermediate	Routine	Manual	Service	Unemployed	Inactive
Origin	Professional	69.1	10.9	6.4	5.5	0.4	0.7	2.2	4.9
	Managerial	7.3	57.3	8.8	11.3	1.4	5.3	2.8	5.9
	Intermediate	6.0	8.7	62.0	10.5	0.4	3.8	2.2	6.6
	Routine	5.0	7.1	4.8	64.8	2.2	4.1	4.0	8.0
	Manual	0.6	3.9	1.3	10.5	74.5	1.7	4.6	3.0
	Service	3.2	8.5	7.4	8.2	0.4	49.7	4.3	18.2
	Unemployed	6.1	3.2	6.3	15.5	3.4	8.0	33.7	24.0
	Inactive	6.0	2.9	3.7	5.8	0.6	8.9	7.3	65.0

Table 6.4 Estimated occupational mobility probabilities from routine occupations (values in per cent)

Decline in routine occupations	Professional	Managerial	Intermediate	Service	Unemployed	Inactive
Level 2 academic (GCSEs)						
NCDS 0%	0.6	2.0	0.7	0.3	0.1	0.2
10%	1.6	4.7	1.6	0.6	0.4	0.5
BCS 0%	3.8	7.0	2.3	0.5	1.0	0.4
10%	3.4	7.5	3.0	0.8	0.4	0.5
Level 2 academic +level 4 vocational						
NCDS 0%	1.7	2.9	1.3	0.3	0.2	0.2
10%	4.4	6.5	3.1	0.7	0.4	0.5
BCS 0%	10.0	9.8	4.3	0.5	1.1	0.4
10%	8.9	10.4	5.7	0.9	0.4	0.5
Level 3 academic (A-levels)						
NCDS 0%	1.1	2.2	0.7	0.2	0.2	0.2
10%	2.9	5.0	1.6	0.4	0.4	0.5
BCS 0%	6.8	7.5	2.3	0.3	1.1	0.4
10%	6.0	8.0	3.1	0.5	0.4	0.5
Level 4 academic (degree)						
NCDS 0%	3.0	3.1	1.3	0.2	0.2	0.2
10%	7.8	7.0	3.1	0.4	0.4	0.5
BCS 0%	17.0	10.4	4.4	0.3	1.1	0.4
10%	15.3	11.0	5.8	0.5	0.4	0.5

status at age 23 (1981 and 1993, respectively), looking at employment shares of the total population and then graduates separately. We class an individual as a graduate if they had achieved a university first or higher degree by the age of 26. For those in jobs, there is some decline in routine employment between the two cohorts. However, graduate employment in these types of jobs increases, reflecting the shift towards a higher supply of graduates in the labour market. In 1981, 9.1 per cent of 23-year-olds had completed a degree, while in 1993 this figure had risen to 15 per cent.

Table 6.5 also shows that employment shares rose in both higher-level and lower-level non-routine jobs; however, these increases are marginal – the largest increases were found in lower skilled service and non-routine manual occupations. Comparing this to the results in the previous section, it suggests that the 'room at the bottom', created by the decline of routine work, has a much greater effect on new entrants than it does on those already in work. This includes a sizeable number of university graduates – the share of graduates in these types of jobs more than doubles between the two cohorts. Meanwhile, a smaller proportion of the total supply of graduates finds employment in the better non-routine jobs.

To analyse these transitions more thoroughly, we model the probability of being in each of the occupational groups at age 23, controlling for gender, educational attainment and cohort. In addition, given that the relationship between qualifications and entry into the labour market may have changed over time, we look at the interactions between cohort and educational level. For simplicity, we reduce educational attainment to academic qualifications at level 3 and above, and vocational qualifications at level 3 and above. This reduces the possible number of interaction terms to more manageable numbers. The results of these regressions are shown in Table 6A.2.

Table 6.5 Early employment outcomes (values in per cent)

	Employment share at age 22/23		Employment share of graduates at age 22/23		Proportion of graduates in occupation	
	NCDS	BCS	NCDS	BCS	NCDS	BCS
Of those in employment:						
Professional	10.1	10.5	49.4	41.7	43.0	51.3
Managerial	12.1	13.4	18.2	14.8	13.2	14.3
Intermediate	14.0	13.0	13.5	19.1	8.5	19.0
Routine	45.7	41.7	15.1	16.3	2.9	5.0
Non-routine	6.4	7.1	0.2	0.7	0.3	1.4
Non-routine service	11.7	14.4	3.6	7.4	2.7	6.6
Of the total population:						
Unemployed	7.5	4.9	5.7	4.9	7.1	15.1
Non-employed	18.3	15.3	23.6	26.5	11.9	25.9

Source: NCDS and BCS data and author's own calculations.

Cohort effects (including the interaction between cohort and qualification levels) indicate something about the demand for young workers in different occupations relative to the supply of suitable job candidates. Our results show that while higher qualifications are correlated with a higher likelihood of entering a top occupation across both cohorts, the highly qualified in the younger cohort have a lower probability of doing so than those in the previous cohort, which reflects the growing supply of such individuals in this cohort. This pushes them into intermediate non-routine and routine occupations. Less-qualified individuals have benefited from the growing supply of managerial occupations even while graduates are increasingly competing for similar jobs. This might include those who left education earlier but worked up to such positions within a firm or internal labour market. Finally, those with higher vocational qualifications alone seem to have done worst of all, with their probability of entering all occupations, apart from low-skilled service work, decreasing between the two cohorts. Figure 6.1 illustrates the size of these changing prospects.

Earnings

Up to this point, the analysis has focused on occupational grouping, where the assumption is that increases in employment in good non-routine jobs represent an improvement in labour market outcomes. However, recent analysis of cross-sectional UK earnings data (Holmes and Mayhew 2013) has argued that

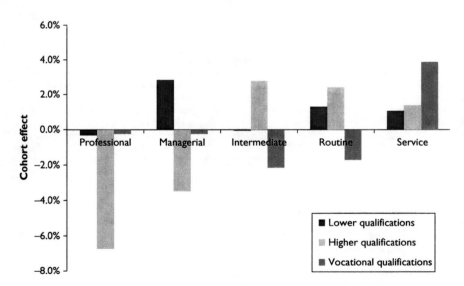

Figure 6.1 Differences in early employment occupational probability between cohorts.

the good non-routine jobs being created fall into two categories. Some are found right at the top of the distribution, while many others have wages that are at the low end of the group historically, and are near the middle of the overall earnings distribution of the whole labour force. In this section, we examine how earnings have been affected across the two cohorts as a result of a shift towards non-routine employment.

Figures 6.2 and 6.3 show how the real earnings distribution of good non-routine jobs has evolved between the two cohorts at comparable points in their careers. In both figures, we compare this to changes of pay across the distribution of routine occupations. Figure 6.2 looks at how wages changed within a particular occupational group between each cohort at a point early in the working life – we look at the NCDS data in 1981 (when the cohort was aged 23) and the BCS data in 1996 (when the cohort was aged 26). During this time period, good non-routine jobs enjoyed greater wage growth than routine occupations, which likely reflects both the declining demand for those skills and the decline of union bargaining power during the 1980s. This means that the shift towards non-routine jobs in the 1980s and early 1990s had some positive effects through a widening of relative wages – this can be thought of as a 'between-group' effect. However, Figure 6.2 also shows how those working in good non-routine jobs became increasingly heterogeneous over the time period (a 'within-group' effect). The bottom 50 per cent of these jobs did not experience any increase in real wages,

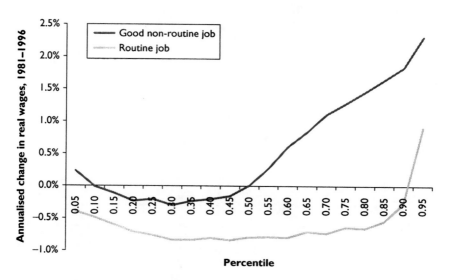

Figure 6.2 Real earnings growth for entry-level employment.

Note: Earnings distributions measured in 1981 (NCDS) and 1996 (BCS). Earnings weighted using RPI.

while earnings growth increases further up the distribution. This means that the rewards to changes in the occupational structure were felt most by those in the top non-routine jobs, whereas wage rewards lower down the distribution were far more muted.

Similarly, Figure 6.3 compares pay for cohort members in their mid-30s (aged 33 for the NCDS cohort and aged 34 for the BCS cohort). Earnings growth is far higher during this period for all occupations, possibly partly reflecting greater economic prosperity and stability during the late 1990s and 2000s. Again, we observe a widening of pay within good non-routine jobs, particularly between the bottom and top thirds. What is also striking here is that the relative pay of many apparently good non-routine jobs fell compared to the remaining routine occupations, while all experienced real wage growth of about 5–6 per cent during this time period.[6]

Therefore, as a result of both a widening of pay within these occupations, and some evidence of a lowering of pay relative to routine occupations, a significant proportion of workers in good non-routine jobs experience a less favourable position than if we focused purely on occupational titles.

Finally, we briefly examine wage mobility and, because we are interested in the expanding 'room at the top', we will focus on absolute mobility (the level and growth of earnings) rather than relative mobility (the position in the distribution). Using the NCDS data, we look at whether there are improvements in earnings associated with transitions from routine occupations to 'good' non-routine occupations. In these data, wages are measured at four points in time – 1981, 1991, 1999 and 2004. We look at gross earnings in high-skill non-routine

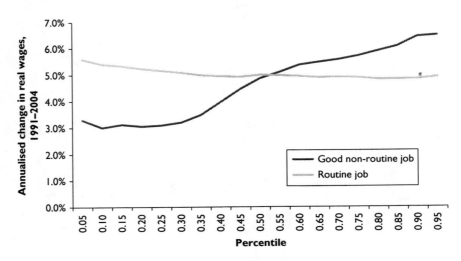

Figure 6.3 Real earnings growth for later employment.

Note: Earnings distributions measured in 1991 (NCDS) and 2004 (BCS). Earnings weighted using RPI.

occupations, and control for educational attainment, gender, age, year-specific shocks and the occupational group five years earlier. We therefore omit earnings data in 1981. In addition, gaps in data on hours mean that we have a relatively small number of individuals moving between occupations with recorded hourly earnings data. In order to increase the sample size, we analyse weekly earnings.

The results of the regression are included in the Appendix, Table 6A.3. The main result shown in this table is that even controlling for observable demographic and educational differences between workers, those who transition into these jobs from routine work (as well as from service occupations, unemployment or non-employment) tend to experience lower wages in those occupations. This is not purely the result of a premium on experience within an occupation – the results show that those who move into managerial or intermediate occupations from other higher-skilled non-routine occupations do not experience lower wages. Therefore, part of the widening gap within good non-routine jobs can be attributed to the lower earnings of those who move from lower-level jobs. Although our data does not let us explore what the reason for this might be, it might reflect unobservable ability differences between different groups of workers, or differences in available progression routes.

Conclusion

This chapter has looked at what the changes in occupational structure – in particular, the decline of routine occupations – have meant over the past 30 years for labour market outcomes. We have shown that the growing number of jobs in higher-level occupational categories has increased intragenerational upward mobility, but that this has diminished over time, suggesting that recruitment into these jobs is increasingly coming from new entrants rather than existing workers. In addition, increases in the supply of the highly qualified has outpaced the number of higher-level jobs, meaning than many new entrants are entering the labour market at lower levels than before, including low-skilled service work. Finally, the earnings of those who do manage to enter good non-routine jobs are becoming increasingly spread out. Compared to the highest earners, many individuals obtain wages that become relatively closer to the middle of the distribution.

These concerns have important implications for current policy on social mobility, which has largely focused on raising the numbers of individuals with various higher-level qualifications. Policymakers should be more sceptical about the view that there is, and will continue to be, 'room at the top'. There is also 'room at the bottom', and even the well-educated face increased risks of ending up there. Moreover, even for those who do access the top occupational groups, only a proportion are rewarded highly for their educational investments, while many jobs in these categories are increasingly found lower down the pay spectrum. This is often masked by focusing on the average premium on acquiring higher qualifications over those at lower levels. It suggests, however, that there are important demand-side constraints to the ability of the labour market to continually create high-wage jobs as the supply of well-educated workers increases.

Where might employer engagement in education fit into these conclusions? One issue would be if any of these outcomes was being driven by specific shortages of certain skills. In this case, there might be a mismatch between what the education and training system delivers and what employers actually want. Greater involvement of employers across all levels (including education and training before labour market entry, initial work-based training and continuing skill development while in work) would help to realign supply and demand, moving more workers towards higher skill, higher paid employment and probably raising social mobility in the process.

There is a very real concern, however, that if this were indeed the problem, then it would already be in employers' interest to become more involved in the education of their future workforce. There are two reasons why they might not. First, there needs to be some form of mechanism through which employers engage with educators, which might be missing. Similarly, there might be a collective action problem – each individual employer does not have enough of an incentive to act because doing so is costly and the benefits of doing so might accrue to free-riding rival employers. This gives a clear role for policymakers to facilitate greater engagement in education and training to drive the desired changes. Alternatively, the problem might be more deep-seated if the production processes of some employers lead to fixed skill demands regardless of how well qualified prospective workers are. As well as the growth of low-skill service work, we discussed how many supposed graduate jobs have become increasingly deskilled by employers applying Taylorist production processes to what would once have been called knowledge work. In this case, it is not necessarily in employers' interests to engage with the education sector. Their skill needs are already being met, increasingly by new labour market entrants, leaving less opportunity for progression from those already in work. To make any significant improvements, policymakers need to find new ways to encourage more employers to develop higher-skill production processes. While greater employer engagement in education might be a consequence of this, it would only be one part of a wider industrial strategy.

Appendix: Regression estimations

Table 6A.1 Logit regression on probability of moving to non-routine occupations from routine occupations[a]

	Professional	Managerial	Intermediate	Service	Unemployed	Inactive
Female	-0.966***	-0.672***	-0.100	1.904***	-0.330**	1.869***
Non-White	0.159	-0.152	-0.421*	-0.216	0.402*	0.024
Age	0.017	0.012	-0.001	0.037***	0.011	-0.043***
Routine exp.	-0.038	-0.034	-0.160**	-0.178***	-0.353***	-0.312***
Age × routine exp.	-0.001	-0.001	0.002	0.003*	0.006**	0.007***
Cohort	1.881***	1.301***	1.266***	0.614***	1.925***	0.830***
Displacement	10.012***	8.599***	9.097***	8.321***	10.033***	12.193***
Displacement × cohort	-11.316***	-7.961***	-6.224***	-3.148*	-20.125***	-9.571***
Voc. level 0	-0.096	-0.076	-0.024	0.429***	0.189	0.277***
Acad. level 0	-1.430***	-0.794***	-0.991***	0.405**	0.573***	0.139
Voc. level 1	0.166	0.026	-0.187	0.199	0.142	0.406***
Acad. level 1	-0.897***	-0.395***	-0.367***	0.543***	-0.061	-0.155
Voc. level 2	0.021	-0.264*	-0.250	0.157	0.126	0.202
Acad. level 2	-0.612***	-0.068	-0.017	0.507***	-0.043	-0.012
Voc. level 4	0.680***	0.295**	0.324**	0.059	-0.217	0.030
Acad. level 4	1.030***	0.361**	0.657***	0.095	0.047	-0.026
Voc. level 5	0.913***	1.001***	0.114	0.313	-1.087	-0.662**
Acad. level 5	1.437***	-0.141	0.952***	-0.563	0.633	0.021
Constant	-4.796***	-3.968***	-4.17765***	-6.577***	-4.997***	-3.683***
N	19,878	19,878	19,878	19,878	19,878	19,878
Pseudo R^2	0.1439	0.0668	0.0728	0.1013	0.0621	0.1259

Note
a *, **, and *** indicate significance at the 10%, 5% and 1% levels, respectively. Standard errors are omitted for reasons of space.

Table 6A.2 Logit regression on occupational group of initial employment[a]

	Professional	Managerial	Intermediate	Routine	Service
Female	-0.461***	-0.586***	0.251***	-0.325***	1.323***
	(-8.57)	(-12.28)	(5.36)	(-10.65)	(23.92)
Non-White	-0.273**	-0.196	-0.163	-0.032	-0.135
	(-1.83)	(-1.46)	(-1.23)	(-0.39)	(-1.00)
Cohort	-0.086	0.280***	-0.009	0.053	0.203***
	(-0.88)	(4.54)	(-0.13)	(1.49)	(3.73)
Acad. level 3–5	2.380***	0.728***	0.502***	-1.212***	-1.029***
	(25.03)	(7.99)	(5.18)	(-15.1)	(-7.22)
Voc. level 3–5	0.834***	0.238**	1.037***	-0.097	-0.480***
	(6.61)	(2.30)	(12.06)	(-1.52)	(-3.94)
Cohort × acad. level 3–5	-0.242*	-0.527***	0.270**	0.104	0.357**
	(-1.92)	(-4.51)	(2.25)	(1.05)	(2.14)
Cohort × voc. level 3–5	0.055	-0.304*	-0.150	-0.125	0.636
	(0.25)	(-1.66)	(-0.98)	(-1.09)	(3.45)***
Acad. level 3–5 voc. level 3–5	-1.223***	-0.208	-0.473***	0.395***	0.243
	(-7.06)	(-1.21)	(-3.00)	(2.78)	(0.84)
Cohort × acad. level 3–5 × voc. level 3–5	0.712**	0.167	-0.053	-0.201	-1.201***
	(2.60)	(0.60)	(-0.22)	(-0.93)	(-2.91)
Constant	-3.125***	-2.181***	-2.607***	-0.309***	-2.941***
	(-41.1)	(-41.3)	(-46.5)	(-9.82)	(-49.0)

Note
a *, ** and *** indicate significance at the 10%, 5% and 1% levels, respectively.

Table 6A.3 Earnings regressions[a]

		Destination occupation	
		Managerial	Intermediate
	Gender	−0.597***	−0.561***
		−(18.26)	−(20.27)
	Non-White	−0.104	0.087
		−(1.23)	(1.30)
	Age	0.021***	0.020***
		(7.57)	(7.88)
Original occupation	Professional	0.144**	0.089
		(1.96)	(0.99)
	Managerial		0.088
			(1.26)
	Intermediate	−0.090	
		−(1.26)	
	Routine	−0.150***	−0.201***
		−(2.86)	−(3.68)
	Manual	−0.070	−0.108
		−(0.37)	−(0.53)
	Service	−0.585***	−0.392***
		−(6.24)	−(5.18)
	Unemployed	−0.634***	−0.338**
		−(2.96)	−(2.27)
	Inactive	−0.414***	−0.388***
		−(4.36)	−(7.24)
	Voc. level 0	0.072	0.015
		(1.75)*	(0.35)
	Acad. level 0	−0.410***	−0.184***
		−(6.53)	−(2.93)
	Voc. level 1	0.096	0.005
		(1.46)	(0.08)
	Acad. level 1	−0.425***	−0.148***
		−(7.61)	−(2.73)
	Voc. level 2	0.070	−0.138**
		(1.15)	−(2.35)
	Acad. level 2	−0.295***	−0.118***
		−(6.88)	−(3.14)
	Voc. level 4	0.119**	0.082*
		(2.27)	(1.81)
	Acad. level 4	0.026	0.025
		(0.56)	(0.61)
	Voc. level 5	0.208***	0.170***
		(3.99)	(3.39)
	Acad. level 5	0.155**	0.096
		(2.03)	(1.19)
	Constant	4.970***	4.697***
		(46.21)	(45.59)

Note
a *, ** and *** indicate significance at the 10%, 5% and 1% levels, respectively.

Notes

1 Erikson and Goldthorpe (2010) criticise the over-reliance on this single statistic from a relatively small sample in recent policy discussion. They argue that earnings, unlike social class classification, are far more susceptible to transitory shocks, and that the biases created by these shocks in the estimation of these correlations may have driven this result. Results from Nicoletti and Ermish (2008) using the British Household Panel Study further support this – they find little change in intergenerational earnings mobility for cohorts born between 1950 and 1972.

2 This is consistent with other studies, which find that future prospects can have long-term damage for those who work for some time in lower-skilled work, especially where individuals are overqualified for these jobs, even if they then move away from these occupations (see Booth *et al.* 2002; Scherer 2004).

3 They use a Poisson distribution-based model, which predicts the conditional probability of observing a given number of transitions in a particular period. The probability is conditional on factors relevant to either the origin or destination occupation (such as employment share growth or the mean wage), relative factors (such as the skill difference between the two occupational groups) and other factors (such as the proportion of moves within the public sector and geographic information).

4 The method used here is logistic regression. For more details on the estimation methodology, see Holmes (2011) and Holmes and Tholen (2013).

5 Logistic regression is a nonlinear model, so the overall effect size of one variable depends on the other variables. In the interest of space, Table 6.4 shows the estimated effects for a 28-year-old male who had five years' experience working in a routine job. The table then illustrates the educational attainment and overall decline in routine work for such an individual in each cohort.

6 A consequence of this is that the bottom 40 per cent of good non-routine jobs earn less, in absolute terms, than the bottom 40 per cent of routine jobs for this age group in 2004. In all earlier distributions, all good non-routine jobs had higher earnings than routine occupations at similar points on their respective distributions.

References

Blanden, J., Gregg, P. and Machin, S. (2005). Educational inequality and intergenerational mobility. *In:* S. Machin and A. Vignoles, eds. *What's the good of education?* Princeton, NJ: Princeton University Press.

Booth, A., Francesconi, M. and Frank, J. (2002). Temporary jobs: stepping stones or dead ends? *The Economic Journal,* 112 (480): F189–F213.

Brown, P., Lauder, H. and Ashton, D. (2011). *The global auction.* Oxford: Oxford University Press.

Bukodi E. (2009). *Education, first occupation and later occupational attainment: cross-cohort changes among men and women in Britain.* CLS Cohort Studies Working Paper, 2009/4, London: Centre for Longitudinal Studies, Institute of Education, University of London.

Bukodi, E. and Goldthorpe, J. (2009). *Class origins, education and occupational attainment: cross-cohort changes among men in Britain.* CLS Cohort Studies Working Paper, 2009/3, London: Centre for Longitudinal Studies, Institute of Education, University of London.

Erikson, R. and Goldthorpe, J. (2010). Has social mobility in Britain decreased? Reconciling divergent findings on income and class mobility. *British Journal of Sociology,* 61: 211–230.

Goldthorpe, J. (2012). *Understanding – and misunderstanding – social mobility in Britain: the entry of the economists, the confusion of politicians and the limits of educational policy.* Barnet Papers in Social Research No. 1/2012.

Goos, M. and Manning, A. (2007). Lousy jobs and lovely jobs: the rising polarization of work in Britain. *The Review of Economics and Statistics,* 89 (1): 118–133.

HM Government. (2011). *Opening doors, breaking barriers: a strategy for social mobility.* London: Cabinet Office.

Holmes, C. (2011). *The route out of the routine: where do the displaced routine workers go?* SKOPE Research Paper No. 100. Cardiff: SKOPE.

Holmes, C. and Mayhew, K. (2013). *Have earnings distributions polarised? Wage growth and dispersion in the hourglass labour market.* Unpublished working paper.

Holmes, C. and Tholen, G. (2013). *Occupational mobility and career paths in the 'hourglass' labour market.* SKOPE Research Paper No. 113. Cardiff: SKOPE.

Leontaridi, M. (1998). Segmented labour markets: theory and evidence. *Journal of Economic Surveys,* 12 (1): 103–109.

McNabb, R. (1987). Testing for labour market segmentation in Britain. *Manchester School,* 55: 257–723.

Mayhew, K. and Rosewell, B. (1979). Labour market segmentation in Britain. *Oxford Bulletin of Economics and Statistics,* 41 (2): 81–115.

Nicoletti, C. and Ermish, J. (2008). Intergenerational earnings mobility: changes across cohorts in Britain. *The B.E. Journal of Economic Analysis and Policy,* 7 (2): 1–36.

Rhein, T. and Trübswetter, P. (2012). Occupational mobility and the change in the occupational structure in Britain and Germany, 1993–2008. *Applied Economics Letters,* 19 (7): 653–656.

Scherer, S. (2004). Stepping-stones or traps? The consequences of labour market entry positions on future careers in West Germany, Great Britain and Italy. *Work, Employment and Society,* 18 (2): 369–394.

Thurow, L. (1975). *Poverty and discrimination.* Washington, DC: The Brookings Institute.

Tomkins, J. and Twomey, J. (2000). Occupational mobility in England. *Applied Economics,* 32 (2): 193–209.

Chapter 7

Local labour markets

What effects do they have on the aspirations of young people?

Ralf St Clair, Keith Kintrea and Muir Houston

It seems inevitable on a common sense level that where somebody grows up is going to affect what they will think about doing when they are older. It would be surprising if a young person in Manchester grew up with the ambition of being a shepherd in Mongolia. On a more subtle level, it would seem probable that not very many affluent young women in Chelsea grow up wanting to work in a chip shop. And, in fact, this is one of those instances where common sense is backed up with evidence. What young people see around them, and the broader environment they experience, does make a difference to what they want to do.

What is harder to explain is why. It is easy to talk in big terms about forces such as 'class' or 'environment', but it is extremely difficult to provide an explanation of how these forces might work. Yet as discussed in Chapter 1 by Archer, policymakers in recent years have homed in on the idea of aspirations, or what young people want to do when they are adults. The general assumption has been that young people living in areas of disadvantage tend to develop lower levels of aspiration than those in more advantaged areas. The study described in this chapter, funded by the Joseph Rowntree Foundation, set out to explore this idea and assess how much truth there was to it (Kintrea *et al.* 2011).

In this chapter, we discuss the idea of aspirations, the findings of our study and what they mean for public policy. In particular, we believe our study shows that the hopes of young people are not completely constrained by their experiences growing up, and that employer involvement can help to shape education in ways that will allow young people to act more effectively on their hopes. The key to avoiding the loss of so much talent is helping young people to understand both what options are available to them and the concrete steps needed to get there – areas where employer expertise is critical.

Understanding aspirations

There is a high degree of interest among politicians and policymakers in aspirations. It is assumed that policy can raise aspirations and that, in turn, this will help to increase educational achievement, bring about greater equity in access to good jobs and enhance the UK's economic competitiveness by ensuring that talent can rise to the top. Aspirations were a key theme of many of the Labour Government's policy papers about children and young people up to 2010, including *The Children's Plan* (Department for Children, Schools and Families (DCSF) 2007), and *Aiming High for Young People* (HM Treasury and DCSF 2007).

The Conservative/Liberal Democrat Coalition Government elected in May 2010 has continued this theme. For example, in his speech to the Conservative Party Spring Conference in March 2013, David Cameron claimed:

> We are building an aspiration nation, a country where it's not who you know or where you come from, but who you are and where you are determined to go. My dream for Britain is that opportunity is not an accident of birth but a birthright.
>
> (Cameron 2013)

But in spite of the political interest in raising aspirations, the links between aspirations, educational outcomes and the labour market are not well understood, and neither are the best ways to raise aspirations. There is a presumption in policy thinking that high aspirations implies a sense of career direction and a belief that upward mobility can be achieved through learning. The portrayal of aspirations can sometimes suggest that they are essentially an individual choice. And that low aspirations are the reason for people remaining at the bottom of the social hierarchy. However, the Social Exclusion Task Force's conclusion that aspirations may vary systematically by place (Cabinet Office Social Exclusion Task Force 2008) and the range of institutional factors acting as barriers to the professions for working-class young people featured in the Milburn report (Panel on Fair Access to the Professions 2009) argue for fuller recognition of the importance of social, economic and cultural context.

The influence of place is a key dimension of some policy thinking. The *Schools White Paper* (Department for Education (DfE) 2010) notes the differences in attainment between groups of young people and attributes a lack of aspiration in predominantly working class environments as a key reason for this. Similarly, the coalition's strategy for social mobility (Cabinet Office 2011) shares a desire to raise aspirations, particularly among children from disadvantaged areas, as a route to educational and career success.

Research interest has tended to centre on young people who belong to groups typically marginalised from education and high status occupations, and there has been a degree of tension between the view that aspirations lead directly to final outcomes and a more nuanced perspective that challenges causative claims. Quaglia and Cobb offer a clear definition of a student's aspirations as their 'ability to identify and set goals for the future, while being inspired in the present to work towards those goals' (Quaglia and Cobb 1996: 130). However, the controversy around the causes and effects of aspirations, and indeed the extent to which they can be considered as a consistent and reliable concept, continues (St Clair and Benjamin 2011).

The implicit theory of aspirations applied in the majority of research is based on the idea that people from more deprived backgrounds tend to have lower aspirations and this leads to lower achievement. But it is very difficult to support rigorously the argument that low aspirations *causes* low achievement. It is relatively simple to imagine a scenario where young people who dislike school, for example, tend not to score well in tests or exams and become disengaged and unambitious. In this case, low aspiration is an outcome of low achievement, not its cause.

The majority of literature assumes that higher aspirations – a desire for more education, higher income and occupational status – are more positive. One problem with this is that having a large proportion of the population with lofty ambitions could lead to a situation where few actually fulfil those aspirations. The other side of this argument is that unless people aspire to some form of success, it is guaranteed that they will fail.

However, it is also possible for low aspirations to be a rational response to circumstance. Educational sociologists can sometimes be sceptical about aspirations because family and parental history, home culture and community context can contribute to a deep alienation from education that individuals cannot simply choose to change. 'Low' aspirations may be a strategic move on the part of the educated to avoid negative outcomes (Furlong *et al.* 1996; Perry and Francis 2010).

There are many studies that demonstrate aspiration formation. Wigfield and Eccles (2000) suggest that aspirations are composed of two components: the expectation of success and the subjective value of that success. Any given outcome might have a low expectation of success but a sufficiently high value to pursue. Alternatively, an outcome may be achievable but have little value. The balance of expectation of success and value of success affects the 'achievement-related choices' (Wigfield and Eccles 2000: 69) made by the individual. This suggests that aspirations are not created in a vacuum, but reflect a person's situation and their resources (Furlong and Cartmel 1997). In other words, aspirations can be seen as the active constructions of individuals using the resources that they find around them.

Eccles and Wigfield have warned against over-rationalisation of aspirations and emphasise the way expectations change and how much they reflect different situations: their empirical evidence suggests that 'even during the very early elementary grades children appear to have distinct beliefs about what they are *good* at and what they *value* in different achievement domains' (Eccles and Wigfield 2002: 75). As they get older, young people become less positive about their achievements; they become more 'realistic'. In essence, children construct a worldview where they are aware both of what they are good at and how much worth this ability has, and as they age they bring this awareness into their aspirations.

The notion that raising aspirations will lead to enhanced outcomes is approaching the status of a common-sense truism. What appears to be missing is an explanation of why some aspirations are better than others and, even more fundamentally, how aspirations actually affect outcomes. A recent study for the Joseph Rowntree Foundation (Goodman and Gregg 2010) analysed four large-scale datasets to build a strong evidence base for the importance of aspirations at key stages of children's lives. Both children's and parents' aspirations and expectations were powerfully related to outcomes.

Our study

From 2006 to 2011 the authors conducted research to try to understand more about how aspirations reflect the places that young people live in. We focused on understanding more fully how the varying influences found in different places manifest in aspirational pathways for young people between 13 and 15 years of age.

Three types of aspirations were considered in this research:

1   *Ideal.* What the individual would do for a job if there were no real-world constraints.
2   *Realistic.* What the individual expects to be able to do for a job given the circumstances within which they live.
3   *Educational.* What the individual anticipates regarding their educational career.

The difference between ideal and realistic aspirations is an important one. Ideal aspirations can tell us a great deal about the general direction of a young person's ambitions, even if they may be, by definition, unrealistic. Realistic aspirations reflect perceived individual and structural constraints, though the two types tend to be highly correlated (Andres *et al.* 1999).

Data was collected in a two-stage survey of young people in three secondary schools, plus surveys of parents and semi-structured interviews with staff in the schools and people in the local communities. The schools were used as a point of access to a cohort of young people living mainly in disadvantaged areas, set within three distinctive labour markets:

- *London.* A city with great cultural and ethnic diversity, substantial educational and labour market disparities and localised concentrations of poverty, but a buoyant economy in recent years. The research was conducted in East London in an area with very high proportions of first- and second-generation immigrants where residents mainly held low-status jobs.
- *Nottingham.* A city with moderate cultural and ethnic diversity, but continuing challenges of inequality, segregation and labour market adjustment despite recent economic improvements. The study area was, in many ways, a traditional White working-class location.

- *Glasgow*. A city with extensive worklessness and associated deprivation. Educational attainment remains much lower than anywhere else in Scotland. The study school had a large majority of White Scottish students, but from a more varied economic background, and broader catchment area, than the other cases.

At stage 1, the young people were interviewed in school year 2007–2008 (referred to as '13-year-olds'). Most of the same students were then re-interviewed in 2010 ('15-year-olds'). For the second round of interviews, the young people in the English schools were in Year 10 and had not yet taken any GCSEs. In Glasgow, students were in S4 and had started Standard Grades (then the Scottish equivalent of GCSEs). Overall, almost 500 young people were interviewed in the first stage and almost 300 in the second (Table 7.1).

The core of the interviews with young people at both stages was their ideal and realistic aspirations. The interviews also collected information from the young people about their home areas, their leisure interests, social interactions and networks, their attitudes to school and learning, and their family backgrounds, including the support they got at home for their aspirations and with their school work. Young people were also asked open questions that probed their reasons for holding particular aspirations and expectations, and, for 15-year-olds, the reasons behind changes since they were 13.

The interviews with young people were supplemented by three focus groups with young people in each school that were designed to explore, in particular, neighbourhood and school influences on aspirations. At both stages, we carried out a telephone survey with parents of the young people who had been surveyed in school and a small number of semi-structured interviews with staff in the schools and with members of the community in which the schools stood. These interviews were designed to better understand the school and neighbourhoods as contexts for the shaping of young people's aspirations.

The research team used the Standard Occupational Classification to analyse occupational aspirations. This divides all occupations into nine classes ranging from high skilled (and generally well rewarded in terms of money and status) to low skilled (and generally low paid and lower status). The young people were also asked if they intended to stay on at school after 16 and go to college or to university.

Table 7.1 Participation by location

	Glasgow	Nottingham	London	Total
Number of pupils/school (2007)	1,200	807	1,300	3,307
Pupil interviews (12)	150	137	203	490
Pupil interviews (15)	66	108	114	288
Parent interviews	77	66	32	175
Teacher and community interviews	13	14	6	33

The occupational aspirations of young people

Even though all the young people in our study were growing up in urban areas where adult labour market outcomes were often poor and there were few models of high status occupations, it was striking how much importance the participants attached to successful employment. Overall, 98 per cent of 13-year-olds agreed or strongly agreed that it was important that they got a job when they left school, and 87 per cent had given some thought to what it might be. The proportion who agreed or strongly agreed that they worried about not being able to get a job when they were older was 70 per cent. Three-quarters of participants worried about leaving school with no qualifications. This challenges the idea that people growing up in low employment areas tend to reproduce what they see around them, in line with previous research (Archer *et al.* 2010).

A very high proportion of young people were highly aspirational regarding their education, as shown in Table 7.2. All of these percentages are a great deal higher than the percentage actually continuing to college or university in England or Scotland. The percentage that wanted to leave school as soon as possible varied substantially, and reflected the vocational aspirations of the three groups of students. In London only 5 per cent wanted to leave as soon as possible, 17 per cent in Nottingham did so, and Glasgow came in the middle with 11 per cent.

When 13-year-olds were asked about their occupational aspirations, 96 per cent could name a specific job that they were hoping to do, and 70 per cent were able to provide a 'realistic' option if their 'ideal' job was not available to them. Figure 7.1 shows the distribution of ideal jobs named by the young people at the age of 13. One notable aspect is the high concentration of aspirations in category 3. This is due to a number of common ideal jobs, such as acting and professional sport, being clustered in this category. In order to check for the effect of this, we ran all of our statistical analysis with these responses dropped out, but found no statistically significant differences from the results with the full dataset.

There were interesting differences between ideal and realistic aspirations at age 13 (Figure 7.2). The 30 per cent of respondents who had no 'realistic' alternative to their 'ideal' aspiration had their 'ideal' response used in this analysis but, still, the proportion in Standard Occupations Classification (SOC) category 3 drops from 47.2 to 32.2 per cent. Mostly the 'realistic' aspirations of those whose 'ideal' is in category 3 appear in lower 'realistic' categories, particularly skilled trades (grows from 6.4 per cent to 14.2 per cent), sales and customer service

Table 7.2 Percentage of pupils aspiring to attend college or university

	London	Nottingham	Glasgow
College	97	91	79
University	87	78	81

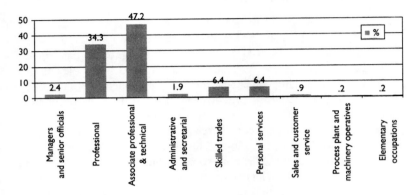

Figure 7.1 Ideal jobs of 13-year-olds by Standard Occupational Classification.

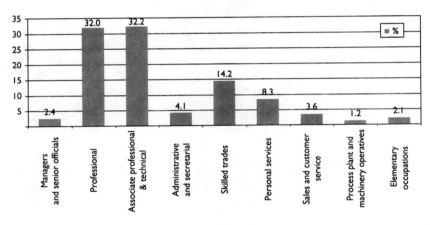

Figure 7.2 Realistic jobs of 13-year-olds by Standard Occupational Classification.

(0.9 per cent to 3.6 per cent) and elementary occupations (0.2 per cent to 2.1 per cent). Overall, the proportion of responses in the top three categories dropped from 84 per cent to 67 per cent, suggesting that the realistic responses did indeed reflect a degree of realism.

Although there were some differences between the respondents from each of the three schools, the consistent picture was of high aspirations. The clear message is that, even at 13, young people have thought about the future, are concerned about getting a good job, have some insight into what might be more or less attainable and are strongly ambitious. The degree to which this data represents high aspirations is illustrated in Figure 7.3. Here the labour market is considered in three segments: SOC categories 1–3, 4–6 and 7–9. The three left-hand columns show that 44 per cent of the UK workforce is employed in the top three categories, with 25 per cent in the bottom three. The ideal aspirations are clearly

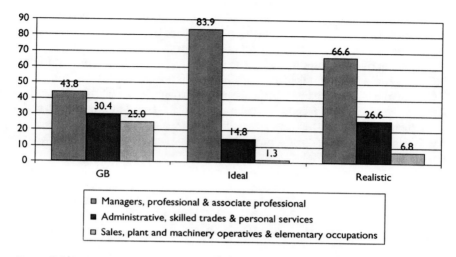

Figure 7.3 Ideal and realistic aspirations compared to the GB labour market by Standard Occupational Classification (values in per cent, rounded).

not aligned with this, and even the realistic aspirations are very different from the actual distribution.

By the age of 15, one-third of young people had revised their aspirations upwards, one-third downwards and one-third had not changed, but overall the mean remained very similar. Figure 7.4 shows the realistic aspirations of the 15-year-olds, and again they are very strong. However, there has been some redistribution. Category 3 represents a smaller proportion than before, although

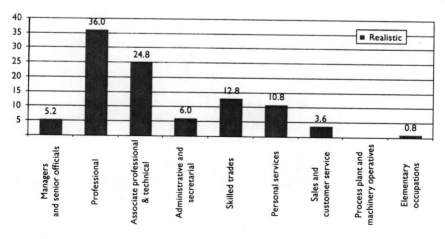

Figure 7.4 Realistic jobs of 15-year-olds by Standard Occupational Classification (values in per cent, rounded).

there has been an increase in aspiring professionals and managers. The proportion naming administrative and secretarial aspirations is up a little, as is personal service jobs. Interestingly, the proportion suggesting they would get jobs in the bottom two categories has fallen from 3.3 per cent to 0.8 per cent. This may be because some of these respondents chose not to respond to the second round of the survey that was undertaken close to their minimum school leaving age.

One of the more striking findings concerns changes in realistic aspirations between 13 and 15. On average for young people surveyed in both rounds, realistic aspirations rose by 0.15 categories. While this is a very small rise, it means that for this group the realistic aspirations of occupational outcomes were robust during this two-year period.

A key aim of the study was to try to understand the reasons behind the patterns of aspirational development. We conducted considerable amounts of analysis to explore the possible effects of family income, housing tenure, gender, ethnicity and similar dimensions on aspirations, but found no consistent relationships even in multivariate models. However, there were strong differences between the three locations.

Local influences on aspirations

The Nottingham school was located in a traditional working-class neighbourhood. The school was heavily protected with entry systems and high fences, and focused on discipline as the way to resolve many educational issues. The school's approach was apparently more divisive than the other schools. Young people recognised that there was a group of students that was strongly supported by the school to be high achievers but that there was also a more problematic group that was subject to heavy discipline. Aspirations in Nottingham were the lowest of the three areas, and occupational aspirations were much more inclined towards traditional trades (for boys) and personal care (for girls) than in the other locations.

In the case of the London school, many children were part of immigrant families, and overall they were the most aspirational of the three groups; the London data drives the positive change in realistic aspirations over the period of the study. The London school was very supportive of high aspiration, but in doing so it was working with a momentum that was already remarkably positive. Here the survey evidence showed high and rising aspirations between 13 and 15, and this was backed up by interview data with the young people. Parents were also highly ambitious for their children's futures.

In Glasgow, with a mixed catchment area, aspirations fell over the period of the study. This school was the most laissez-faire of the three and there was a much greater sense that young people were ambitious of their own accord, rather than because the school expected it. There was also a tendency for occupational aspirations to move towards the middle over this two-year period, so while those with the highest aspirations at 13 dropped them little at 15, those with the lowest aspirations at 13 were now aiming a little higher. This perhaps suggests that comprehensive schools with students from mixed backgrounds may have a levelling effect.

In all three areas, young people's aspirations showed weak links, if any, to local labour markets. Few were definitely interested in the types of jobs thought to be available locally (21 per cent overall) and there was little correspondence between the structure of local labour markets and job aspirations. While there were many in London who aspired to professional and managerial jobs (of which there are many in the London labour market), there was no evidence that these aspirations had been driven by specific local job market knowledge. The inclination towards traditional working-class jobs in Nottingham seemed to be more a product of local tradition than a concrete impact of today's labour market, with even fewer in Nottingham than elsewhere saying that the type of job available locally was of interest. Across the three locations, the majority of young people did not want to stay in their present locations as adults.

Families were a much more important source of specific job ideas (see Archer in Chapter 1 of this volume). Many cited family members as an influence on their preferred job: either there was someone in the family who already had that job ('one of my granddads was a doctor'; 'my cousin is a computer tech'; 'some of my cousins are security guards') or the idea for the job came from parents ('Mum wants me to be one'; 'my dad's dream(is) for this'; 'my dad would like me to be a doctor and repay my parents . . .').

Finally, the data showed consistent mismatches between vocational aspirations and educational aspirations. It was quite common for young people to be unaware that a particular vocational outcome required university study, for example, or more specifically that the choice of subjects studied could restrict future options.

Conclusions

This study set out to better understand the relationship between young people's aspirations in relation to education and jobs, and the context in which they are formed. Many of the key findings are not consistent with the policy claims about poor neighbourhoods as sources of low aspiration. The aspirations that young people have for education are generally to stay on in school and go to university, in far higher proportions than the numbers who actually attend from all social backgrounds. The aspirations that they have for jobs are generally to get professional and managerial jobs, again in proportions far greater than actually exist in the labour market, especially in their immediate areas.

What is more, young people's aspirations do not diminish over time: they were high at age 13 and they remained high at age 15. The desire to go to university increased, not decreased. Young people's individual job aspirations have often shifted, but across the sample, this has happened in both directions; some have raised their aspirations and others have lowered them, with the overall picture at age 15 being much the same as at 13.

Findings of earlier studies, which suggested that aspirations were associated with possibilities in the local labour market, were not closely supported by the study, except perhaps in a residual, cultural way in one location (Nottingham). It might be expected that living amid relatively depressed labour markets would generate a degree of fatalism among young people. In fact, the opposite seemed to be true: their aspirations for higher education and a good job can be seen as a defence against a tough labour market. However, the job aspirations of many young people were not formed with the active knowledge of what the labour markets offered or close knowledge of the educational requirements of particular occupations.

Although aspirations were high, they were not equally high across the three locations. The research locations are quite different in their social make-up and in the resources on which young people can draw in shaping their lives. Place, therefore, is important but place represents a particular nexus of class, ethnicity and institutions set against existing experiences in education and the labour market, and not just a position on the indexes of multiple deprivation. To explore this further needs a more nuanced and locally sensitive approach than the assumption that deprived areas drive low aspirations. We have researched three locations only; it is reasonable to assume that others would throw up equally distinctive patterns of aspiration formation.

These findings have strong implications for policymakers who are interested in aspirations as a policy instrument. The first is that any approach that begins with an assumption of aspirational deficit among young people living in deprived communities must be treated with a lot of caution. The research did not compare aspirational levels in more and less deprived communities, but the consistent message is that aspirations are very high – indeed far higher than the labour market can support. This is consistent with other recent studies carried out in the United Kingdom (e.g. Goodman and Gregg 2010) and is open to two interpretations. The first is that recent policy measures to increase aspirations have been effective, although this is challenged by the Scottish case, where aspirations are high in the absence of any clear policy focus. We also found that the approach of schools to aspirations tended to be consistent with the underlying patterns of aspirations in the communities they served, as place, family and schools tend to coalesces around particular approaches to future options and reinforce each other. The second interpretation is that underlying aspirations are very high and that the policy challenge for young people in deprived communities is not raising aspirations but achieving them.

There are several significant clues that this may be the case in the study. One is the disparity between named occupational aspirations and the educational aspirations associated with them. It was not at all unusual for somebody to want to be a lawyer and to attend university, but not to be taking the appropriate GCSE examinations to go on to the next stage. The lack of knowledge of the pathways to achieve high aspirations was an important issue: for example, only 60 per cent of young people, who were all approaching critical examinations, said they had received useful careers advice at school, and only 46 per cent said that that advice had shaped their aspirations. The evidence in this study points clearly towards a lack of knowledge of pathways as a reason why the young people with high aspirations in disadvantaged areas may not achieve them.

The study points to better support for young people's aspirations at a level of detail that is necessary to make informed decision about future pathways. The findings suggest that there is a need for young people to be exposed to a greater range of occupations and to promote a better understanding of job content, for example by stronger engagement with employers, sector skills councils and individuals who have taken up particular career paths. Given the importance of families in shaping aspirations – and the lack of knowledge among many families about routes to particular occupations – supporting aspirations also means working with parents more closely, especially where parents face disadvantages themselves.

References

Andres, L., Anisef, P., Krahn, H., Looker, D. and Thiessen, V. (1999). The persistence of social structure: cohort, class and gender effects on the occupational aspirations of Canadian youth. *Journal of Youth Studies*, 2: 261–282.

Archer, L., Hollingworth, S. and Mendick, H. (2010). *Urban youth and schooling*. Milton Keynes: Open University Press.

Cabinet Office. (2011). *Opening doors, breaking barriers: a strategy for social mobility*. London: Cabinet Office.

Cabinet Office Social Exclusion Task Force. (2008). *Aspirations and attainment amongst young people in deprived communities: analysis and discussion paper*. London: Cabinet Office.

Cameron, D. (2013). Speech to Conservative Party Spring Conference. *Daily Telegraph*, 16 March 2013. Available from: www.telegraph.co.uk/news/newsvideo/9934683/David-Cameron-We-are-building-an-aspiration-nation.html [accessed 15 July 2013].

Department for Children, Schools and Families (DCSF). (2007). *The children's plan*. London: DCSF.

Department for Education (DfE) (2010). *The importance of teaching: Schools White Paper CM7980*. London: DfE.

Eccles, J. and Wigfield, A. (2002). Motivational beliefs, values and goals. *Annual Review of Psychology*, 53: 109–132.

Furlong, A. and Cartmel, F. (1997). *Young people and social change: individualisation and risk in the age of high modernity*. Buckingham, UK: Open University Press.

Furlong, A., Biggart, A. and Cartmel, F. (1996). Neighbourhoods, opportunity structures and occupational aspirations. *Sociology*, 30 (3): 551–565.

Goodman, A. and Gregg, P. (2010). *Poorer children's educational achievement: how important are attitudes and behaviour?* York: Joseph Rowntree Foundation.

HM Treasury and Department for Children, Schools and Families (DCSF). (2007). *Aiming high for young people: a ten-year strategy for positive activities*. London: HM Treasury and DCSF.

Kintrea, K., St Clair, R. and Houston, M. (2011). *The influence of parents, place and poverty on educational attitudes and aspirations*. York: Joseph Rowntree Foundation.

Panel on Fair Access to the Professions. (2009). *Unleashing aspiration: the final report of the panel on fair access to the professions.* London: Cabinet Office.

Perry, E. and Francis, B. (2010). *The social class gap for educational achievement: a review of the literature.* RSAProjects. Available from: www.thersa.org/__data/assets/pdf_file/0019/367003/RSA-Social-Justice-paper.pdf [accessed 15 July 2013].

Quaglia, R. and Cobb, C. (1996). Toward a theory of student aspirations. *Journal of Research in Rural Education,* 12 (3): 127–132.

St Clair, R. and Benjamin, A. (2011). Performing desires: the dilemma of aspirations and educational attainment. *British Educational Research Journal,* 37 (3): 501–517.

Wigfield, A. and Eccles, J. (2000). Expectancy-value theory of achievement motivation. *Contemporary Educational Psychology,* 25: 68–81.

Chapter 8

The impact of financial and cultural capital on FE students' education and employment progression

Emma Norris and Becky Francis

Introduction

Social class[1] remains the strongest predictor of educational achievement and life outcomes,[2] undermining government claims to meritocracy, and strongly impeding both social mobility and social justice. This chapter reports on research investigating the barriers that Further Education (FE) students and their teachers believe disadvantaged students face when engaging in FE and their related education-to-work routes. The research was carried out as part of a social justice agenda at the Royal Society for the Encouragement of Arts, Manufactures and Commerce (RSA).[3] It focused on the FE sector because (a) this is where a majority of young people from low-income groups are concentrated in their post-16 studies, and (b) because the sector itself is seen as lacking social capital. But also, the FE sector and its courses are often specifically targeted to vocational engagement. Our findings concerning the cultural and financial impediments disadvantaged students face often relate directly to a lack of access to work experience, opportunities and information.

Background

The continuing impact of social class has been well documented by sociologists (see e.g. Savage 2007; Sayer 2005; Reay *et al.* 2001). In relation to school-to-work trajectories, this impact has been underlined by the continued scale of the socio-economic gap for attainment (Francis and Wong 2013), and in recent debates about internships and university fees, highlighting how difficult it can be for young people with limited cultural capital and financial means to progress in education and employment. Although the socio-economic gap is a widespread international phenomenon, the United Kingdom has a particularly high degree of social segregation and is one of the nations with the most highly differentiated results among Organisation for Economic Co-operation and Development (OECD) countries (OECD 2007).

There is a range of explanations for the inequalities in school-to-work routes and outcomes; however, many relate to inequalities of financial and cultural capital. Existing research demonstrates that capitals of various kinds significantly impact life chances: a raft of research in education and sociology demonstrates how this works (e.g. Bourdieu 1986; Reay 2001; Archer *et al.* 2007). Cultural capital refers to the non-financial advantages that many middle-class parents can use to further their children's ambitions. These include general inculcation into a middle-class 'habitus' and set of assumptions; large networks of professional and social contacts; detailed knowledge of how the education system works; and transferable experience in soft skills such as interview manner. There is a considerable body of research highlighting the impact of social and cultural capital in education that shows how middle-class parents are better able to 'play the game' (Reay 2001; Reay and Lucey 2003) and ensure that their children experience smooth progression routes in education and the workplace (Walkerdine *et al.* 2001). Students from lower socio-economic backgrounds on the other hand, find progression more complex and alienating (Walkerdine *et al.* 2001; Reay *et al.* 2001; Archer *et al.* 2007). In this chapter, we draw out some particular examples of how a lack of cultural and social capital in relation to school-to-work routes disadvantages many FE students, and we make recommendations as to how this might be addressed.

The FE sector has sometimes been branded 'the Cinderella sector' due to its comparative underfunding and lack of political attention and status in comparison to other sectors, such as higher education (and – at least until recently – school sixth forms). Employers and politicians often have little understanding of the sector and too often perceive it and its students as 'second division' (Learning and Skills Council (LSC) 2007). FE colleges work with more young people than schools and independent sixth forms combined: in 2008/2009 there were over one million learners under 19 years old participating in government-funded further education. Many of these young people have struggled in education and are from disadvantaged backgrounds: 56 per cent of FE learners are from the bottom three socio-economic groups, compared with only 22 per cent in maintained school sixth forms (Buddery *et al.* 2011). Working with these groups presents challenges in terms of learner support, attendance and attainment, but it also means the sector has a huge opportunity to promote and sustain social mobility.

Methods

The research reported was based on a review of the literature on social inequalities in young people's post-14 trajectories and focus groups with FE staff and students. Eight focus groups were conducted with staff and students in four case study colleges in London (×2), Nottingham and Leicester. A total of 30 staff and 32 students took part in the research. Each focus group lasted approximately 1.5 hours. Senior management in participating colleges identified young people and staff members to take part. Recruitment also occurred via 'snowballing' (where students would invite their friends or acquaintances in college).

Cultural capital

Parental guidance

When making decisions about progression in education and employment, young people often rely either directly or indirectly on their parents or guardians for direction (Tough and Brooks 2007; see also Chapter 1 in this volume by Louise Archer). Parents indirectly influence their children by modelling, and directly influencing their children's decisions by giving them advice about the future. Middle-class parents are able to use their experience and knowledge of education and careers (their cultural capital) to provide their children with such advice. In contrast, a number of students that participated in our research said they would be unlikely to approach their parents for progression advice because of their parents' limited experience of post-16 education. Others had only a few family members who they would confidently approach:

> I wouldn't go back to my parents for advice, just because they're from different backgrounds.
>
> (FE student, Nottingham)

> I mean whoever actually works in your family is the one you're actually going to pick [to ask for advice].
>
> (FE student, London)

Parents with limited experience of the education system want the best for their children but lack knowledge about how to help them (Kintrea *et al.* 2011). This high aspiration but lack of information/experience bore particular risks in relation to elite routes because working-class families did not understand the competition for places in higher education or elite careers. Staff worried that students were not being given realistic notions of how challenging and competitive particular progression routes are, or the level of dedication, and often financial, commitment that these routes entail. Staff were not necessarily worried about the abilities of young people, but rather that the young people concerned did not have realistic and accurate knowledge about some progression routes.

> There [are] also some [students] that have unrealistic expectations that often come from the parents. These parents have actually got very few qualifications themselves, but they just have this fixed idea that their son or daughter, they're doing science and therefore they must be able to go to university and do medicine and that's what will happen without much work or effort. They're just totally unrealistic. I think in many cases it's just that parents don't know what is available and they don't know what the processes are, what grades are needed in what subjects, they don't understand education, they don't understand what sort of routes are best for their kids.
>
> (FE practitioner, Leicester)

Clearly we would want to avoid an understanding of parents from low-income groups as 'inadequate' in this regard: indeed, as we have said, these perceptions of working-class parents as wanting the very best for their children refutes the image of such parents often presented by policymakers (as lacking aspiration). What our findings demonstrate, however, is that these parents urgently need to be provided with proper sources of information in order to support their children in their decision-making (see Wolf 2011).

Less commonly, a few young people reported that their parents' own negative or limited educational experiences prevent them from providing their children with support and encouragement when studying in FE. According to research participants, this is because their parents' negative experiences of education have alienated them from their children's education (see e.g. Reay 1998; Lucey and Reay 2002; Department for Children, Schools and Families (DCSF) 2008).

> My mum just doesn't get it. Like, she isn't against me going, although she said 'why aren't you getting a job?' when I first went [to FE] . . . You know my dad left school when he was 14.
>
> (FE student, Leicester)

Confidence and experience

FE students from lower socio-economic backgrounds also appeared less likely to feel confident and self-assured about their ability to 'fit in' in higher education and elite progression routes (see e.g. Archer *et al.* 2007). This relates to identities and 'habitus' (see Archer *et al.* 2007), but also to broader issues of cultural capital and connected (lack of) familiarity. Disadvantaged young people are less likely to have been exposed to professional work settings before or to have family experience of higher education that helps them understand what to expect, whereas middle-class young people already possess this capital, which is crucial to their progression.

> It's completely, you know, they don't know to turn up in your smart attire . . . and that is your interview and things like that, but they don't understand.
>
> (FE practitioner, Nottingham)

> [Working-class young people] get to university and lecturers say 'This what I'm going to say' and they do a big lecture and then you have to leave and there's no questions, there's no 'Can you repeat that please?', there's none of that and [working-class young people] find that really difficult.
>
> (FE practitioner, Nottingham)

Staff told us that low confidence and a lack of experience sometimes results in young people either becoming extremely risk-averse and unlikely to try to pursue ambitious routes or finding it hard to compete with their more affluent counterparts who are naturally at ease in these settings and situations.

Networks

Previous research shows that middle-class parents are able to harness their networks to support the progression of their children (Perry and Francis 2011). When faced with decisions about progression, middle-class children are able to draw upon their parents' professional and other contacts to mobilise information and expertise (Horvat *et al.* 2003). Parents also use their contacts to gain valuable work experience opportunities for their children (Francis *et al.* 2005; Hatcher and Le Gallais 2008; Milburn 2012). Most FE students lack access to the kinds of social networks that facilitate high-level work experience and, as such, are excluded from experiences and advocacy that would help inform their decisions about progression and make them more attractive candidates in higher education and the workplace. One FE practitioner in our research complained that none of her students studying for a law National Vocational Qualification (NVQ) were able to access any local placements with employers because they lacked the social capital necessary to secure them.

> Law students suffer significantly in [the college] because in Nottingham we have two tremendously wonderful law schools . . . so our students don't stand a chance. Yet these are the students that actually need those placements more and they haven't got the networks, the connections, parents, have they?
>
> (FE practitioner, Nottingham)

Cultural expectations

FE practitioners and students who participated in our research suggested that students from lower socio-economic backgrounds did not feel comfortable using cultural and social capital to further their own ends. A number of students talked about 'making your own way' or 'making it by yourself'. There appeared to be a strong aversion among students to the idea of using contacts, family connections or other networks in order to progress in education or the workplace. For these students, conceptions of success appeared grounded in discourses of independence and narratives of 'self-made' men and women. Using anything but your own ability and luck was considered 'cheating'.

> I want to be able to hold my head up and say 'I've found my own way here . . .' and it's not through people that I know.
>
> (FE student, London)

> When I'm doing dance and shows, you know I want people to notice me because I'm good at it. Sometimes when we go on trips we get to talk to the dancers and so we do have [contacts] I suppose . . . but it doesn't mean as much to bother them does it?
>
> (FE student, Leicester)

The 'belts and bootstraps' and 'rags to riches' narratives which appeared to underpin such assertions evoke both a different cultural approach, but also a complete lack of recognition of the networking practices adopted by others. Middle-class students have no need of such ideals of independent 'rags to riches' achievements because they have no gap to traverse: they simply have to replicate their parents' achievements.

Economic capital

> These kids don't have a financial back-up.
>
> (FE practitioner, Nottingham)

Money had a direct and negative impact on disadvantaged young people in both the short and long term. It restricted their participation in FE courses and influenced their decisions about progression, especially with regards to higher education (see also Archer *et al.* 2003, 2010). The importance of money among FE students is unsurprising because the majority are from low-income families. Education Maintenance Allowance (EMA) take-up figures show that in 2010 at least 643,000 16–18-year-olds in education came from families with less than £31,000 annual income. As a result, the prospect of moving straight into the workplace and being able to contribute to family income or live independently often feels more realistic and attractive than other progression routes.

The basics

Many of the students we spoke to struggled to afford the most basic items necessary for their education. This included uniform, stationery and educational trips. Struggling to afford basic items compromised their enjoyment of study and forced them to miss valuable educational experiences. In extreme cases, some young people even found it difficult to afford enough food, which meant they were tired and found it difficult to concentrate. A number of recent research studies have similarly found that poverty can force students from low-income backgrounds to forgo items that most of us consider essential (ATL (Association of Teachers and Lecturers) 2011).

> Students that were timetabled for four days – they couldn't afford the bus fare for that many days. Now we bring them in on big long days, to save them the bus fare. The students want it squashing into two or three days so they can work alongside it. We're designing our timetables around their money concerns.
>
> (FE practitioner, London)

Transport costs were singled out by the young people we spoke to, especially if they lived far away from college. According to the ATL (2011) study, 66 per cent of education staff said that unaffordable transport costs caused absences from classes. The problem has become so acute that two of the colleges we spoke to have redesigned college timetables to limit transport costs for students, squashing a week's worth of lessons into two days. While this saved students money, it damaged concentration levels because their days were often extremely long and full. It also put a strain on colleges' teaching resources and classroom facilities because so many students were in college at particular points, rather than attendance being evenly spread throughout the week.

Debt aversion

Financial concerns presented a barrier not only in the immediate term but also for progression to higher education. The students we spoke to were very concerned about the recent decision to lift the cap on top-up fees, and said it would cause many of them to reassess the viability of higher education.

There is a considerable body of research to demonstrating how cost is a strong factor in the decision as to whether to pursue higher education (HE), and that students from lower socio-economic backgrounds are more likely than those from affluent families to be deterred by the costs of HE (Connor *et al.* 2001; Forsyth and Furlong 2003) – as are mature students in contrast to younger students (Ross *et al.* 2002). This latter is pertinent for FE, which caters for a broader age range than school-maintained sixth forms. In addition, several of these studies cite debt and the prospect of building up large debts, particularly student loan debt, as a deterrent to university entrance among qualified students from low-socio-economic groups (Archer *et al.* 2003; Forsyth and Furlong 2003). Rather than representing ignorance or lack of commitment, this aversion commonly reflects first- or second-hand experience of the potentially devastating consequences of debt, and the proportional impact of fees on a far smaller family resource (in comparison to middle-class families).

Limiting choice

Financial expediency continues to influence the decisions of those students who do want to progress to higher education. Studying at a local institution was an attractive option among the FE students that participated in our research because it enabled them to continue living at home and limit their outgoings. This is part of a broader trend for students (particularly those from lower socio-economic backgrounds) to choose to live at home, a decision strongly influenced by debt aversion. However, this constrains students' choices and prospects:

> Actually I was planning to go to [an HEI] near the house, it's not far from there, like half an hour from the bus so I was thinking, you know, I don't have to move to nowhere which is actually very cheap. And you're still in contact with your friends and family.
>
> (FE student, Leicester)

The local kids can't get into their local universities – Nottingham – not a chance. And yet they can't afford to live away from home, even more so with the new fee system that's coming in.

(FE practitioner, Nottingham)

FE: institutional lack of capital?

Our findings highlighted two areas which FE institutions need to develop further in order to help young people with progression: (1) information, advice and guidance (IAG) and work experience, and (2) employer engagement.

Information, advice and guidance

Our conversations with learners and their teachers reinforced how valuable informed and impartial IAG is for progression (Hooley *et al.* 2012). Despite its importance, some of the students who participated in our research had encountered difficulties with careers advice in their FE colleges. In FE, more than schools, learners are looking for specific and detailed advice and information. Alison Wolf touches on this in her report on vocational education, emphasising that students need detailed data about entry qualifications and destinations of students on particular courses to help them understand what qualifications are really needed to qualify for particular courses and careers (Wolf 2011). The students we spoke to did not feel that such detailed advice was available, and observed that one-stop careers services in colleges were, by nature, generic.

Staff acknowledged that, in place of approaching the careers service, students would often look to their teachers for advice. This is seen as problematic by FE staff, who feel too distant from industry and the workplace to provide high-quality and accurate advice. Staff also felt that students needed *realistic* advice, but felt that their ability to provide this was compromised in two ways. First, by the approach to IAG that Alison Wolf has described as 'well-meaning attempts to pretend that everything is worth the same as everything else' (Wolf 2011), meaning that there is not a culture of honesty about which qualifications are likely to help students access particular routes and which are not. This is a real problem for young people from lower socio-economic backgrounds who, as discussed, are not always able to fall back on the experiences of their parents to provide realistic guidance about which courses are well regarded and which are not.

Second, there was concern among some FE practitioners that students are not fully aware of the diversity of jobs available in different sectors, leading them to develop aspirations that are neither determined by their ability nor based on a comprehensive understanding of the types of jobs available. FE students need careers advice that does not constrain or dampen their ambitions, but rather enhances their understanding of options that are available.

Work experience

As discussed, affluent young people are often able to secure placements and experience though parents or wider social networks. Young people from low-income families are less likely to have this advantage and are more reliant on FE colleges to provide these opportunities for them. The staff we spoke to acknowledged how important their role in facilitating work experience is, but said there is a range of difficulties in delivering this.

Most colleges have formal work experience programmes organised, administered and delivered by in-house careers advisers. However, both staff and students said that – like careers advice itself – such placements tend to be generic and often bear little relation to the qualifications and careers that learners are studying towards. This leads to students relying on practitioners as a source for relevant opportunities. As with careers advice, staff said that they find it very difficult to maintain the contacts necessary for more bespoke work placements. Busy in the classroom, many simply do not have the time to nurture professional networks.

Employer engagement

The content and structure of courses was a final area of challenge, with students and staff maintaining that FE is not yet sufficiently grasping the opportunity to work closely with employers and provide 'cutting-edge' qualifications. Staff said that NVQ qualifications tended to trail behind what is required in the workplace, with provision failing to anticipate what is attractive to industry or provide a real taste of the types of projects that learners will encounter in the workplace.

> New jobs we need to identify and this is one of the issues really in the curriculum or how do we keep up with new skills, you know, a simple working example: soon 25 per cent of European car sales will be hybrids. Well, who is teaching hybrid technology? It should be FE.
>
> (FE practitioner)

> NVQs can be a little bit long in the tooth – employers accept them, but they do need updating.
>
> (FE practitioner)

Implications for policy and practice

Our research with FE students and staff has highlighted the numerous barriers that young people from lower socio-economic backgrounds face when considering education and employment progression. Many of these relate to cultural and social capital, both of which present meaningful obstacles to optimal progression. In particular, we found that FE students have a limited awareness of the reality of local labour market demand, and of the variety of occupational opportunities and the specific routes through which these might be accessed. Moreover, we found that FE colleges lack institutional capital to remedy these disadvantages.

As had been found in previous education research, young people from disadvantaged backgrounds often lack the middle-class 'habitus' and other forms of social and cultural capital that dominate higher education and elite career paths. This was strongly illustrated in our research with young people and their teachers, who talked about the lack of role models and the social networks that allow students to easily progress. This was alongside discussion about a broader sense of alienation and inability or unease about replicating middle-class modes of behaviour that are beneficial and even necessary to certain types of progression. We suggest a number of ways to limit the disadvantage this causes young people from low-income backgrounds:

- *Find innovative ways to transmit educational cultural capital* to young people from disadvantaged backgrounds. FE colleges must build relationships with organisations that have high cultural capital. The ability of civil society and professional organisations to share their cultural capital is currently not utilised.
- More work needs to be done on *how the 'capital' of low-income families can be made valuable in progression.* At the moment, it disadvantages young people from lower socio-economic backgrounds and contributes to feelings of alienation.

Young people from lower socio-economic backgrounds continue to be negatively affected by a lack of financial capital and were particularly concerned about the withdrawal of the EMA, and the costs of HE. Hence:

- consistent and accessible financial support is necessary to ensure disadvantaged students can access the FE and HE sectors and successfully progress;
- accurate and early information about financial support must be made available to disadvantaged students to help counter the negative impact of debt aversion.

Our research also revealed that FE students are at an institutional disadvantage when it comes to progression due to lack of access to high-quality careers advice and institutional networks and inadequate employer engagement. These had disproportionately negative consequences for students from lower socio-economic backgrounds because they rely on the networks of their educational institutions for advice and opportunities in the absence of personal connections. FE colleges could have a positive institutional impact on the progression of disadvantaged students through improved employer engagement. By working closely with employers, the FE sector can ensure its provision is meeting the needs and demands of local and national economies, making its students as competitive as possible. Employer engagement also extends the influence of colleges outside of their buildings by giving teachers and assessors the opportunity to work directly with the local community. As the Foster Review of FE (Foster 2005), the National Employers Skills Survey (LSC 2005), the FE White Paper (DfES 2006) and the Leitch Review (Leitch 2006) have all suggested, the employer engagement agenda is vital for providing further education with a clearer mission and focus by addressing the educational needs of local people and businesses while also addressing the wider economic and social challenges of up-skilling learners for what industry will require of them.

Suggested routes forward include the following:

- FE students will need improved, face-to-face *careers advice* in addition to the offer provided by the all-age careers service recently introduced in England by the UK Coalition government. This should include detailed advice on the range of occupations available in different areas of interest, and the various qualification routes and other aspects needed to access these various occupations.
- *The FE sector needs to strengthen its networks and contacts.* FE practitioners could take some responsibility for maintaining these networks and contacts if they are provided with CPD opportunities that facilitate this. Building relationships with local employers needs particular attention in order to ensure FE provision is sensitive to their needs. This could be achieved by rejuvenating employer advisory boards that are subject-specific.

Evidently, the FE sector alone cannot address the social inequalities that underpin different levels of social and cultural capital in relation to high status learning and career routes, or indeed remedy the very real structural barriers that preclude equality of opportunity. However, some of the constraints for disadvantaged students identified in this chapter *are* possible to tackle. By better aligning FE provision to local and national economic needs, by providing new means of transferring capital and valuing working-class capital itself, and by providing timely information and support around financial hardship, these students can be better supported. In these ways, the FE sector can realise its potential in driving forward social mobility and provide its students with the chances they need and deserve.

Notes

1 'Social class' remains a controversial concept, with some commentators arguing that social class distinctions have faded or rapidly changed in recent decades, and others pointing out that inequalities and distinctions according to socio-economic background have grown greater than ever. Sociologists argue for a retention of the concept of 'class' because it incorporates cultural as well as financial factors (see e.g. Reay 1998; Savage 2007). For simplicity, we usually refer to young people from 'low-income backgrounds' in this chapter.

2 See e.g. National Equality Panel (2010), Lupton *et al.* (2009) and Sodha and Margo (2010).
3 See e.g. www.thersa.org/action-research-centre/learning,-cognition-and-creativity/ education/reports-and-events/social-justice [accessed 6 February 2014]. The chapter draws on a longer research report authored by Norris (2011), www.thersa.org/__data/ assets/pdf_file/0017/410039/RSA-Education-Not-enough-capital1.pdf [accessed 6 February 2014].

References

Archer, L. (2003). *Higher education and social class: issues of exclusion and inclusion.* London: RoutledgeFalmer.

Archer, L., Halsall, A. and Hollingworth, S. (2007). Class, gender, (hetero) sexuality and schooling: paradoxes within working-class girls' engagement with education and post-16 aspirations. *British Journal of Sociology of Education*, 28 (2): 165–180.

Archer, L., Hollingworth, S. and Mendick, H. (2010). *Urban youth and education.* Buckingham: McGraw Hill.

ATL. (2011). *80 per cent of education staff work with students who live in poverty in the UK.* ATL Press Release: 11 April 2011.

Bourdieu, P. (1986). The forms of capital. *In:* J. Richardson, ed. *Handbook of theory and research for the sociology of education.* New York, NY: Greenwood, 241–258.

Buddery, P., Kippin, H. and Lucas, B. (2011). *The further education and skills sector in 2020: a social productivity approach.* London: 2020 Public Services Hub.

Connor, H., Dawson, S., Tyers, C., Eccles, J., Regan J. and Aston J. (2001). *Social class and higher education: issues affecting decisions on participation by lower social class groups.* Research Report RR 267, London: Department for Education and Employment.

Department for Children, Schools and Families (DCSF). (2008). *The impact of parental engagement of children's education.* London: DCSF.

Department for Education and Skills (DfES). (2006). *Further education: raising skills, improving life chances.* London: DfES.

Forsyth. A. and Furlong A. (2003). *Losing out? Socioeconomic disadvantage and experience in further and higher education.* Bristol: Policy Press/JRF.

Foster, A. (2005). *Realising the potential: a review of the role of further education colleges.* London: DFES.

Francis, B. and Wong, B. (2013). *What is preventing social mobility? A review of the evidence.* Leicester: ASCL.

Francis, B., Osgood, J., Dalgety, J. and Archer, L. (2005). *Gender equality in work experience placements for young people.* Occupational Segregation: Working Paper Series No. 27. Manchester: Equal Opportunities Commission.

Hatcher, R. and Le Gallais, T. (2008). *The work experience placements of secondary school students: widening horizons or reproducing social inequality?* Birmingham, UK: Birmingham City University.

Hooley T., Marriot, J., Watts, A. and Coiffait, L. (2012). *Careers 2020: options for future careers work in English schools.* London: The Pearson Think Tank.

Horvat, E. M., Weininger, E. B. and Lareau A. (2003). From social ties to social capital: class differences in the relation between school and parent networks. *American Educational Research Journal*, 40 (2): 319–351.

Kintrea, K., St Clair, R. and Houston, M. (2011). *The influence of parents, places and poverty on educational attitudes and aspirations.* York: Joseph Rowntree Foundation.

Learning and Skills Council (LSC). (2005). *National employer skills survey: key findings.* Coventry: LSC.

Learning and Skills Council (LSC). (2007). *The status and reputation of the further education system.* Coventry: LSC.

Leitch, S. (2006). *Prosperity for all in the global economy: world class skills.* London: DfES.

Lucey, H. and Reay, D. (2002). A market in waste: psychic and structural dimensions of school-choice policy in the UK and children's narratives on 'demonised' schools. *Discourse,* 23: 23–40.

Lupton, R., Heath, N. and Salter, E. (2009). Education: New Labour's top priority. *In:* J. Hills, T. Sefton and K. Stewart, eds. *Towards a more equal society? Poverty, inequality and policy since 1997.* Bristol: Policy Press, 71–90.

Milburn, A. (2012). *Unleashing aspiration: the final report of the panel on fair access to the professions.* London: Cabinet Office.

National Equality Panel. (2010). *Report of the National Equality Panel.* London: CASE/Government Equalities Office. Available from: http://sticerd.lse.ac.uk/dps/case/cr/CASEreport60_executive_summary.pdf [accessed 6 February 2014].

Norris, E. (2011). *Not enough capital: exploring education and employment progression in further education.* London: RSA.

Organisation for Economic Co-operation and Development (OECD). (2007). *PISA 2006: science competencies for tomorrow's world executive summary.* Available from: www.pisa.oecd.org [accessed 14 October 2010].

Perry, E. and Francis, B. (2011). *The social class gap for educational attainment: a review of the literature.* London: RSA.

Reay, D. (1998). *Class work.* London: UCL Press.

Reay, D. (2001). Finding or losing yourself? Working-class relationships to education. *Journal of Education Policy,* 16 (4): 333–346.

Reay, D. and Lucey, H. (2003). The limits of choice: children and inner city schooling. *Sociology,* 37, 121–143.

Reay, D., Davies, J., David, M. and Ball, S. (2001). Choices of degree or degrees of choice? Class, 'race' and the higher education choice process. *Sociology,* 35: 855–874.

Ross, A., Archer, L., Thomson, D., Hutchings, M., Gilchrist, R., Joh C. and Akantziliou (2002). *Potential mature student recruitment in HE.* Research Report RR 385. Nottingham: DfES.

Savage, M. (2007). Changing social class identities in post-war Britain: perspectives from mass-observation. *Sociological Research Online,* 12 (3): 6.

Sayer, A. (2005). *The moral significance of class.* Cambridge, UK: Cambridge University Press.

Sodha, S. and Margo, J. (2010). *A generation of disengaged children is waiting in the wings.* London: DEMOS.

Tough, S. and Brooks, R. (2007). *School admissions: fair choice for parents and pupils.* London: Institute for Public Policy Research.

Walkerdine, V., Lucey, H. and Melody, J. (2001). *Growing up girl.* London: Macmillan.

Wolf, A. (2011). *Review of vocational education: the Wolf Report.* London: Department for Education.

Part 3

Equity and access in the experience of employer engagement

The views of young Britons (aged 19–24) on their teenage experiences of school-mediated employer engagement

Anthony Mann and Elnaz T. Kashefpakdel

Introduction and methodology

In 2004, education ministries in England, Scotland and Wales each introduced new requirements on state schools to provide pupils, specifically at the age of 14–16, with a minimal exposure to work-related learning within their learning experiences (QCA 2003; Scottish Executive 2004, 2007; Welsh Assembly Government 2004, 2008). With work-related learning described in England by way of example, as learning about work, for work and through work, it was expected by policymakers that the requirement would provide young people with enhanced opportunities to come into contact with employers. National administrations, in explicit guidance, encouraged engagement between employers and young people through such activities as short periods of work experience, provision of careers information, business mentoring and enterprise competitions (DCSF 2009). In doing so, it was the intention of policymakers that participation in such activities would help young people improve their transitions from education into employment (Mann and Percy 2013; Jamieson and Miller 1991).

This chapter presents the findings from a survey of young adults who were invited to look back on the experiences of employer engagement they received during their schooling. Whereas a number of surveys record the extent to which pupils still in the education system had participated in employer engagement activities at the point of questioning (QCA 2004, 2007; Ipsos MORI 2009; YouGov 2010), no comparable survey is known to have been undertaken of young adults after they had completed their secondary education. Importantly, the chapter investigates whether those young people who experienced these interactions with employers believed, in later life as young adults, that these interactions had enhanced their school-to-work transitions. In particular, respondents were asked whether employer engagement experiences were useful to them in relation to three kinds of outcome: getting a job after education; deciding on a career; and getting into higher education. Recent research and policy literature have claimed that there are relationships between participation in employer engagement activities and these outcomes. For example, the UK Commission for Employment and Skills (UKCES) has argued that engagement 'with businesses [while in school] improves the prospects of young people when seeking employment' (UKCES 2012: 16). Jones argues in Chapter 11 of this collection that work experience forms an important element within UK higher education admissions. Reports from both the Organisation for Economic Co-operation and Development (OECD) and from Harvard Graduate School for Education have argued that the involvement of employers is essential to effective careers advice within successful transitions from education to employment (OECD 2010; Symonds *et al.* 2011). The survey reported on in this chapter reveals the perceptions of young adults as to whether their exposure to employers while in school had, on reflection, provided such benefits to them subsequently.

The survey was undertaken by YouGov, an opinion pollster, on behalf of the British charity Education and Employers Taskforce. YouGov questioned 985 young British adults resident in England, Scotland and Wales who were drawn from a panel of 280,000+ individuals. An email was sent to a random sample of young adults aged 19–24. The achieved sample was evenly divided with respect to age and gender and can be understood as representative of this cohort. The results presented in this report relate to a subset of the sample: those 773 young people who attended the same form of schooling (non-selective state education, selective state education or independent education) at both 14–16 and 16–18. In so doing, it allows comparisons to be drawn between former pupils of the three different types of schooling who stayed in education after the age of 16. Aged between 19 and 24 years, the survey participants would have been aged between 12 and 17 in 2004 when official expectations of schools with respect to work-related learning were codified. In the discussion that follows, results from the survey in relation to four specific types of employer engagement activity (work experience, careers advice, business mentoring, enterprise competitions) are given. Data on the extent of recalled engagement, segmented by school type attended, is given alongside data on perceptions of the ultimate utility of the experience in relation to three dimensions of effective school-to-work transitions: deciding on a career, getting a job after education and getting into university. The data are further considered by school type attended, allowing comparison by age (at which the activity was undertaken), highest qualification level obtained (at the time of the survey) and between the experiences and perceptions of young adults who had attended independent schools (which have been under no obligation to engage with employers or to provide work-related learning) and their peers in the state sector. The data analysis for this chapter was carried out using SPSS and appropriate testing for statistical significance was carried out. The level of statistical significance testing has been denoted in the tables. Descriptive tables of the full survey and subsample respondents are in the Appendix.

Work experience

Work experience has long been assumed to be the most popular employer engagement activity experienced in the British educational setting (Mann 2012; QCA 2004; Miller *et al.* 1991) and, as Table 9.1 shows, nearly 90 per cent of young

British adults recalled undertaking short work experience placements while they were at school or college between the ages of 14 and 19. The sample size was sufficient to explore whether variations existed between former pupils of non-selective state schools/colleges, grammar schools and independent schools. The survey notably records a very high level of participation by the former pupils of independent schools, providing a validation for limited existing research into the behaviour of these institutions (Huddleston *et al.* 2012; YouGov 2010). Given that such independent institutions would have been under no requirement to provide such experiences to their pupils, the behaviour is suggestive of a very broad willingness of British educationalists to incorporate periods of workplace exposure into the school experience of young people. However, statistical testing does show significant variance with the recalled experiences of former pupils of other school types, indicating that school type attended has a non-trivial relationship with an individual's likelihood of having experienced work experience placements.

Unpacking data by age at which work experience was undertaken, however, does show an important, and statistically significant, variation between the sectors (see Table 9.2). In the state sector, in keeping with state demands, majorities undertook periods of work experience between the ages of 14 and 16: 91 per cent in the case of former pupils of non-selective schools and colleges, and 72 per cent in the case of former grammar school pupils. By contrast, only half (52 per cent) of the former pupils of independent schools undertook a placement at 16 years or younger. Such an emphasis on placements being undertaken at an older age within the independent sector would be in keeping with findings reported by Huddleston *et al.* and Jones (in Chapters 10 and 11 of this collection, respectively). These authors show that work experience in the independent sector takes place at an older age and is more closely associated with supporting entry into higher education.

Table 9.1 Participation in work experience segmented by school type attended[a]

Did you ever do a work experience placement? This is where you would spend some time with an employer (possibly a week or two weeks) to get experience of the workplace	School type attended 14–19			Total (all)
	A non-selective state comprehensive or academy	Grammar/ state selective school	An independent school	
Yes	498	119	77	694
	91%	88%	84%	90%
No	38	16	15	69
	7%	12%	16%	9%
Not sure	9	1	0	10
	2%	1%	0%	1%
Total	545	136	92	773
rounded	100%	100%	100%	100%

Note
a P-value: 0.019 at 10% significance level.

Table 9.2 Work experience – age placements undertaken segmented by school type attended[a]

How old were you when you did your work experience placement(s)?	School type attended 14–19			Total
	A non-selective state comprehensive or academy	Grammar/ state selective school	An independent school	
16 or younger	81%[b]	58%	30%	498 (72%)
Between 16 and 19	8%	27%	48%	111 (16%)
Did work experience at both ages	10%	14%	22%	82 (12%)
Don't know	–	1%	–	3
Total	498	119	77	694

Note
a P-value: 0.000 at 10% significance level.
b Values in per cent are rounded.

Contemporaneous surveys of young people undertaking work experience typically show high proportions of young people agreeing that their placements were of real value to their future progression. A 2007 survey of 15,025 young people after their return from work experience placements by the National Support Group for Work Experience on behalf of the English Department for Children, Schools and Families (DCSF) found high proportions of respondents agreeing that their placements had helped them to refine their career aspirations and to develop skills and insights of value to future employment. Some three-quarters of respondents agreed (37 per cent agreeing strongly) that they were now 'clearer about what I want to do in my future education and career' while upwards of 90 per cent of young people agreed (42 per cent agreeing strongly) that they returned from their placement with a better understanding of the skills employers are looking for (34 per cent strongly agreeing) and having developed 'some new skills that employers value' (National Support Group for Work Experience 2007).

As Jones argues in Chapter 11 of this collection, work experience placements are commonly referred to in the applications of young people to study in higher education (see also Mann *et al.* 2011) and Massey provides evidence from employers in Chapter 15 that work placements can help some young people get a job. This survey sought to test these claims by asking whether young adults believed that their own experiences of school-mediated work placements were useful to getting a job after education, deciding on a career or getting into university. The results are given in Table 9.3. In this table, as in those that follow, the first number reports the combined total of all respondents positively agreeing that, as an activity, work experience was of use to them in relation to an area of impact, whether 'a little' or 'a lot'. The remaining survey participants reported that the activity was 'not at all' useful to them. The second figure, in parentheses,

Table 9.3 Work experience – perceptions of utility

How useful was it to you in later life?	Total	Non-selective state school	Selective state school	Independent school	P-value	Work experience undertaken only pre-16	Work experience undertaken only post-16	Work experience undertaken at both ages	P-value	L0–L2 highest qualification	L3–L5 highest qualification	P-value
Getting a job after education	27% (9%)	25% (9%)	30% (10%)	36% (13%)	0.000	22% (6%)	39% (16%)	43% (23%)	0.000	38% (15%)	26% (9%)	0.414
Deciding on a career	58% (20%)	53% (17%)	64% (23%)	83% (39%)	0.000	50% (14%)	78% (37%)	82% (41%)	0.000	53% (9%)	59% (21%)	0.347
Getting into HE	27% (7%)	23% (7%)	31% (13%)	43% (14%)	0.010	17% (3%)	54% (22%)	51% (21%)	0.000	21% (9%)	27% (9%)	0.709
Number	694	498	119	77		498	111	82		34	646	

gives the figures for respondents reporting the activity to be 'a lot' of use to them. By way of illustration, as set out in Table 9.3, 25 per cent of the former pupils of non-selective state schools agreed that work experience was of some use (whether 'a little' or 'a lot') in helping to get a job after education and 9 per cent felt it was 'a lot' of use.

Table 9.3 is striking in its variations. The survey shows young adults to value work experience most highly in terms of career decision-making and this is found across all segmentations. Strikingly, it is former pupils of independent schools who consistently report the highest benefits from their work experience placements, reporting perceived utility levels of up to almost twice those reported by the alumni of non-selective state schools and colleges. The finding is relevant to pieces in this collection by Huddleston *et al.* (Chapter 10) and Le Gallais and Hatcher (Chapter 12), which explore relationships between socio-economic status and access to work experience placements, and it supports the conclusions of Jones (Chapter 11) who argues that privately educated young people are better placed to draw on workplace experiences to support university admission than their comprehensively educated peers. The poll also addresses issues raised in Massey's chapter on the timing of work experience. A significant recent change to the delivery of work experience in English education, driven by the Wolf Report (Wolf 2011), has been to increase the age from 14–16 to 16–19 at which the Department for Education encourages or requires it to be undertaken. This survey shows later work experience to be perceived to have been of considerably higher benefit than pre-16 placements across all three outcome areas. Comparison of the responses of young people who undertook work experience at both ages and only at post-16 suggests that later timing, in and of itself, may well contribute considerably to higher perceptions of utility. However, whereas delivery of work experience is well understood at pre-16 (Hatcher and Le Gallais 2008; Francis *et al.* 2005; Miller *et al.* 1991), it has been subject to comparatively little attention at post-16, indicating that results given here should be considered with some caution. It may well be, for example, that pupils undertaking post-16 work experience, as well as being closer to transition points into employment or continuing education and so arguably better placed to identify placements relevant to their hardening future ambitions, are also more likely to have opted into a placement, increasing likelihood of perceived value. The survey also highlights an interesting, but not statistically significant, variation in perceptions of the utility of work experience for getting a job by highest level of qualification. Young adults whose highest qualification was five GCSEs A*–C or lower reported perceived utility values some two-thirds higher than more highly qualified peers in terms of getting a job after education. The finding speaks to the view of British policymakers over recent years of the desirability of programmes of study aimed at lower achievers, including strong elements of work-related learning, in order to facilitate direct entry into the labour market (Raffo 2003, 2006; Golden *et al.* 2006) and is again deserving of further research.

Careers advice from an employer/employee volunteer

Half of those surveyed recalled receiving careers advice directly from employers, for example through a careers fair, as part of their educational experiences (see Table 9.4). For only 13 per cent of the sample in total, however, was this more than a rare intervention that happened just once or twice. Variation in participation levels by school type are statistically significant: one-quarter of those former pupils of independent schools experienced three or more such sessions compared to one in ten of those attending non-selective state schools/colleges.

Young adults who recalled such sessions valued them particularly highly when they heard from three or more employers compared to just one or two, a statistically significant variation. The comparatively high levels of value ascribed support the view, widely reported, that young people are particularly attentive to advice coming from working professionals (Lord and Jones 2006; Mann and Caplin 2012; Deloitte UK 2010). The responses in terms of 'deciding on a career' are particularly striking, with more than half of young adults agreeing that the career talk had influenced their decisions. Career decision-making has been shown to contribute to successful transitions from education into work; a significant array of recent longitudinal studies report that teenage certainty and/or realism about career aspirations as being linked (statistically significantly) with later employment related outcomes (Sabates *et al.* 2011; Ashby and Schoon 2010; Gutman and Schoon 2012; Yates *et al.* 2011). The findings reported here (see Table 9.5) endorse the proposition that many young people perceive that they gain

Table 9.4 Employee careers advice – extent of experience by school type attended[a]

How often, if ever, did you ever get careers advice directly from local employers or business people (e.g. careers fairs, careers talks, CV/interview workshops)?	School type attended 14–19			Total
	A non-selective state comprehensive or academy	Grammar/ state selective school	An independent school	
Just once or twice	204	48	33	285
	37%	35%	36%	37%
More often than this	54	22	23	99
	10%	16%	25%	13%
Never	250	59	33	342
	46%	43%	36%	44%
Don't know	37	7	3	47
	7%	5%	3%	6%
Total	545	136	92	773
rounded	100%	100%	100%	100%

Note
a P-value: 0.004 at 10% significance level.

Table 9.5 Employee careers advice – perceptions of utility

How useful was it to you in later life?	Total	Non-selective state school	Selective state school	Independent	P-value	Careers talks undertaken only pre-16	Careers talks undertaken only post-16	Careers talks undertaken at both ages	P-value	L0–L2 highest qualification	L3–L5 highest qualification	P-value
Getting a job (1–2 times)	33% (4%)	32% (2%)	35% (12%)	36% (6%)	0.303	28% (3%)	39% (5%)	38% (5%)	0.002	27% (9%)	33% (4%)	0.143
Getting a job (3+ times)	54% (16%)	54% (20%)	54% (4%)	52% (17%)		53% (0%)	52% (19%)	57% (20%)		75% (37%)	53% (15%)	
Deciding on a career (1–2 times)	55% (8%)	51% (5%)	60% (15%)	73% (18%)	0.000	47% (5%)	62% (10%)	62% (10%)	0.001	45% (9%)	56% (8%)	0.741
Deciding on a career (3+ times)	84% (28%)	81% (26%)	82% (14%)	92 (48%)		73% (7%)	92% (29%)	77% (37%)		87% (37%)	85% (28%)	
Getting into HE (1–2 times)	32% (6%)	29% (4%)	44% (15%)	27% (9%)	0.156	27% (5%)	38% (8%)	33% (7%)	0.043	18% (9%)	32% (6%)	0.268
Getting into HE (3+ times)	52% (20%)	57% (24%)	41% (0%)	52% (30%)		40% (7%)	56% (25%)	54% (20%)		62% (38%)	52% (18%)	
Number (1–2 times)	285	204	48	33		95	112	68		11	268	
Number (3+ times)	99	54	22	23		15	48	35		8	88	

something of long-term value from their school-mediated careers sessions with employers. The analysis raises the question of how this kind of careers advice impacts upon employment. A possible answer may lie in Mark Granovetter's conception of the 'power of weak ties', whereby economic advantage is conferred through extensive social networks, which give first-hand access to trusted information relating to labour market opportunities (Granovetter 1973; Jokisaari and Nurmi 2005).

Business mentoring

Studies on the character of teenage engagement in mentoring activities arranged through schools and colleges commonly begin with a lament over the imprecision and variation with which the word 'mentoring' is defined and used (Hall 2003). The term is used, for example, to describe employer engagements as varied as the provision of primary school non-expert employee volunteer reading partners through to periods of extended work experience (Miller *et al.* 2011; Linnehan 2001, 2003). Narrower, more widely accepted definitions of mentoring focus on the creation of new relationships, sustained over a period of time, between young people and adults who are neither family members nor teachers. Within this narrower definition, interest is focused on such relationships best described as 'business mentoring', which connect non-specialist, largely untrained working adults with pupils (Miller 1998; Bartlett 2009).

The survey's finding that some 19 per cent of young adults recalled some form of mentoring experience while in school aligns with findings from snapshot surveys of teenagers in state education that places the extent of mentoring at 10–20 per cent of the pupil cohort (YouGov 2010; Ipsos MORI 2009). Table 9.6 provides what appears to be the first published assessment of the extent of mentoring across the main three school types experienced by teenagers, finding very comparable levels of engagement across the private, selective and

Table 9.6 Business mentoring – participation by school type[a]

Experience of some form of mentoring		Type of school attended 14–19			Total
		A non-selective state comprehensive or academy	Grammar/state selective school	An independent school	
	Yes	106	27	16	149
		19%	20%	17%	19%
	No	439	109	76	624
		81%	80%	83%	81%
Total		545	136	92	773
		100%	100%	100%	100%

Note
a P-value: 0.117 at 10% significance level.

non-selective state sectors – the variation between institutional types is statistically insignificant.[1]

Studies of the impact of business mentoring have largely focused on evidence of impact upon pupil engagement in education and attainment (Green and Rogers 1997; Miller 1998; Linnehan 2001, 2003). Some studies have identified changes in pupil attitude and behaviour linked to personal confidence and communication skills relevant to employment (Bartlett 2009; Rose and Jones 2007). In Table 9.7, experiences of business mentoring are disaggregated to consider three common types of mentoring experience: 1–2–1 mentoring, which might be seen as a standard form of the activity whereby relationships will be created between individual pupils and individual adults; group mentoring, where two or more pupils would typically engage with a single individual mentor; and e-mentoring, where 1–2–1 relationships are created and sustained through electronic mail and web-based communication tools. The disaggregation of results inevitably leads to small numbers of pupil experiences being considered, but does provide insight into very different activities and allow for significance testing. The results cast a rare light on the perceptions of young adults of the value of the mentoring they encountered. Of the three forms, e-mentoring is noticeably the most highly valued form of mentoring. Very low numbers (11 individuals), however, prevent reliable conclusions from being drawn; the consistently high values ascribed, however, demands further investigation. Strikingly, pupils' perceptions are evenly split on whether 1–2–1 or group mentoring provides greatest help across the three outcome areas. The finding echoes that of Miller's 1998 study into the impact of business mentoring at key stage 4 on pupil attainment. Based on a small sample, Miller was able to provide some comparisons of the experiences of young people mentored 1–2–1 and in group, arguing:

> Small group mentors had the advantage of allowing more students to participate. It was 'less embarrassing' for some students to be in a group and they were able to make new friends. The main disadvantages were the lack of time available for each student and the problem of discussing individual needs.
>
> (Miller 1998: 3)

Investigating relationships between mentoring and attainment, Miller found that in 'the school which had a group mentoring scheme there were no significant differences between the mentored and the control groups for either boys or girls' (Miller 1998: 3). In the current survey, significant variation is identified in relation to age at which mentoring is undertaken and by type of school attended.

Enterprise competition

Like mentoring, the meaning of 'enterprise education' has been subject to some contention. Definitions have varied considerably along a spectrum from a broad

Table 9.7 Business mentoring – perceptions of utility

How useful was it to you in later life?	Total	Non-selective state school	Selective state school	Inde-pendent	P-value	Mentoring undertaken only pre-16	Mentoring undertaken only post-16	Mentoring undertaken at both ages	P-value	L0–L2 highest qualification	L3–L5 highest qualification	P-value
Getting a job (1–2–1 mentoring)	51% (12%)	44% (13%)	75% (12%)	80% (0%)	0.314	28% (11%)	62% (15%)	50% (10%)	0.000	40% (20%)	52% (10%)	0.104
Getting a job (Group mentoring)	48% (11%)	43% (9%)	60% (20%)	54% (8%)		30% (0%)	55% (14%)	60% (30%)		100% (33%)	44% (10%)	
Getting a job (E-mentoring)	82% (45%)	83% (67%)	75% (25%)	100% (0%)		–	75% (25%)	100% (100%)		100% (100%)	78% (33%)	
Deciding on a career (1–2–1 mentoring)	63% (22%)	57% (20%)	75% (37%)	100% (20%)	0.039	44% (6%)	76% (26%)	50% (40%)	0.002	40% (20%)	63% (23%)	0.781
Deciding on a career (Group mentoring)	71% (16%)	62% (9%)	85% (35%)	84% (15%)		52% (9%)	76% (14%)	80% (40%)		100% (33%)	69% (16%)	
Deciding on a career (E-mentoring)	100% (45%)	100% (50%)	100% (50%)	100% (0%)		–	100% (25%)	100% (100%)		100% (50%)	100% (44%)	
Getting into HE (1–2–1 mentoring)	57% (16%)	52% (17%)	62% (25%)	100% (0%)	0.007	22% (11%)	70% (18%)	70% (30%)	0.000	40% (20%)	58% (17%)	0.496
Getting into HE (Group mentoring)	47% (12%)	41% (5%)	55% (35%)	61% (8%)		17% (0%)	61% (16%)	50% (20%)		68% (0%)	44% (12%)	
Getting into HE (E-mentoring)	71% (16%)	83% (17%)	75% (50%)	100% (0%)		–	75% (12%)	100% (67%)		50% (0%)	89% (33%)	
Number (1–2–1 mentoring)	67	54	8	5		18	34	10		5	60	
Number (Group mentoring)	89	56	20	13		23	51	10		3	83	
Number (E-mentoring)	11	6	4	1		–	8	3		2	9	

approach to education, based upon project learning and using real-life learning resources to a very narrow focus on activities which present young people with entrepreneurial challenges (Coiffait *et al.* 2012). It was the latter, narrow definition that was the focus of our survey questions related to enterprise competitions where pupils are commonly brought into contact with employee volunteers acting as coaches and/or judges. The survey distinguishes between 'short' and 'long' competitions. A 'short competition' is typically experienced as an event lasting a few hours or perhaps a single day with pupils competing in teams to develop proposals for a product or service to be judged in an ultimate competition. In the 'long competition', an example of which would be the Young Enterprise company programme, teams of young people compete over a period of many months within and then between schools to develop a product or service that is taken to market. In short competitions, commonly whole classes or years will participate in the activity, whereas for long competitions, typically the activity is optional and presented as an opt-in extra-curricular activity.

A number of authors have suggested that involvement in enterprise competitions is particularly common in the independent sector (Huddleston *et al.* 2012; Athayde 2012) and the survey results (see Table 9.8) suggest that this is the case, with statistical variation significant at the 5 per cent level. Grammar school pupils were more likely to have engaged in enterprise competitions than alumni of the non-selective state sector.

Since 2001, enterprise education has been a priority of successive British governments in the belief, in large part, that by providing young people with opportunities to experience entrepreneurial activities while still in education they will then become more likely to seek out entrepreneurial opportunities in adult life and be more likely to succeed in them (Davies 2002). Policymakers in the United Kingdom and internationally have reasoned that by providing young people with opportunities to experience competitive business environments they would

Table 9.8 Enterprise competitions – participation by school type[a]

Did you undertake any enterprise activities involving employers?	Type of school attended 14–19			Total
	A non-selective state comprehensive or academy	Grammar/state selective school	An independent school	
Yes	177	56	39	272
	33%	41%	42%	35%
No	368	80	53	501
	67%	59%	58%	65%
Total	545	136	92	773
	100%	100%	100%	100%

Note
a P-value: 0.050 at 10% significance level.

develop abilities, attitudes and aspirations for future self-employment. 'The fact remains', however, as Rosemary Athayde argues, 'that considerable investment of public money has been made to provide enterprise education [in an entrepreneurial sense] in secondary schools in the UK, and the evidence on which this investment has been made is weak' (Athayde 2012: 711).

The literature on the effectiveness of school-age enterprise projects provides a mixed picture. Two rigorous studies have tracked young participants in longer-duration enterprise competitions over time, comparing development of attitudes and vocational interests to those of reasonably constituted control groups, using statistical analysis to test for variation in outcomes. The studies reach conflicting conclusions. Athayde's 2012 study of Young Enterprise participants in London found evidence of improved entrepreneurial competencies as measured against a control group. By contrast, Oosterbeek et al.'s 2008 Dutch study found no evidence that participation within long-duration enterprise competitions had any significant influence on individual entrepreneurial capabilities as measured by a survey tool widely used by Dutch banks to determine the enterprising character of potential entrepreneurs.

The survey considered here explored the question of perceived impacts across the three outcome areas (see Table 9.9). The results reveal distinctions in attitude between short and long competitions. More than twice as many young people who undertook short competitions felt that the experience was very useful in informing their career ambitions than peers who undertook longer-duration activities. One interpretation of the result is that in contrast to long duration competitions, where perhaps the more entrepreneurially minded opt into the activity and have their existing vocational ambitions confirmed, greater opportunity exists in shorter competitions for young people to broaden their understanding of potential career paths. Modest variation is seen in perceived impacts of the different type of enterprise competition by age undertaken and school type attended. Further research is warranted in understanding the difference in delivery, including relative costs, and impacts of short and long duration competition.

Conclusion: comparative perceived value of activities

The survey finally allows comparisons to be made of the value of different employer engagement activities across the three outcome areas. Table 9.10 presents the percentages of young adults agreeing, on average, that the activities they undertook were of any use at all or very useful in getting a job after education, deciding on a career or getting into higher education. The table presents low and high volume career talks, and short and long duration enterprise competitions separately and, given lower response rates, combines attitudes towards all types of mentoring. A notable finding of the table is that the most commonly experienced, and typically longest duration, employer engagement activity – work experience – undertaken by young people is often perceived by young adults as being of less

Table 9.9 Enterprise competitions – perceptions of utility

How useful was it to you in later life?	Total	Non-selective state school	Selective state school	Independent	P-value	Enterprise undertaken only pre-16	Enterprise undertaken only post-16	Enterprise undertaken at both ages	P-value	L0–L2 highest qualification	L3–L5 highest qualification	P-value
Getting a job (short)	25% (5%)	22% (5%)	33% (3%)	25% (8%)	0.380	24% (2%)	28% (8%)	25% (8%)	0.021	20% (20%)	25% (4%)	0.210
Getting a job (long)	34% (7%)	30% (7%)	47% (6%)	31% (8%)		28% (0%)	37% (8%)	40% (10%)		100% (50%)	34% (6%)	
Deciding on a career (short)	35% (8%)	29% (7%)	47% (10%)	50% (8%)	0.420	26% (6%)	46% (10%)	50% (8%)	0.085	40% (20%)	34% (7%)	0.649
Deciding on a career (long)	50% (3%)	51% (5%)	56% (0%)	42% (4%)		44% (0%)	54% (3%)	60% (10%)		100% (0%)	50% (3%)	
Getting into HE (short)	28% (4%)	26% (4%)	27% (3%)	42% (8%)	0.357	21% (2%)	38% (5%)	42% (8%)	0.000	40% (20%)	26% (4%)	0.265
Getting into HE (long)	50% (8%)	47% (5%)	44% (9%)	65% (11%)		40% (0%)	54% (8%)	60% (20%)		50% (0%)	50% (8%)	
Number (short)	141	99	30	12		84	39	12		5	134	
Number (long)	119	61	32	26		25	78	10		2	114	

Table 9.10 Comparative perceptions of utility of four different
employer engagement activities

Type of activity	Percentage of all young adults undertaking	Getting a job after education	Deciding on a career	Getting into HE
Work experience	90%	27% (9%)	58% (20%)	27% (7%)
Career talks (1–2 times)	37%	33% (4%)	55% (8%)	32% (6%)
Career talks (3 and over)	13%	54% (16%)	84% (28%)	52% (20%)
Mentoring (All types)	19%	60% (23%)	78% (28%)	62% (18%)
Enterprise (Short)	18%	25% (5%)	35% (8%)	28% (4%)
Enterprise (Long)	15%	34% (7%)	50% (3%)	50% (8%)

use to them than other activities. In terms of the three questions, it is ranked as less useful than three or more career talks and mentoring, and as being similarly useful to enterprise competitions. The high regard in which higher volumes of career talks are held is striking. The UK Chartered Institute of Personnel and Development, a professional body representing tens of thousands of British employees working in human resources, has surveyed members on how 'taxing' different employer engagement activities are on them as employers and found the least demanding activity to be 'staff going in to schools to talk about their organisation or the job they do'. By contrast, the most demanding activity listed was work experience (CIPD 2012: 20). With its requirements for child safeguarding checks, training and long duration, mentoring equally is a high demand activity. It would be beneficial for further research to explore questions of comparative demand, on both school and employer, and value to participating young people (see Mann and Dawkins 2014). The tables also reveal that young adults felt that many of the employer engagement activities which they undertook while in school were 'not at all useful' to their school-to-work transitions. More than half of those who took part in work experience placements and enterprise competitions, notably, perceived no relationship between the activities and getting a job after education, deciding on a career or getting into higher education. These results should be considered with care. As young adults go through school-to-work transitions increasingly characterised by complexity, undertaking a growing number of different jobs in different vocational areas and training/education courses (OECD 2010), the point at which it becomes possible for an individual to say with any certainty that their educational experiences were of no use to their transitions is likely to be delayed. Second, the survey provides no information on the perceived quality of the employer engagement activities undertaken. It would be of strong interest to practitioners and policymakers to know why different young people responded in different ways to their experiences and if young people's perception of quality during and after their engagement in an activity is positively associated with later perceived utility. A question for researchers is how intensity and/or duration of employer activities impacts upon such perceptions. Finally, it must be remembered that the activities addressed in this survey are commonly delivered by schools for a multitude of reasons and there are many potential outcomes: greater engagement with education, in attainment, in development of problem-solving or team-working skills or in general personal maturation. Consequently, any consideration of the full value of participation in different activities should consider the breadth of potential outcomes.

A decade after ministries of education in Scotland, Wales and England called on schools to increase employer engagement within the educational experiences of young people aged 14–16, this chapter sets out the recalled experiences of young adults and their perceptions of the value of such experiences across three primary outcome areas. The data, in keeping with previous studies, reveals considerable variation in the extent of participation young people might have expected across the four types of employer engagement examined. Whereas the great majority undertook short work experience placements, participation in career talks, enterprise competitions and business mentoring was less common. The survey presents evidence that young people educated in the independent sector (where ministries of education have little control) participated in employer engagement activities at high levels, although lower than their peers educated in the state sector and in some respects in distinctive ways. Young people educated in the private sector, for example, were much more likely to have undertaken work experience at an older age and to have taken part in enterprise competitions. Perceptions of the utility of different types of activity also show variation linked to school type attended, age at which activities were undertaken and highest level of qualification. The variation observed suggests that perceptions of the later utility of common employer engagement interventions can and do vary, suggesting that different modes of delivery could improve outcomes and that particular outcomes might be targeted with particular interventions.

Appendix

Table 9A.1 Description of survey respondents: by age

Age	#Main sample	#Subsample
19	164	134
20	164	131
21	163	135
22	163	127
23	165	124
24	166	122
Total	985	773

Table 9A.2 Description of survey
respondents: by gender

Gender	#Main sample	#Subsample
Male	498	382
Female	487	391

Table 9A.3 Description of survey respondents:
by highest level of qualification

Highest qualification	#Main sample	#Subsample
No qualification	3	1
Level 1	20	6
Level 2	68	34
Level 3	531	434
Level 4	260	218
Level 5	72	62
Others	31	14

Note

1 Huddleston *et al.* (2012) surveyed 20 high-performing English private schools and reported that 25 per cent offered some forms of mentoring to at least some pupils.

References

Ashby, J. S. and Schoon, I. (2010). Career success: the role of teenage career aspirations, ambition value and gender in predicting adult social status and earnings. *Journal of Vocational Behavior*, 77: 350–366.

Athayde, R. (2012). The impact of enterprise education on attitudes to enterprise in young people: an evaluation study. *Education and Training*, 54 (8/9): 709–726.

Bartlett, J. (2009). *Mentoring programmes, aspirations and attainment.* London: DEMOS.

Chartered Institute of Personnel and Development (CIPD). (2012). *Learning to work: survey report.* London: CIPD.

Coiffait, L., Dawkins, J., Kirwan, R. and Mann, A. (2012). *Enterprise education: value and direction – an interim report.* London: Education and Employers Taskforce & Pearson.

Davies, H. (2002). *A review of enterprise and the economy in education.* London: HM Treasury.

Deloitte UK. (2010). *Helping young people succeed: how employers can support careers education. Increasing and improving employer involvement in providing young people with careers education, information, advice and guidance.* London: Education and Employers Taskforce.

Department for Children, Schools and Families (DCSF). (2009). *The work-related learning guide.* 2nd ed. London: DCSF.

Francis, B., Osgood, J., Dalgety, J. and Archer, L. (2005). *Gender equality in work experience placements for young people.* Manchester: Equal Opportunities Commission.

Golden, S., O'Donnell, L., Benton, T. and Rudd, P. (2006). *Evaluation of increased flexibility for 14–16 year olds programme: outcomes for the second cohort.* London: Department for Education and Skills.

Granovetter, M. (1973). *Getting a job – a study of contacts and careers.* Chicago, IL: University of Chicago Press.

Green, J. and Rogers, B. (1997). Roots and wings community mentoring: an evaluation from the manchester pilot. *Mentoring & Tutoring: Partnership in Learning*, 5: 26–38.

Gutman, L. S. and Schoon, I. (2012). Correlates and consequences of uncertainty in career aspirations: gender differences among adolescents in England. *Journal of Vocational Behavior*, 80: 608–618.

Hall, J. C. (2003). *Mentoring and young people: a literature review.* Glasgow: University of Glasgow.

Hatcher, R. and Le Gallais, T. (2008). *The work experience placements of secondary school students: widening horizons or reproducing social inequality?* Birmingham: Birmingham City University.

Huddleston, P., Mann, A. and Dawkins, J. (2012). *Employer engagement in English independent schools.* London: Education and Employers Taskforce.

Ipsos MORI. (2009). *Young people omnibus 2009 – Wave 15. A research study on work-related learning among 11–16 year olds on behalf of the Qualifications and Curriculum Authority, January–April 2009.* Coventry: QCA.

Jamieson, I. and Miller, A. (1991). History and policy context. *In:* A. Miller, A. G. Watts and I. Jamieson, eds. *Rethinking work experience.* London: Falmer Press, 3–15.

Jokisaari, M. and Nurmi, J. E. (2005). Company matters: goal-related social capital in the transition to working life. *Journal of Vocational Behavior*, 67: 413–428.

Linnehan, F. (2001). The relation of a work-based mentoring program to the academic performance and behavior of African American students. *Journal of Vocational Behavior*, 59: 310–325.

Linnehan, F. (2003). A longitudinal study of work-based, adult youth mentoring. *Journal of Vocational Behavior*, 63: 40–54.

Lord, P. and Jones, M. (2006). *Pupils' experiences and perspectives of the national curriculum and assessment – final report of the research review.* Slough, UK: National Foundation for Educational Research.

Mann, A. (2012). *Work experience – impact and delivery.* London: Education and Employers Taskforce.

Mann, A. and Caplin, S. (2012). *Closing the gap: how employers can change the way that young people see apprenticeships.* London: Education and Employers Taskforce and PriceWaterhouseCoopers.

Mann, A. and Percy, C. (2013). Employer engagement in British secondary education: wage earning outcomes experienced by young adults. *Journal of Education and Work*, doi:10.1080/13639080.2013.769671.

Mann, A. and Dawkins, J. (2014). *Employer engagement in education: a users' guide.* Reading: CfBT Education Trust.

Mann, A., Spring, C., Evans, D. and Dawkins, J. (2011). *The importance of experience of the world of work in admissions to Russell Group universities: a desktop review of admissions criteria for six courses.* London: Education and Employers Taskforce.

Miller, A. (1998). *Business and community mentoring in schools*. London: Department for Education and Skills.

Miller, A., Watts, A. G. and Jamieson, I. (1991). *Rethinking work experience*. London: Falmer Press.

Miller, S., Connolly, P. and Maguire, L. (2011). *A follow-up randomised controlled trial evaluation of the effects of business in the community's Time to Read mentoring programme*. Queen's University, Belfast: Centre for Effective Education.

National Support Group for Work Experience. (2007). *Students' perceptions of work experience*. London: Department for Children, Schools and Families (DCSF) and National Education Business Partnership Network.

Oosterbeek, H., van Praag, M. and IJsselstein, A. (2008). *The impact of entrepreneurship education on entrepreneurship competencies and intentions: an evaluation of the Junior Achievement Student Mini-Company Program*. Jena Economic Research Papers 2008-027, Friedrich-Schiller University Jena, Max-Planck Institute of Economics.

Organisation for Economic Co-operation and Development (OECD). (2010). *Learning for jobs*. Paris: OECD.

Qualifications and Curriculum Authority (QCA). (2003). *Work-related learning for all at key stage 4 – guidance for implementing the statutory requirement from* 2004. Coventry: QCA.

Qualifications and Curriculum Authority (QCA). (2004). *Work-related learning – baseline study 2004*. Coventry: QCA.

Qualifications and Curriculum Authority (QCA). (2007). *Work-related learning at key stage 4: first replication study: a QCA-commissioned report on the development of work-related learning in the three years since September 2004*. Coventry: QCA.

Raffo, C. (2003). Disaffected young people and the work-related learning curriculum at key stage 4: issues of social capital development and learning as a form of cultural practice. *Journal of Education and Work*, 16 (1): 69–86.

Raffo, C. (2006). Disadvantaged young people accessing the new urban economies of the post-industrial city. *Journal of Education Policy*, 21 (1): 75–94.

Rose, R. and Jones, K. (2007). The efficacy of a volunteer mentoring scheme in supporting young people at risk. *Emotional and Behavioural Difficulties*, 12 (1): 3–14.

Sabates, R., Harris, A. L. and Staff, J. (2011). Ambition gone awry: the long term socio-economic consequences of misaligned and uncertain ambitions in adolescence. *Social Science Quarterly*, 92 (4): 1–19.

Scottish Executive. (2004). *Determined to succeed – enterprise in education*. Edinburgh: Scottish Executive.

Scottish Executive. (2007). *Determined to succeed: three years on*. Edinburgh: Scottish Executive.

Symonds, W. C., Schwartz, R. B. and Ferguson, R. (2011). *Pathways to prosperity: meeting the challenge of preparing Americans for the 21st century*. Cambridge, MA: Harvard Graduate School of Education.

UK Commission for Employment and Skills (UKCES). (2012). *Business and schools: building the world of work together*. London: UKCES.

Welsh Assembly Government. (2004). *Learning pathways 14–19 guidance*. Cardiff: Welsh Assembly Government.

Welsh Assembly Government. (2008). *Careers and the world of work: a framework for 11 to 19 year olds in Wales*. Cardiff: Welsh Assembly Government.

Wolf, A. (2011). *Review of vocational education: the Wolf Report*. London: Department for Education.

Yates, S., Harris, A., Sabates, R. and Staff, J. (2011). Early occupational aspirations and fractured transitions: a study of entry into 'NEET' status in the UK. *Journal of Social Policy*, 40(3): 513–534.

YouGov. (2010). *EDGE annual programme of stakeholder research: business in schools*. London: Edge Foundation.

Chapter 10

'That aroma of where they are likely to go'

Employer engagement in high-performing English independent schools

Prue Huddleston, Anthony Mann and James Dawkins

Introduction

Given the weight of influence that high-performing independent schools have in discourses surrounding social mobility (Panel on Fair Access to the Professions 2009; Sutton Trust 2012; Devine 2004), they have been subjected to remarkably little serious study. Literature investigating whether and how fee-paying schools engage with employers to support their school-to-work transitions is slight, but is consistently suggestive that employer engagement is typical of school life.

A brief review of careers practice in three independent schools for the National College for School Leadership in 2011 identified a range of activities which would provide pupils with direct insight in the workplace through engagement with employers/employees – workplace visits, work experience, enterprise competitions, careers advice – and highlights use of alumni networks to support such activities, but does not critique behaviour or consider its typicality beyond schools observed (Gilbank 2011). The use of alumni and senior managers from local employers to provide advice to pupils on their careers and progression choices, and to provide mock interviews, is also observed in Pugsley's 2003 study of careers provision in a single Welsh private school. Writing elsewhere in this collection (see Chapter 11), Steven Jones's analysis of UCAS personal statements suggests strongly that pupils attending fee-paying schools gain access to a wide range of work placement experiences often of high relevance in admissions to undergraduate degrees of choice. A 2009 survey of 105 secondary level teachers from British independent schools found levels of engagement with businesses over the preceding two years comparable to the state sector, with high levels of engagement in work experience (63 per cent), enterprise projects (40 per cent), workplace visits (48 per cent), mock interviews (46 per cent), 'presentations' (47 per cent) and mentoring (16 per cent) (YouGov 2010: 66). Comparable levels of engagement are found in survey data provided by young adults considered by Mann and Kashefpakdel in Chapter 9 of this collection. This study drills down into the experiences of a subset of independent secondary schools – those whose pupils attain the highest levels of qualifications – and asks for the first time whether they too engage systematically with employers and, if they do, why that is the case and how they go about it.

Methodology

Given the ambition of the research to test the level and character of employer engagement in high-performing fee-paying English schools, an approach to selection was adopted that combined purposive and convenience sampling. The *Sunday Times* 2009 Secondary and Further Education league tables combined GCSE and A-level results, ranking schools with sixth-form provision and creating opportunity for insight into pre- and post-16 engagement. The full list of 20 schools is listed in Table 10.1 in order of attainment ranking by the newspaper. Researcher contacts were used to gain access to six schools in total, reflecting the characteristics of the sector (three girls' schools and three boys' schools; three located in London and three outside London; three boarding and three day schools).

The websites of all 20 schools were examined for evidence of employer engagement across six specific activities commonly found within the state sector (careers advice from employers as in careers fairs or networking events, work experience, business mentoring, enterprise activities, workplace visits, visiting speakers). Desk research allowed an assessment of activity across the 20 schools, and subsequently informed interviews with a sample of six of the schools randomly drawn from the list in Table 10.1.

Following discussions with head teachers, six semi-structured in-depth interviews were arranged. Most interviews took place with two or more members of the school's staff, as nominated by the head teacher. Interviewees included heads of careers, directors of learning, classroom teachers and senior leadership team members, including head teachers. Interviews were recorded and transcribed, subject to the agreement of the respondents. Fieldwork was carried out between November 2010 and June 2011. In keeping with standard ethical research guidelines, participating schools have been made anonymous in this report.

In terms of analysis, the transcripts were initially examined and a coding framework developed in relation to the three overarching research questions. The data was thematically segmented, coded and then interrogated (using Ethnograph V6.0 computer assisted qualitative data analysis program). The approach permitted the research team to drill down into the data and generate over a dozen relevant categories, which aided the understanding of the extent to which, why and how independent schools engage with employers to support pupil learning and progression (Dohan and Sanchez-Jankowski 1998). Textual validation was also employed and consisted of sending the final draft of the report to all the interviewees for review. They were given a two-week window to respond, after which their comments were reviewed by the report's authors and the necessary amendments made (Shenton 2004).

Table 10.1 Participation in employer engagement activities: 20 high-performing English independent schools

Institutions	Types of employer engagement activity					
	1 Careers IAG	2 Work experience	3 Business mentoring	4 Enterprise activities	5 Workplace visits	6 Visiting speakers
Withington Girls' School	✓	✓		✓		✓
Westminster School	✓	✓	✓	✓		✓
North London Collegiate School	✓	✓		✓	✓	✓
St Paul's School	✓	✓		✓		✓
Magdalen College School Oxford	✓	✓	✓	✓	✓	✓
St Paul's Girls' School	✓	✓		✓		✓
Stephen Perse Foundation/ Perse Girls'	✓			✓	✓	✓
Wycombe Abbey School	✓	✓		✓		✓
Royal Grammar Schools Guildford	✓	✓		✓		✓
City of London School for Girls	✓	✓		✓	✓	✓
Lady Eleanor Holles School	✓	✓	✓	✓	✓	✓
Eton College	✓	✓	✓	✓		✓
King's College School, Wimbledon		✓		✓	✓	
Sevenoaks School	✓	✓		✓		✓
Guildford High School for Girls					✓	
Haberdashers' Aske's School for Girls	✓	✓		✓	✓	✓
Haberdashers' Aske's Boys' School	✓	✓	✓	✓		
Oxford High School GDST	✓	✓		✓	✓	✓
Winchester College	✓	✓	✓	✓	✓	✓
South Hampstead High School GDST		✓		✓		✓

Findings

Q1. Do high-performing independent schools engage with employers to support the learning and progression of pupils?

The desktop review provided results in line with previous studies of the private sector, indicating that employer engagement is commonplace across high-performing independent schools. As Table 10.1 indicates, 80 per cent or more of the 20 schools under consideration engaged employers to provide pupils with opportunities to take part in enterprise activities, careers advice, work experience placements and visiting speakers. Evidence found that 45 per cent of schools undertook workplace visits and 25 per cent of schools worked with employers to provide pupils with business mentors.

Such levels of engagement would be characteristic of state schools showing high levels of engagement with employers (YouGov 2010: 66). As illustrated elsewhere in this collection (see Mann and Kashefpakdel, Chapter 9 in this volume), such levels of engagement may also be towards the higher end of behaviour across English independent schools.

Q2. Why do high-performing independent schools engage employers?

Employer engagement can perhaps best be seen as a process through which schools access specialist resources to help pupils clarify, confirm and support identification of career aspirations and routes towards securing them. A number of common themes emerge from the evidence collated. Schools were driven to engage with employers in order to:

- help young people decide on career goals and work positively towards achieving them;
- enable access to university courses of choice;
- help develop pupils' personal and social skills, including at times explicitly employability skills;
- help pupils develop networks of value to them after leaving school; and
- help stimulate a culture of expectation and aspiration.

The focus of independent school activity is on enabling the successful progression of pupils through access to useful information, networks and experiences. Engagement with employers is seen as relevant to wider learning outcomes (such as employability skills), but is rarely used as a means to contextualise learning or embedded within classroom activity.[1] Unlike the state sector, where employer engagement is often seen as an effective means of increasing the motivation of pupils to achieve academically, independent school interviewees argued that this was rarely relevant because pupils were commonly already highly motivated.

Independent schools perceived their engagement with employers as essential in helping pupils decide on and achieve their chosen career destinations. Activities such as work experience, visiting speakers and careers advice from employers were viewed as opportunities for individual pupils to obtain insights into career options and pathways to achieving them. Embedded within personalised approaches to careers advice and guidance, employer engagement activities, over the duration of secondary education, were used to clarify, confirm and support the intended career destinations of pupils.

> . . . what I hope is that they see the range of possibilities. I don't know if that sounds ambitious enough for them, but . . . I want them to realise that there's all sorts of options that they can consider; they don't need to be limited.
>
> (Head of Careers reflecting on value of careers fair to pupils,
> Girls' School A)

Careers-related employer engagement was typically delivered through a combination of workplace visits, theme days and careers fairs/talks.

> . . . careers education really starts in Year 8 . . . 'take our daughters to work day' . . . earlier than many schools; because the school is very selective and very academically successful we've tried to adapt the programme to reflect the needs and ambitions and aspirations of the children . . . and I think the girls get a great deal from that 'take our daughters to work day'. Again, we've got a very supportive parent body, we're very fortunate with [that], and they all go on a placement.
>
> (Head of Careers, Girls' School A)

> . . . there are careers days when we have visiting speakers, many of them boys who have been at school here, who are able to come down to the school and tell current pupils what work there is like and how they got into it, what qualifications and experience they need, and that's a complete day, I think for . . . Year 11 and Year 12 . . . so we may have 20 or 30 speakers here and they choose what they want to go to and they go and listen to these speakers . . . before their A-level choices. . . . We like to get them thinking . . . careers testing.
>
> (Registrar, Boys' School F)

> Obviously each department will only invite their own guests . . . from the science department they will invite people in the field of physics, biology etc. . . . and they will also have people [from the arts] . . . we try and be as forward as possible, we invite as many people as we can from a variety of different careers and then we have [them] give their little talks . . . they often gather over in the school where the boys have the opportunity to meet them and talk on a one to one basis.
>
> (Head of Careers, Boys' School F)

So why do we engage with employers? Because I suppose that's the most obvious way of giving them that aroma of where they are likely to go.

(Teacher, Boys' School E)

As is commonly found in the state sector (Lord and Jones 2006), pupils attending independent schools were felt to be especially attentive to advice that came directly from professionals working in a field of interest.

> . . . some girls themselves have aspirations which aren't suited to their particular skill set, and part of our role is to try and encourage them to understand why there isn't that match and what might be a better route for them . . . you know, I can tell them a hundred times that their strengths are in particular areas . . . When they talk to people who are in those professions and they talk with them directly: 'What are you good at?' 'What are your skills?' it has a bigger impact than anything we can tell them second hand . . . Having that opportunity to speak to people who have made a career in a particular area which will either motivate them: 'this is definitely want I want to do' or make them think, 'oh, actually, this isn't what I want to do' for whatever reason, and they can believe it fully because it's from someone who is living it.
>
> (Head Teacher, Girls' School C)

All six independent schools emphasised the importance of engaging with employers in order to help pupils gain entry to undergraduate courses of choice, and more specifically to a university or university college of choice. Interviewees were keenly aware that work experience, in particular, was often highly desirable or an essential requirement for influencing successful admission to highly competitive university courses. Interviewees noted that where undergraduate courses related closely to a specific vocation, for example medicine, work experience (and other employer engagement activity) could provide excellent opportunities for pupils to show insight and commitment to careers linked to intended courses of study.

> [In supporting pupils to secure work experience] . . . We focus on the ones who we know need it for their particular careers, so all the medics will be doing it and the engineers because it's a requirement for their course. I mean, some vets have to do 11–13 weeks of work experience before they can apply . . . and the medics need to have done a variety of things . . . they need to have done some hospital type work, they need to have done some voluntary work, they need to demonstrate that they've got a real understanding of what it is they're getting into . . . and I think for some university courses which inevitably lead into a particular career you can only do that with work experience beforehand. The engineers are actively encouraged to take a year off between school and university and it's even better if they've got a clear idea that that's what they want to do before they embark on it.
>
> (Head of Careers, Girls' School B)

Interviewees consistently argued that relevant work experience would often make a difference to the success of applications and cited first-hand advice from Russell Group university admissions tutors who commonly visited schools to speak to pupils. Courses linked to medical, dental and veterinary degrees were particularly cited. Consequently, schools worked hard to ensure that pupils were aware of the importance of securing attractive and relevant work experience and that they presented it effectively within their personal statements in UCAS applications. Work experience was seen as less relevant to successful admission to what were described as academic courses, such as History or Classics, but not irrelevant.

A number of the interviewees explicitly noted the desirability of equipping pupils with employability skills, which were understood by respondents in ways that would be familiar within the state sector. They were recognised as the sort of personal skills necessary to be effective in the workplace, for example team-working, problem-solving, communication. Respondents saw employer engagement in general and work experience in particular as a means of developing the personal effectiveness of pupils in different social settings. Consequently, employer engagement was seen as a means of enhancing the maturation of pupils and often discussed in relation to other activities designed to secure similar outcomes, such as volunteer working, community engagement and extra-curricular activities. Such activities were described in terms of developing 'more rounded pupils', which all schools knew would help to create a stronger university application and ultimately put alumni at an advantage in the job market. A number of respondents identified 'employability skills' to be gained from employer engagement activities (and work experience in particular), which would be readily recognisable in the state sector.

> Emphasising the sorts of skills that [employers] are interested in, like leadership skills, your team work . . . how you use the things like Young Enterprise to show the sorts of skills you have, key communication skills. Improving employability . . . not just an academic [qualification] but things you need alongside that. I think it's very useful . . . it's important for them to be able to reflect on all the things they do.
>
> (Head of Careers, Girls' School B)

Other respondents focused on broader aspects of personal development and life planning.

> I think it does their self-esteem quite a lot of good and I think in a school where you've got very high-achieving girls, confidence can sometimes be an issue . . . I think actually getting out into the work environment makes them realise that they are intelligent in slightly different ways and that [pupils who] sometimes aren't praised in a high-achieving environment suddenly feel, 'well, actually, I'm good at this' when dealing with people or whatever

it might be; it's a moment where different sorts of students can find strengths that aren't celebrated in the same environment.

(Head of Careers reflects on the value of work experience, Girls' School B)

There's no good shying away from it, you've got to address [the issue of women balancing careers with family responsibilities] and the more women that you can get in who have dealt with it and can talk about it openly, makes it a lot easier for girls to make those hard decisions.

(Development Director, Girls' School C)

We want to give them as many experiences as we possibly can . . . you have got to remember this is a bit of a goldfish bowl and it can be quite insular . . . they play on the field with each other, they stay in the boarding house and so on and so forth . . . we do try and encourage them to branch out and then rather than being within their own little bubble they are actually able to communicate with a broad range of people from different social backgrounds.

(Head of Careers, Boys' School F)

Helping pupils to develop networks of value was another common reason for engaging with employers. Interviewees understood that having connections with these individuals/institutions played important roles in securing work experience placements and helping them to make a transition into the world of work after leaving education. To a great extent, it was expected that useful relationships with alumni and other adults of influence, particularly family connections, would develop informally without the direct involvement of the school. One school, however, adopted a more directive stance.

. . . a girl who's got an interest in engineering, for example, we'd be able to put in touch with a former pupil who's now working as an engineer who might be able to offer her work experience. But even if she couldn't, she could certainly be a sounding board for ideas, not just in her applications for work or in her applications for university, but beyond. Hopefully their careers would move in parallel so there would always be an older mentor in that sort of area.

(Head Teacher, Girls' School C)

All schools interviewed invited visiting speakers, often of very high national profile and sometimes, but by no means always, alumni, to speak to pupils. Typically, speakers would address issues related to their profession, often providing insight into topical questions of public interest of relevance to academic study. While the content of speeches would at times be discussed in related classroom activity, the purpose of inviting visiting speakers was not particularly curriculum related. Rather, it provided pupils with insights into the worldviews of individuals occupying elite positions, privileging them as insiders with whom confidences could be shared. Such events were often attended by a relatively small number of interested pupils (dozens rather than hundreds) and often followed by a dinner or lunch to which interested pupils would be invited, often acting as hosts. Consequently, excellent opportunities were presented to build social connections and explore career aspirations in detail. Visiting speakers, in particular, were seen to reinforce thoughtful, serious approaches to considering relevant questions rooted in public life.

> Social networks are very important, very interesting, the way external involvement creates a culture of expectation, a culture of achievement, a learning environment.
>
> (Teacher, Boys' School D)

> . . . we run a thing called the [XXXX] Society and that happens every Wednesday and it's open to sixth formers. We have really notable people from all walks of life, so we'll have MPs, media people, bankers, people who have done something very, very interesting, and many of them quite well-known, will come back and give a lecture. Again our sixth formers get to know the life of someone who has been very successful and perhaps what it took for them to get there, what luck they had, what bad luck they had, things in life where we can't always predict where we're going . . . so they get a nice insight into the grown-up world into professions and achievements and that happens every week . . . so we get at least 25 of these a year.
>
> (Teacher on the value of high-profile visiting speakers meeting with pupils, Boys' School E)

Q3: How do high-performing independent schools engage with employers?

The respondents had a clear understanding of the importance and impact that employer engagement had upon the career choices and destinations of their pupils. Consequently, they endeavoured to build and sustain productive working relationships with employers upon which they drew when organising engagement activities.

One of the most common methods used to engage employers is alumni networks. Interviewees saw former pupils as valuable conduits into the world of work; their details were held on alumni databases. These were used to track the career pathways of alumni for the purpose of identifying work placements aligned with the career aspirations of their pupils. Parental and teacher/governor networks were used to make contact with employers. In particular, they were used to support pupils who encountered difficulties in securing their own work placements. Employers were also engaged directly by pupils who would negotiate and arrange their own work placements. This approach proved effective in most cases and was encouraged by the schools' staff. One school in this study made limited use of intermediaries such as Connexions; however, this practice was atypical and was not used in any of the other five schools. Engagement also occurred in the form of direct approaches from employers to the schools, several of whom commented upon the constant attention they had received from high-profile investment banks.

All six independent schools made effective use of alumni networks to engage employers with their pupils. Schools maintained alumni directories and databases and networked primarily for fundraising, but also used these networks to provide work experience placements for current pupils. The utility of such connections was optimised as current pupils commonly aspired to both the higher education pathways and the professional occupations of alumni (medicine, law, military service and business/accountancy).

> It's such a good network through the old boys' association, and the parents; we have sent out a blanket request and people will say 'yes, I'm happy to help.'
>
> (Registrar, Boys' School F)

> One of the aspects of privilege is not about how much money you've got, but how you have this contact . . .
>
> (Teacher, Boys' School E)

Two of the schools visited described the creation of online networking sites connecting alumni with current pupils. As schools that routinely approached alumni to raise funds, the costs in connecting with former pupils were perceived to be minimal. Schools described being overwhelmed by interest from alumni in supporting the learning and progression of current pupils, leading staff to view such engagement as a positive addition to their approaches to secure the interest of alumni in the ongoing life of the school.

Interviewees also commonly identified the parents of current pupils as resources drawn upon for employer engagement activities. As well as providing first-hand support – one interviewee described a barrister taking five girls with him on Take Your Daughter to Work Day – others provided a way to access employers who were potentially able to offer attractive work experience.

> I try and find a way, and usually I can find it through a parent contact. If you just call from outside, who are you going to speak to? They don't have a full-time work experience organiser so it's usually personal.
>
> (Head of Careers, Girls' School A)

Governors' networks were also used to engage employers in providing work experience placements. School governors occupy positions of influence in places of direct relevance to the career aspirations of pupils and can be called upon to provide access to desirable workplace experiences.

One of our governors, professor X, is very senior at an NHS foundation trust . . . we had a meeting and wanted [pupils] to go in and do some work [experience], and they did quite a lot of work and they produced presentations to the board, to the CEO, in the foyer of [large London hospital] . . . all their photographs, all their recommendations and they have to do that and they have to stand up and give a speech about it. Now that is putting them on the spot; it may be a bit uncomfortable, they have to do the work . . . but it's going to resonate far more if they do that than if they shadowed [someone] . . . I want to produce more things like that.

(Teacher, Boys' School E)

Some pupils actively sourced their own placements often using school-arranged activities, such as visiting speakers, to approach employers and negotiate placements.

I think also our girls are very astute at taking advantage of opportunities. When we took them down to the 'XXXX' competition . . . one of our girls negotiated her own media work experience with the person who shot our video . . .

(Head of Economics, Girls' School C)

A number of interviewees, particularly from girls' schools, reported that direct, unsolicited approaches from employers, typically of national or international prominence, were common. In contacting schools, employers would invite participation in activities raising awareness about careers in their sector.

Sometimes an investment bank approaches us wanting to come and talk about their internship scheme . . . I said, 'That's lovely; come and do that but could you do something on CV writing with our senior girls?' and then while they were here I said, 'Oh, by the way, what about having some girls [on work experience placements]?' . . . You know, why not talk to the younger ones because actually if you want to get investment banking on the horizon you need to be talking to girls who are much younger [before] they've chosen their A-levels. So we were looking at things which they could do for us and we could do for them; they were always looking for very bright women, most of these companies . . . in fact, I'm always being approached by investment banks because they have various programmes that they run . . . but I wish they would do something slightly more co-ordinated . . . they get in touch with you as if you have never heard of an investment bank . . . well actually you're the third investment bank this week!

(Head of Careers, Girls' School B)

Conclusions

Data gathered through this study suggest clearly that high-performing independent schools undertake considerable engagement with employers – a finding in keeping with comparative levels of reported engagement of former state and independent pupils reported by Mann and Kashefpakdel (Chapter 9 in this volume). Like maintained schools, independent schools usually offer work experience, careers advice and enterprise activities, although other forms of employer engagement are less common, for example curriculum projects, mentoring and Industry Days. The use of visiting speakers appears to be more prevalent in the independent sector than in the maintained sector, based on this sample, although within the maintained sector 'classroom visitors' who provide specific subject input may not always be regarded as 'visiting speakers'. The important point to be made is that while there is widespread evidence of employer engagement within the maintained and independent sectors, the focus of employer engagement activity often differs markedly between them.

The high-performing independent schools in this sample see employer engagement as a means of identifying, confirming and supporting higher education aspirations and related career trajectories. Engaging employers provides access to careers advice, high-quality work experience and communities of practice where pupils can meet and engage with successful professionals, many of whom have been pupils at their own schools. Through these constructed social networks, pupils are provided with insights, role models, encouragement and experiences designed to support a successful navigation of the transition from education into employment.

The emphasis on successful higher education admission is foregrounded in the types of employer engagement, such as Year 12 work experience, in which the independent sectors typically participate. This is understandable given that the overwhelming majority of pupils studying in the sixth forms of high-performing independent schools aspire to gain entrance to higher education and, if not to Oxbridge colleges, then certainly to Russell Group institutions. For pupils in these independent schools, future destinations are largely presumed and, therefore, work experience needs to be more aligned with the process of university admission and ultimate career destination and, it has to be said, to parental expectation.

The evidence from the fieldwork overwhelmingly supports the conclusion that employer engagement within high-performing independent schools is designed to enable pupils to succeed in terms of admission to their university of choice by providing them with relevant experiences within their chosen field of study and eventual career destination. This process is strongly supported by specialist school staff who assist pupils in identifying appropriate placements and ensuring that such placements are highlighted within UCAS personal statements. In addition, other forms of employer engagement, for example visiting speakers, reinforce career development by providing pupils with role models of successful men and women from the professional and business world.

In undertaking this approach, young people can be observed travelling through a school-to-work transition at the heart of which is a socialisation to distinctive adult cultures. In such a way, the experiences observed evoke those commonly described in vocational education and the language of apprenticeship; in the axiomatic French vocational education and training ambition, for example, to lead a young person through a transitional process of *savoir – savoir faire – savoir être*. The evidence provided by our sample of high-performing independent schools appears to confirm such a desired, and actual, trajectory.

Note

1   For a fuller discussion of the purposes of work experience more generally, see Huddleston (2012).

References

Devine, F. (2004). *How parents help their children get good jobs.* Cambridge, UK: Cambridge University Press.

Dohan, D. and Sanchez-Jankowski, M. (1998). Using computers to analyse ethnographic field data: theoretical and practical considerations. *American Review of Sociology*, 24: 477–499.

Gilbank, C. (2011). *Provision for CEIAG in the independent sector.* Nottingham, UK: National College for School Leadership.

Huddleston, P. (2012). Pupil work experience. *In:* P. Huddleston and J. Stanley, eds. *Work-related teaching and learning – a guide for teachers and practitioners.* Abingdon, UK: Routledge, 67–84.

Huddleston, P., Mann, A. and Dawkins, J. (2012). *Employer engagement in English independent schools.* London: Education and Employers Taskforce.

Lord, P. and Jones, M. (2006) *Pupils, experiences and perspectives of the national curriculum and assessment – final report of the research review.* National Foundation for Educational Research.

Panel on Fair Access to the Professions. (2009). *Unleashing aspirations: final report.* London: HM Government.

Pugsley, L. (2003). Choice or chance: the university challenge – how schools reproduce and produce social capital in the choice process. *In:* G. Walford, ed. *British private schools – research on policy and practice.* London: Woburn Press, 202–216.

Shenton, A. K. (2004). Strategies for ensuring trustworthiness in qualitative research projects. *Education for Information*, 22: 63–75.

Sutton Trust. (2012). *The educational backgrounds of the nation's leading people.* London: Sutton Trust.

YouGov. (2010). *EDGE annual programme of stakeholder surveys report.* London: Edge Foundation.

Chapter 11

The role of work experience in the UK higher education admissions process

Steven Jones

Introduction

The purpose of this chapter is to approach the issue of work experience from a new perspective – that of access to leading UK universities. I have two related aims: first, to quantify differences in the work-related activity reported by applicants from a range of educational backgrounds; and, second, to consider the ways in which work experience is conceptualised within the higher education admissions, both by applicants and within the sector, with a view to assessing wider implications for social mobility and social justice.

In the United Kingdom, the agency responsible for processing admissions is the Universities and Colleges Admissions Service (UCAS). As part of the admissions process, a 4,000-character personal statement is submitted. The statement is a 'free response' composition, meaning that applicants are able to write about themselves and their suitability for higher education in an unrestricted fashion. This contrasts with the US equivalent, the Common Application, in which applicants must respond to one of five set questions.[1] Following Jones (2013), the personal statement is used here as a means to learn more about young people's work-related activity. UCAS prompts applicants to 'give details of any relevant work experience, paid or unpaid' (see www.ucas.ac.uk) and responses reveal much about the differing levels of activity to which they have had access. However, personal statements also provide an insight into the ways in which young people understand the role of work experience and are able to articulate what they have gained from it.

The backdrop for this research is the Wolf review of Vocational Education (2011), which proposed that work experience for under 16s should no longer be a statutory requirement,[2] arguing that 'virtually everyone stays on post-GCSE, and an overwhelming majority participate to age 18' (Wolf 2011: 9). The focus of the Wolf Review is on young people following 'occupational' routes and those at risk of Not in Employment, Education or Training (NEET) status – not on those looking to enter higher education. This chapter considers the consequences of shifting opportunities for work-related activity from pre-16 to post-16, particularly among academically able students who rely on their school to facilitate experiences. Specifically, it explores whether a move from universal engagement to a policy focused more on those planning immediate entry to the labour market may leave some young people further disadvantaged in the higher education admissions process.

I begin with a brief summary of the literature to contextualise this research. I then outline how data were collected and analysed. Finally, I summarise the key findings of the chapter and offer a number of observations about young people's opportunities, both to access meaningful, professionalised work experience and, partly as a result, to access the UK's leading universities.

Background

The body of research into work experience is beginning to grow, as this collection attests. Some of this research examines the role of work experience in the higher education admission process, e.g. Neilson and McNally (2010) in relation to nursing degrees or Hodgkinson and Hamill (2010) in relation to civil engineering. However, the focus has mostly been on the value of work experience in helping young people gain employment. This is not surprising: vocational qualifications are often seen as an alternative to academic progression (e.g. Wolf 2011) and do, of course, provide many young people with the skills and experience needed to move directly into the labour market. However, work-related activity plays another key role in shaping young people's futures: many competitive undergraduate programmes use non-academic indicators, such as the personal statement, to distinguish between equal achievements candidates, and work-related activity forms a central part of this statement. Indeed, many programmes require candidates to demonstrate relevant experience as part of the selection process (Mann et al. 2011). Work-related activity can therefore make a real difference to a young person's chances of attending a leading university and may provide a partial explanation for reported differences in success rates among equal attainment applicants of different socio-economic backgrounds and school types (Boliver 2013).

Indeed, with rising pressure on universities to widen access (Milburn 2012), questions arise about whether a focus on non-academic indicators, such as work experience, brings greater fairness to the admissions process, as some commentators have suggested,[3] or whether it actually has the reverse effect, shutting some high-achieving students out of top courses because – through no fault of their own – they have not enjoyed the same opportunities or benefited from the same guidance.

According to the Institute for Public Policy Research (IPPR), in the year since most GCSE-equivalent vocational qualifications were removed from school performance league tables as a result of Wolf's recommendations (2011), '60 per cent of school leaders said their school had either already reduced the number of level-two vocational qualifications on offer or was planning to do so' (Muir 2013: 1). Those who lose out on work experience opportunities, either because formal qualification routes are closed or because other work experience opportunities are limited, lose out on the know-how, skills, practices and understanding of the world of work. They are less able to make informed opinions about their own careers and less attuned to the unspoken demands of the workplace (Mann 2012). As noted by John Hayes, the then UK Minister for Further Education, Skills and Lifelong Learning, during the second reading of the Further and Higher Education (Access) Bill, 'it is not aspiration or ambition but wherewithal that limits working class people from achieving what they might' (Hansard, 4 March 2011).[4] However, this chapter argues that 'wherewithal' is also crucial in the university admissions process; without access to meaningful work-related activity, academic opportunities for less-advantaged young people are restricted further.

How are UK university applicants assessed?

The primary way in which universities select students is through academic achievement, typically A-level grades; however, when competition is high, or when several candidates are equally qualified, universities often turn to non-academic indicators. In the United Kingdom, this can involve interviews or, occasionally, assessed work; however, the most ubiquitous non-academic indicator is the personal statement.

Admissions tutors may examine statements for fluency of writing and relevant extra-curricular activity and, as Jones (2013) noted, there is strong evidence that school type is a key predictor of both features. For example, applicants from sixth form colleges were found to make almost three times as many clear linguistic errors (misused apostrophes, run-on sentences, etc.) as their equal attainment private school counterparts. More qualitatively, whereas the hobbies listed by sixth-form college applicants often have little value in the admissions process ('sometimes I just go on walks and listen to my iPod'), those listed by private school applicants reflected more exclusive cultural capital ('I did a Cordon Bleu cookery course at the Tante Marie School in London'). The focus of this chapter, however, is on work-related activity: how it varies between applicants of different educational backgrounds; how it is understood and articulated by young people; and how it may advantage some applicants more than others in the higher education admissions process.

Data and method

Previous research into the personal statement is scant, as noted by GlenMaye and Oakes (2002) and Brown (2004), among others. Where statements have been examined, evidence has not pointed towards them being accurate predictors of future performance (Pelech et al. 1999; Ferguson et al. 2000; Norman 2004). No research has been undertaken into the ways in which work experience, in particular, is described. Therefore, although the methods used here build on previous studies where possible, improvisation was often required.

The dataset is the same as that used by Jones (2013: 309) – personal statements all submitted to a leading UK university by applicants who would subsequently achieve identical A-level results, and each tagged according to the applicant's school type. In order to arrive at this sample, all 5,276 applications made to one department within one Russell Group UK university for 2010 entry were accessed.[5] To control for academic attainment, only those personal statements submitted by students who went on to achieve A-level grades of BBB[6] (excluding General Studies) were included. School type was then noted: comprehensive school (88 applicants), sixth form college (83), grammar school (45) and independent school (93).[7] To ensure anonymity, details of the host university and department are not made public, applicants remain fully anonymous, and where text from a personal statement is cited, sensitive information is omitted or modified.

Distributions of work-related activity

When applying to university, most young people follow UCAS advice to 'include details of jobs, placements, work experience or voluntary work, particularly if it's relevant to your chosen course(s)'. This section assesses the quantity and the quality of the work-related activity that applicants from different educational backgrounds draw upon, and looks at how they characterise it in the personal statement.

Quantification of individual, work-related activities is difficult because applicants include full-time jobs ('I work full-time at Aviva Insurance as a commercial claims advisor') and school-based initiatives ('I help mentor Year 8 maths students'), as well as more typical work experience placements ('I spent a week in a City reinsurance broking firm shadowing one of the brokers'). However, to begin with, all-inclusive counts were undertaken (by the author and, independently, by a second coder). These counts took in paid employment, voluntary work, internships, work experience or shadowing, day trips to industry/workplace visits, and anything else that related to the applicant's work-based, non-academic profile. The totals, per school type, are recorded in Figure 11.1.

At first glance, the distribution seems fairly equitable: approximately 3.63 activities per personal statement are mentioned by independent school applicants, fractionally more than those listed by grammar school applicants, about 15 per cent more than those by comprehensive school applicants and about 30 per cent more than those from sixth form colleges. However, this global similarity masks important differences in the nature of the activities, as can be seen when the quality of work-related activity is compared.

To do this, all of the work-related activities were subcoded as either a 'job' or an 'experience' (again, by the author and, independently, by a second coder). The primary criterion was whether or not the activity was (likely to be) paid: if so, it was coded as a 'job'; if not, it was coded as an 'experience'. The purpose of the exercise was to distinguish stereotypical 'Saturday jobs', often undertaken to finance studying, from genuine 'work experience', undertaken to enhance one's

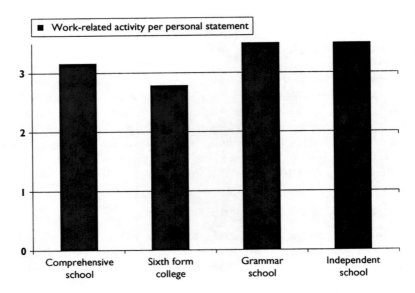

Figure 11.1 Distribution of work-related activity, per personal statement, by school type.

prospects and learn more about possible careers. Examples of each activity type are given in Table 11.1.

A correlation clearly arises between the nature of the activity and the level of skill and prestige involved. In general, the 'jobs' are low prestige and low skill, while the 'experiences' tend to be higher prestige and higher skill. However, it should be noted that some exceptions arise. For example, independent school applicants sometimes report 'jobs' of a different kind from the retail and clerical work generally experienced elsewhere (e.g. 'research assistant for a management consultancy firm' or 'lettings negotiator' in the table). Conversely, not all 'experiences' are high prestige and high skill. For example, some state school applicants report visits to local businesses, taster days and roles undertaken internally for the benefit of the schools.

When all work-related activity is subcoded as a 'job' or an 'experience', a more polarised picture emerges. Contrasting ratios show that although the total amount of work-related activity reported by applicants is not greatly different, the nature of the activity is. While applicants from sixth form colleges report twice as many 'experiences' as 'jobs' per personal statement, those from independent schools report over five times as many. In absolute terms, independent school applicants rely much less on paid work than their state-educated counterparts[8] and much more on voluntary activity. Indeed, some personal statements contain as many as nine instances of meaningful experiences of the workplace, and some applicants (from private schools in particular) are able to reel off a

Table 11.1 Examples of 'jobs' and 'experiences'

'Jobs'	'Experiences'
'I have a part-time paid job as a customer checkout assistant at Tesco PLC.' (SFC)	'I work-shadowed a stockbroker at the London office of the Credit Suisse Group.' (IND)
'I work part-time at a kitchen sales company where I am a telephone salesperson.' (SFC)	'I have arranged a week's work experience in July to shadow Kate Hoey, a Labour MP in the House of Commons.' (IND)
'I am currently employed in a newsagents.' (COMP)	
'Since leaving Abingdon School in Oxfordshire in 2009, I have been working as a research assistant for a management consultancy firm called Berkeley Partners Ltd on behalf of the Carbon Trust.' (IND)	'My fervour for economics has led to organised work placements in a leading bank in India and accountancy firm in New York.' (IND)
	'I have also been on a PriceWaterhouse-Coopers taster day; I was able to see how economics plays such an imperative role in the firm.' (SFC)
'Out of school I have employment as a lettings negotiator.' (IND)	'At school I was co-editor of the school newspaper and part of the team that created the Yearbook.' (SFC)

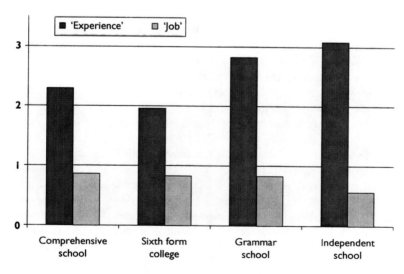

Figure 11.2 Distribution of work-related activity, per personal statement, subcoded as 'job' or 'experience', by school type.

long list of high-prestige placements undertaken with a range of sought-after employers.

The next section reports on what Figure 11.2 means in practice, and suggests that equal attainment applicants from different school types may not be competing on a level playing field when it comes to work-related activity. I begin by looking at one argument often put forward in defence of asking applicants to discuss their work-related activity as part of the university admissions process: that it is not the quantity of the experience that is important, but what the candidate has been able to learn from the experience.

Conceptualisations of work-related activity

The purpose of this section is to consider how applicants talk about the work-related activity that they have accumulated. It could be argued that, in an ideal university admissions process, admissions tutors would all be consistently and equally sensitive to the disparate distributions of work experience opportunities, and would carefully contextualise every application so as to make offers according to future potential, not past achievement. Unfortunately, those activities with the highest prestige tend also to be the ones that allow the candidate to advertise their suitability for a particular course with the greatest ease. For example, consider how the independent school applicants in examples (1) to (3) are able to make their experience relevant.

1   'Having obtained a work placement at an accountancy firm, Grant Thornton UK, I was given the task of inputting and interpreting data using accountancy software such as Sage and Iris. My interpersonal and organisational talents were also put to the test, as I was often responsible for scheduling appointments and liaising with clients. At the end of my experience, I was invited for a one-on-one meeting with the manager.' (IND)

2   'I have enjoyed work experience at James Hutchings & Co., a law firm situated in Norwich. I was able to observe the day-to-day running of the business and also, importantly, how to handle opponents and clients. Through work shadowing I had the opportunity to see one particular manager's style – how he dealt with authority and delegation.' (IND)

3   'The two placements I undertook in the summer of 2008 brought the reality of working in a business alive for me. One of them was at Forshaw Asset Management, Brighton, where I attended presentations by EMX (a fund dealing platform) and internal meetings. This enabled me to observe first-hand the intricacies of a small to medium-sized enterprise. I received instruction and practical experience in the trading of shares and I discussed the various aspects of the broader investment climate in the UK, such as the likely impact of the falling GBP/USD rate. I also gained work experience at 7 Essex Court, London. This afforded me an insight into the world of law as a commercial barrister. I spent time with different members of the chambers

at both junior and senior levels. I sat in on a client meeting, attended a small claims civil trial at a county court in Kent and watched as the barrister I was shadowing delivered the case for the claimant.' (IND)

In all three cases, applicants not only have professionalised, high prestige activity upon which to draw, they also have the skills necessary to exploit this activity in the admissions process. Each statement refers to the responsibility that the applicant was given, mentions direct dealings with clients and makes implicit connections with the courses for which they are applying. When state school applicants attempt to do the same, the outcomes are often less convincing, as examples (4) to (6) demonstrate.

4   'I've recently been working as a part-time sales assistant in a local retail out-let. I realise that this job may have little relation to my degree course but I hope this experience will help me appreciate the work of others, no matter what their job or status.' (SFC)
5   'I have had a part-time Sunday paper round job for the last 5 years, which I have enjoyed, and which displays commitment and dedication.' (SFC)
6   'I also work at a call centre, which helped me to work as a team giving me better communication skills with the general public by talking to customers. In addition I made new friends at work and I love meeting new people. Working in a call centre has improved my ICT skills and made me a much faster typist.' (SFC)

In example (4), the applicant presents paid employment as a means of learning to respect co-workers. The lack of relevance to higher education is acknowledged, and a persuasive attempt is made to argue that the benefit is not skills-based, but rather developmental – a greater appreciation for others has emerged. Usually, however, applicants discuss their part-time jobs in more practical ways – talking about self-discipline ('I've learnt how to get up on time'), hard work ('the shifts I do can last all night') and financial self-awareness ('I now understand the value of money'). Note that the applicant in example (5) cites 'commitment and dedication' as the skills associated with their job. In example (6), the value of working at a call centre is expressed in terms of forming new friendships and becoming a 'much faster typist'. Honest responses to UCAS prompts though they may be, it is difficult to imagine independent school applicants being advised to market themselves in such terms.

The role of schools in facilitating work experience

In this section, I argue that state school applicants, unlike their independent school counterparts, are reliant on their educational institutions to provide opportunities for work-related activity. This can make a big difference to their university applications, allowing them to talk about something more than paid, part-time employment, and often helping them to construct a clearer narrative about their decision to study a particular course.

7   'In Year 10 I undertook a week's work experience at a solicitors, specialising in the insolvency department. I was able to see where financial problems had arisen from and how businesses and individuals were affected. This gave me a greater understanding of how businesses need to be run in order to avoid becoming insolvent. This enhanced my organisation skills as well as furthering my understanding of the financial aspects of a business. I feel these are vital elements to understand in the subject.' (COMP)

8   'My interest in studying Economics and Business began during my Year 9 work experience with KPMG insolvency department when I was able to get a small insight into the impact that decision-makers have on a business and on what information these decisions are based.' (COMP)

9   'The work experience I participated in whilst I was in Year 10 is closely related to business. I worked for one week at the Glaxo factory in Cumbria. Whilst I was based here I worked in the accountancy section completing various tasks such as inputting spreadsheet data, researching the business and its aims etc. The experience of working in a successful business with a worldwide profile has given me a better understanding of a business's everyday operations and improved my ICT skills.' (COMP)

When talking about school-mediated work experience, state school applicants begin to express themselves with the confidence and self-assurance associated more with independent school applicants (Hatcher and Le Gallais 2008: 77). Though some state school applicants exert 'considerable personal agency to secure high-quality placements' (Waller *et al.* 2012: 1), for most, school-mediated work experience is the only route to meaningful experience. This experience is therefore vital, not only for their own personal development, but also in order to make an impression on university admissions tutors. For independent school applicants, such facilitation is less important because, as the next section shows, recourse to very different levels of social capital is available.

The role of social capital in gaining experience

It is noticeable in many work-related activities that family and other personal connections play a major part in securing access to the professions. These connections are almost twice as common in the personal statements of private school applicants as those of other applicants. Often, as examples (10) to (12) show, the family ties allow valuable insight into the world of work.

10   'For the majority of the last two years and currently during my gap year, I have worked for my family business in the retail sector. Responsibilities included assisting in sales, stock control and website advertising. Often

accompanying my father on nationwide and international business trips, it has given me an insight into the operations and workings of a business.' (IND)

11 'I am lucky enough to have gained a valuable insight into the business world, as my father is director of a large wholesale and retail company, showing me a useful experience of a commercial environment.' (IND)

12 'I am particularly interested in this field after I met one of my father's friends who has become hugely successful in the financial sector and as I have grown up I have watched his career develop.' (IND)

State-educated applicants also mention family members who have inspired them or provided opportunities for experience. However, not only is the frequency lower, the applicant's ability to make the experience relevant to the programme being applied for is more restricted. For example, one sixth-form college applicant notes 'experience working with my father in Spain, where he runs a property business'; however, no further details are provided and no connection is made to the proposed course of study.

It has long been acknowledged that the family plays a key role in reproducing social advantage (Bourdieu 1996; Hatcher and Le Gallais 2008). Huddlestone *et al.* (Chapter 10 in this volume) report on independent school students benefiting both through reputation, because local employers are keen to be associated with their school, and through alumni, because former pupils want, and are able, to offer relevant and attractive experiences to current pupils. Work-related activity is therefore available, sometimes in abundance, rather than needing to be actively sourced.

Accessing experience: an issue of fairness?

Evidence from personal statements shows that while some young people have the necessary social capital and school type advantage to access a range of activities that are professionalised and high prestige, others have limited access to any relevant experience. Wolf argues that 'vocational education has been micromanaged from the centre for decades' (2011: 9), adding that 'this is a bad idea, and not just because it is inherently ineffective.' However, a system in which young people are reliant on advantages of school type and social capital is equally ineffective if the goal is to conduct university admissions processes in a fair and transparent fashion.

The findings presented here bring to mind those reported by Mann and Kashefpakdel (see Chapter 9 in this volume), showing that independent school students have the widest – and most professionalised – range of work experience to draw on. From the perspective of equity, important questions are raised about the disadvantage faced by state school applicants to higher education because of the nature and quantity of their work-related activity. Referring to a survey of almost 700 young people, Mann and Kashefpakdel (see Chapter 9) note that when asked whether their work experience activity had helped them to secure a place at university, 43 per cent of those who had attended independent schools said yes. The corresponding proportion for those at comprehensive school was only 23 per cent.

The analysis of personal statements presented here is entirely consistent with these findings: state school applicants are unable to access the most prestigious and relevant forms of work-related activity and are also least well guided (Reay *et al.* 2005) when it comes to writing about their experiences in the personal statement. As Waller *et al.* note, 'more effort is needed to push academically-able working class young people towards placements that will increase motivation and widen horizons' (2012: 1).

Conclusion

This chapter has used evidence from a new source – the UCAS personal statement – to confirm that work experience opportunities are unequally distributed among young people in the United Kingdom, and that socio-economic status, as proxied here through school type, is the primary predictor of both the quantity and quality of activity undertaken. It is interesting to note that, in his foreword to the Wolf Report, Michael Gove (the then UK Secretary of State for Education) acknowledges that 'many of the best courses – like those [apprenticeships] offered by BT – hold open the door for further study in higher education' (Wolf 2011: 4). However, the findings reported here suggest that other doors are being closed to many potential university applicants.

The most obvious solution is increase opportunities within the state sector for meaningful, appropriate work experience. The benefits of such opportunities stretch far beyond access to higher education and would allow all young people to make better-informed decisions about their careers. However, an important secondary measure is for the university admissions process in the United Kingdom to reconsider the role that work experience should play in choosing between equal attainment applicants. Both Schwartz (2004) and Milburn (2012)[9] recommended that universities assess applicants 'holistically', and this inevitably involves the use of non-academic indicators, including work experience. However, Boliver (2011, 2013) notes that state school applicants are less likely to apply for leading universities than their identically qualified peers, and less likely to be accepted when they do. Clearly, the explanations for this are complex and several. However, the current system allows those applicants who already enjoy the advantages of school type to profit further from access to more prestigious work-related activity and from better advice on how to capitalise on this activity in the admissions process.

It is vital to remember that the personal statements examined in this research were composed by students of comparable educational attainment. In terms of work-related activity, however, the differences are stark. Some applicants appear to have access to a network of individuals – family members, teachers, careers advisors, alumni, friends, etc. – who can provide top-quality work experience opportunities, as well as valuable advice on the statement itself (Schwartz 2004;

Kirkland and Hansen 2011). Note that not all nations' admissions agencies place as much emphasis on work experience as the United Kingdom's; many are much more cautious and transparent about the use of non-academic indicators of potential (Jones 2014). This is partly because the distribution of work experience opportunities in the United Kingdom 'tends to reflect and reproduce existing patterns of social class inequality' (Hatcher and Le Gallais 2008: 77). The evidence presented in this chapter suggests that such reproduction will continue apace unless opportunities for meaningful work-related activity become more evenly distributed, or the UK university admissions process places less weight on an indicator to which applicants have very different levels of access.

Acknowledgment

The author is grateful to the Sutton Trust for commissioning the research upon which this chapter is based.

Notes

1 The Common Application is used for undergraduate admissions by most leading US universities and colleges.
2 'Government should . . . remove their statutory duty to provide every young person at KS4 with a standard amount of "work-related learning"' (Wolf Report 2011: 17).
3 'British universities have always looked beyond A-level grades to other things such as applicants' CVs, personal statements and their potential to benefit from a particular course. As long as it is done in a very transparent way, these sorts of schemes have the potential to identify talented young people who can really benefit from higher education' (David Willetts, UK's Minister of State for Universities and Science, cited in Paton 2010).
4 Similar arguments are made by Menzies (2013).
5 Applications from overseas students and mature students (aged 22 or older) were not used in this research.
6 The decision to use BBB is arbitrary. However, selecting a trio of identical grades avoids the need to control for higher achievement in a 'preferred' subject (for example, ABB applicants holding an A in Economics may be considered more academically suitable for an Economics degree than ABB applicants holding a B in the subject).
7 The remaining 18 applications were disregarded either because the school type was unknown or because the institution was a tertiary college, special school or agricultural college.
8 Note that Jones (2013) does not attempt to distinguish between selective and non-selective state schools. Work experience opportunities for very low-performing state schools could well be even more limited than Figure 11.2 suggests.
9 Note that Milburn is more guarded: 'Students from more disadvantaged backgrounds are less likely to . . . have opportunities to gain experiences' (2012: 53).

References

Boliver, V. (2011). Expansion, differentiation, and the persistence of social class inequalities in British higher education. *Higher Education*, 61: 229–242.
Boliver, V. (2013). How fair is access to more prestigious UK universities? *British Journal of Sociology*, 64 (2): 344–364.

Bourdieu, P. (1996). *The state nobility: elite schools in the field of power* [translated by L. C. Clough]. Stanford, CA: Stanford University Press.

Brown, R. M. (2004). Self-composed: rhetoric in psychology personal statements. *Written Communication*, 21 (3): 242–260.

Ferguson, E., Sanders A., O'Hehir, F. and James, D. (2000). Predictive validity of personal statements and the role of the five-factor model of personality in relation to medical training. *Journal of Occupational and Organizational Psychology*, 73 (3): 321–344.

GlenMaye, L. and Oakes, M. (2002). Assessing suitability of MSW applicants through objective scoring of personal statements. *Journal of Social Work Education*, 38 (1): 67–82.

Hansard, House of Commons. (2011). *Further and Higher Education (Access) Bill*. Column 597. Available from: www.publications.parliament.uk/pa/cm201011/cmhansrd/cm110304/debtext/110304-0002.htm#11030451000854 [accessed 7 March 2014].

Hatcher, R. and Le Gallais, T. (2008). *The work experience placements of secondary school students: widening horizons or reproducing social inequality?* London: Education and Employers Taskforce.

Hodgkinson, L. and Hamill, L. (2010). Pre-16 school work experience and civil engineering careers. *Proceedings of the ICE – Civil Engineering*, 163 (3): 131–136.

Jones, S. (2013). Ensure that you stand out from the crowd. A corpus-based analysis of personal statements according to applicants' school type. *Comparative Education Review*, 57 (3): 397–423.

Jones, S. (2014). Non-academic indicators and the Higher Education admissions process: a case study of the Personal Statement. *In:* V. Stead, ed. *Handbook of higher education admission policy and practice*. New York, NY: Peter Lang Publishing.

Kirkland, A. and Hansen, B. (2011). How do I bring diversity? Race and class in the college admissions essay. *Law & Society Review*, 45 (1): 103–138.

Mann, A. (2012). *Work experience: impact and delivery – insights from the evidence*. London: Education and Employers Taskforce.

Mann, A., Spring, C., Evans, D. and Dawkins, J. (2011). *The importance of experience of the world of work in admissions to Russell Group universities: a desktop review of admissions criteria for six courses*. London: Education and Employers Taskforce.

Menzies, L. (2013). *Educational aspirations: how English schools can work with parents to keep them on track*. York: Joseph Rowntree Foundation.

Milburn, A. (2012). *University challenge: how higher education can advance social mobility*. A progress report by the Independent Reviewer on Social Mobility and Child Poverty.

Muir, R. (2013). The impact of league table reform on vocational education in schools. Institute for Public Policy Research. Available from: www.edge.co.uk/media/102394/league-tables-vocational_jan2013.pdf [accessed 11 February 2014].

Neilson, G. R. and McNally, J. G. (2010). Not choosing nursing: work experience and career choice of high academic achieving school leavers. *Nurse Education Today*, 30 (1): 9–14.

Norman, G. (2004). The morality of medical school admission. *Advances in Health Sciences Education*, 9 (2): 79–82.

Paton, G. (2010). Universities should select by 'potential' says David Willetts. *The Daily Telegraph*, 22 August. Available from: www.telegraph.co.uk/education/educationnews/7958648/Universities-should-select-by-potential-says-David-Willetts.html [accessed 11 February 2014].

Pelech, W., Stalker C. A., Regehr, R. and Jacobs, M. (1999). Making the grade: the quest for validity in admissions decisions. *Journal of Social Work Education*, 35: 215–226.

Reay, D., David, M. E. and Ball, S. (2005). *Degrees of choice: social class, race and gender in higher education*. Stoke: Trentham Books.

Schwartz, S. (2004). *Fair admissions to higher education: recommendations for good practice*. Available from: www.admissions-review.org.uk/downloads/finalreport.pdf [accessed 11 February 2014].

Waller, R., Harrison N., Hatt, S. and Chudry, F. (2012). Undergraduates' memories of school-based work experience and the role of class and gender in placement choices. *Journal of Education and Work*, 1–27. doi:10.1080/13639080.2012.742183.

Wolf, A. (2011). *Review of vocational education – the Wolf Report*. London: Department for Education.

Chapter 12

How school work experience policies can widen student horizons or reproduce social inequality

Tricia Le Gallais and Richard Hatcher

Introduction

Until 2011, it was the statutory duty of secondary schools to provide some form of 'work-based learning' for all students aged 14–16 years in key stage 4 (KS4) and almost all school students undertook some form of work experience, usually in Year 10 and usually for a duration of two weeks. Following the Wolf Report's (Department for Education (DfE) 2011) recommendation, the government has removed this legal requirement, which may affect schools' decisions to offer work experience in Year 10.

This chapter examines the relationship between the work placements that school students undertake and their social class. It sets out our findings from two research studies: 'The work experience placements of secondary school students' (Hatcher and Le Gallais 2008) and a follow-up study: 'What a person can be they must be' (Le Gallais 2011).

Equal opportunities in Department for Education and Skills (DfES) guidance publications (DfES 2002a, 2002b) on work placements at KS4 has focused exclusively, and in the research literature largely, on gender issues, not on social class. However, research into work placements for post-16-year-olds indicates that social class may be an important dimension of the relationship between allocation and choice processes and the social character of workplaces (Hall and Raffo 2004; Hillage *et al.* 2001).

Our research explores to what extent work experience placements at KS4 confirm patterns of social selection and reproduction or disrupt them. The initial study (Hatcher and Le Gallais 2008) asks four questions. Is the distribution of students to placements differentiated by social class? If so, what are the processes that contribute to it? Are the students' experiences of work placements differentiated by social class? If so, in what ways? The study is based on research into the work experience placements of Year 10 students at five secondary schools in a large urban area in the Midlands. One of the schools, serving a socially deprived area, appeared to have developed a relatively effective policy for widening students' horizons through work placements and this became the subject of a follow-up study (Le Gallais 2011).

The research process

The five schools in the initial study were chosen in order to provide a range in terms of their social composition. We define social class in terms of socio-economic status (SES) for the purposes of this research, and we used eligibility for free school meals (FSM) as a proxy indicator of the SES of the school populations. The percentages of students eligible for FSM at the five schools in 2006 – the year when the student data collection took place – were as follows:

- Avon: 2.0%;
- Bedford: 10.0%;
- Cumbria: 17.0%;
- Devon: 53.8%;
- Essex: 63.1%.

Four of the schools were comprehensive schools; Avon was a grammar school. For analytical purposes, we grouped the schools into three categories as follows:

- high SES school: Avon;
- middle SES schools: Bedford and Cumbria;
- low SES schools: Devon and Essex.

Questionnaires were completed by the Year 10 cohort in each of the five schools, amounting to a total of 740 students, of whom we interviewed 98. The teachers selected the students to be interviewed, chosen to provide a gender mix and a range of ability according to the schools' criteria. One interview was carried out at each school with the teacher or teachers responsible for its work placement programme. Staff from Connexions provided data concerning post-16 education destinations and Education Business Links provided detailed information about the types of work placements undertaken by the students attending the schools involved in the research.

The social class of students and the social status of workplaces

The potential availability of placements was determined by the character of the local economy and also by legislation preventing work experience at KS4 in some workplaces on health and safety and other grounds. There was a perception on the part of some teachers that some employers offering professional placements restricted them to grammar schools and private schools. If true, this would affect the potential work experience placement in socially differentiating ways.

> It just seems that all the vets' jobs and all the high flying jobs, the journalist jobs and things like that, the accountancy jobs and the surveyors' jobs, all the

placements are harder to get because those placements have already gone to grammar school students.

(Teacher A, Cumbria)

We examined the relationship between the social class categories of the schools and the social status of the workplaces in which placements were obtained. Our categorisation of workplaces is based on Rose and Pevalin's Operational Categories of the National Statistics Socio-economic Classification of Occupations, using their three-category model (2001: 20): managerial and professional, intermediate, and lower. Of course, workplaces comprise jobs of different types; for example, 'professional' workplaces may well include functions in the 'intermediate' and 'lower' categories. Conversely, in workplaces with predominantly 'intermediate' and 'lower' work functions, there are likely to be some of 'managerial and professional' status. Nevertheless, we can distinguish between what can be called predominantly 'professional' workplaces, such as banks and medical and legal offices, and predominantly 'intermediate' or 'lower' workplaces, principally shops and other retail businesses, on the basis of the character of the principal and defining work process within them. For the purposes of comparison, we created two subcategories that exemplified professional workplaces: 'medical/pharmaceutical and legal' and 'offices, companies, banks'.

In general, our questionnaire data, confirmed by our interview data, exhibit a clear correlation between the social status of the workplace and the school SES. Avon students obtained a much greater percentage of placements in 'offices, companies, banks' (21 per cent) than students at Bedford (7 per cent), Cumbria (14 per cent), Devon (5 per cent) and Essex (14 per cent). We created the subcategory 'retail including hair and beauty' to exemplify non-professional workplaces. Avon students obtained a significantly lower percentage of such placements (11 per cent) than students at Bedford (26 per cent), Cumbria (21 per cent), Devon (26 per cent) and Essex (31 per cent).

While Essex exhibited a similar pattern to the other lower SES schools in the 'offices, companies, banks' and 'retail including hair and beauty' categories, there was a significant anomaly in 'medical/pharmaceutical and legal' placements. Avon students obtained a significantly higher percentage (22 per cent) than students at Bedford (5 per cent), Cumbria (2 per cent) and Devon (3 per cent), but the 15 per cent figure for Essex students was a far higher proportion than the other lower SES schools and closer to the Avon figure of 22 per cent. How it achieved this is the subject of our follow-up studies.

Our research has demonstrated that, in general, the lower the SES of the school, the less likely it is that placements will be located in managerial and professional workplaces. Our findings confirm those of Hillage *et al.* (2001) and Francis *et al.* (2005). However, for Avon students, whether or not they carry out their work experience in a professional workplace does not relate to widening career horizons because, for the majority, their family background and future university qualifications destine them for managerial and professional careers anyway.

What are the mechanisms by which this pattern of class reproduction at four of the five schools takes place, in spite of the acknowledgement by the schools that widening career horizons is an aim? The distribution of students to work placements was the result of two factors: student choice and school allocation. All schools operated a combination of these two mechanisms, but four of the five schools (the exception is Essex) relied as much as possible on students making their own choices and arrangements. This approach promoted student independence, maximised attendance and minimised the substantial administrative burden.

> Let's be honest, my concern is to get 156 people 156 places . . . But there is not enough time provided to go around and check that everybody has got a super placement.
>
> (Teacher, Avon)

The consequence of student choice was that students from the lower SES schools largely chose non-professional workplaces. Both Devon and Essex serve areas of high social deprivation and relatively high unemployment. Their teachers felt that the students' work experience aspirations were very limited:

> They want to go to the [city centre shopping area], they want to work in a shop and that is pretty much it for a lot of them, or they want to go and work in a garage. They are still quite restricted in their choices.
>
> (Teacher, Essex)

Typically, the principal factors that determined these students' choice of types of workplaces were familiarity, ease of access, relevance to lifestyle and, for some, the possibility of getting future part-time work in them. Retail outlets, such as clothes and record shops, were particularly popular. In contrast, the response from the Avon teacher described a wider range of workplaces and a much higher proportion of students in professional or quasi-professional placements.

> We get very few shop ones, very, very few . . . our turnout for university is huge, and most of them are going to consider themselves getting a degree and then doing something with that degree. They wouldn't see themselves as working in a shop.
>
> (Teacher, Avon)

Influences on student choice

In the questionnaire, students were asked who had influenced them in the choice and arrangement of their placements. Students across the five schools believed overwhelmingly that they made their own decisions but over 60 per cent at each of the schools stated that their parents were key influences upon their choices.

The important issue here concerns the nature of the influence and the extent to which social class was a differentiating factor in it.

The perceptions of the teachers we interviewed were that social class background was a significant factor in the ways in which parents influenced students' work experience choices. The scope of parents' aspirations at Avon was described as follows:

> . . . we have had people going to places like British Aerospace, Lucas Aerospace, working in a drawing office, that sort of thing, and then there is this ceiling of where (the parents) would not want their child to go and experience. The other side of things, as it were, because they would never want them in the manufacturing hands-on side of things.
>
> (Teacher, Avon)

Conversely, at Devon the school's catchment area included an estate with a high level of social deprivation and the teachers interviewed felt that that might lead to low expectations by parents and pupils.

> I don't know to what extent social-economic factors and parental influences are there upon the students, and they're not encouraged to achieve and aim high. We've got [a large council estate] very close and I wonder if the students have a lot of difficult and challenging issues to tackle at home. Sometimes they say their generation is unemployed and there is poverty and they're not expected to aim very high.
>
> (Devon staff)

Parents' social and cultural capital

We do not assume that parents from low SES backgrounds do not have high parental aspirations for their children; however, they may not have the social and cultural capital to translate their aspirations into appropriate work placements. We explored this in our interviews with students. The class differentiation in parents' social capital, which students were able to make use of in finding placements, is indicated by the following data based on interview responses. The anomaly of the Essex school's 15 per cent of students in professional placements is examined in a later section.

It was almost exclusively students from the high SES school who referred to links that parents had with managerial and professional contacts, exemplified by this student at Avon:

> Well, I was interested in law and my dad helped me find a placement. It's because, well, the barrister was a friend of my dad and the judge is a friend of a friend so I got it sort of like that.
>
> (Student, Avon)

Table 12.1 Correlation of percentage of parents in
professional jobs with percentage of students
in professional placements

SES of schools	% parents in professional jobs	% students in professional work experience placements
High SES: Avon	63	22
Middle SES: Bedford	17	5
Middle SES: Cumbria	10	2
Low SES: Devon	0	3
Low SES: Essex	4	15

Our findings from student responses concerning class differences in family and cultural capital were supported by the perceptions of teachers. They felt that parents in higher SES schools were much more likely to have the contacts to arrange placements in professional workplaces (see Table 12.1). At Avon:

> Some will be better placed for experience than others, but it's always the way, isn't it? It's contacts and things like that. Some will move in circles where perhaps parents, we've got a lot of professional parents around and professional sons . . . and they could say 'oh yes, your uncle so and so has got a good place' and others will not be in a position at all.
>
> (Teacher, Avon)

Family contacts are particularly vital to access placements in workplace sectors that are often not on school or broker agency databases. For students at Essex and Devon, managerial and professional placements in general, as well as certain specific employment sectors, were not easily attainable through parental contacts.

Our findings are congruent with the large body of research literature in the field of student choice ranging, for example, from primary school pupils' choice of secondary school (Lucey and Reay 2000) to career choice (Hodkinson and Sparkes 1997), which shows a consistent pattern of social class differentiation in which family cultural and social capital are significant factors. It is for this reason that intervention by the school or other agencies is essential if the work experience placement is to provide students with the opportunity to expand their horizons.

Students at the two lowest SES schools, Devon and Essex, stated that they were influenced by staff very much more than students in the other schools. But a significantly higher percentage of students at Essex found places in professional workplaces than either Devon and or both of the two middle SES schools. How can this be explained? The answer appears to lie in the role of staff in influencing student choice and allocating placements rather than allowing students to choose. Essex has the highest response with regard to the influence of school and careers staff of all the schools, but it was also the form of the influence – its intervention was geared to placing students, who were generally from relatively poor backgrounds, in professional placements. We examine this in more detail in our follow-up study (Le Gallais 2011).

The work experience placement: student roles and responsibilities

The final issue in our initial research concerns the relationship between the social status of the work placement sites and the roles and responsibilities undertaken by students. Attending a managerial and professional workplace does not necessarily mean that the tasks experienced are commensurate. They might be relatively menial routine tasks such as photocopying. Conversely, a non-professional workplace may offer a challenging educational experience. To what extent is there any social class differentiation in the work experience itself?

The data is drawn only from the three schools – Avon (high SES), Cumbria (medium SES) and Devon (low SES) – where interviews were carried out after the students had completed their work experience. There are some striking differences that are class-related. Only 2 per cent of students at Avon identified the type of work they carried out to be 'menial', compared to 21 per cent of Cumbria students and 34 per cent of Devon students. A much higher percentage of students at Avon than at the other schools reported that they had undertaken responsible tasks and work-shadowing and had been treated as a colleague. For example:

> Well, the first week I was in barristers . . . and every day I went to the City crown courts . . . and just saw the work the barristers do. One day we sat in the judge's office with the judge and spoke to the judge and that.
>
> (Student, Avon)

Some placement staff not only spent time teaching new skills to the students on placement with them, they also discussed how the students might progress with their interest in that type of work. This mentoring took place in predominantly professional occupations and was reported disproportionately by Avon students.

> I was talking to the solicitor and he told me all the qualifications that you need. He said well you have to be quite clever as well to take up the job and quite argumentative.
>
> (Student, Avon)

The conclusion of our initial research can be expressed in one sentence: the distribution of students across work placements, and their experience of them, is strongly differentiated by social class. It is consistent with the findings of studies by Hamilton (2003) and Semple *et al.* (2002). (Social class differentiation may be further differentiated by gender and ethnicity, but that was beyond the scope of our research.) There was a significant correlation between the social status of workplaces and the SES of schools – in general, the higher the school SES, the higher the percentage of students who found work experience in 'professional' workplaces. There was also a correlation between school SES and the educational content of the placement. This was the outcome of multiple social processes, which are complex and probabilistic but which have a cumulative effect that powerfully reproduces patterns of social class differentiation. One factor was selection by employers: some 'professional' workplaces only offered places to students from high SES schools, according to the teacher at the Cumbrian school cited earlier. However, the two principal drivers of student distribution to workplaces for work experience were student choice and the influence and allocator role of the school. A major influence on student distribution to placements was the socially differentiated cultural and social capital of parents: parents of students at higher SES schools often had high aspirations and were able to realise them by using family contacts to access work placements in professional workplaces.

The significance of social class reproduction in work placements at KS4 is unclear, because the extent to which work experience actually influences future career choices and destinations is unknown. It requires further research. What is certainly the case, however, is that because it is presently constituted, it often does little to widen students' career horizons by purposefully exposing them to workplace situations beyond those most familiar in terms of their family class backgrounds.

Working to widen horizons in one school

Only one school was effectively working to widen students' career horizons: Essex. Its students accessed more professional placements than the other schools, apart from Avon, in spite of the fact that Essex serves one of the most deprived areas in the country. In 2010, the unemployment rate in the surrounding suburb was almost 28 per cent (compared with the UK average of 5.5 per cent), with 66 per cent of pupils on free school meals and 86 per cent of the pupils having English as a second language.

Essex was the subject of our small-scale follow-up study where 36 students completed questionnaires, of whom five were interviewed. Staff responsible for work experience, together with the head teacher, were interviewed on several occasions throughout 2010–2011 and provided documentary data.

What was distinctive about Essex compared to the other schools was its directive policy regarding the allocation of students to placements: 78 per cent of students said that the school found their placement for them. The head teacher stated that this approach was vital to the Essex school's efforts to fully support their students:

> We have to be the parent for our pupils. Our (pupils') parents are not able or cognisant enough to play the game and the children here make choices

according to bus routes. Our directing them means showing them a different side of life.

(Head teacher, Essex)

Essex had increased the numbers of professional placements in medical and legal fields from 15 per cent in 2008 to 24 per cent in 2011. However, what is equally important is the quality of all placements in terms of how the students were treated and what roles and responsibilities they were given. In our initial research, there was a marked contrast between the experiences on placement of students at the low SES school (Devon) and the high SES school (Avon). The comments of Essex students in 2011 align more with Avon students' experiences than with their fellow low SES school (Devon). Students describe being treated like colleagues (69 per cent) with work-shadowing and mentoring forming part of their experience, and only 9 per cent referring to carrying out menial tasks on placement. High numbers of students speak of improvements in their interpersonal skills and an increased understanding of the world of work, with 70 per cent saying their ideas about future careers had been widened and 50 per cent saying they were now considering a career they never thought they could aspire to.

For the majority of the students there is a marked contrast between their aspirations regarding careers and university and their parental occupations and this is exemplified by the comments of two Essex school students:

No one's been to uni in my family. They're in shop work. I did my placement in the children's hospital and I really want to go to uni because of my placement.

(Student, Essex)

None of my family's been to uni. My work experience was in the city council offices and the staff there encouraged me to consider uni. They treated me well and gave me responsible tasks. I was encouraged to attend meetings and to give my opinion.

(Student, Essex)

It is clear that, for the school, a good placement should encourage students to look beyond the narrow horizons of their neighbourhood. What students do and how they are treated by employers are deemed to be essential ingredients of a quality placement. To achieve this, the school sets high expectations of employers regarding the placements accessed by their students:

When I talk with employers I am clear about what I want for our pupils. In the medical centre, for example, they will sit in with the doctor; at the library in town they will work as librarians; if they are with a solicitor they will go to court every day. One lad working in the hospital was given a research project where he was asking patients about their anti-emetic medication and his report was used by the staff.

(Teacher, Essex)

This was confirmed by the following student's description of her placement the previous year:

I worked at a medical centre. I worked with different nurses and doctors as they taught me how to deal with different patients; how to enter information on the computer and how to carry out injections. My placement has helped me to decide on my career and I want to do something in the medical field. [...] I have far greater expectations for my education and I feel my aspirations are higher.

(Student, Essex)

The head teacher believes that the school's directive approach is vital in its efforts to fully support its students and offer them opportunities to widen their horizons beyond the deprivation and poverty of their local area. In response to a question about the DfES's (2002a) advice regarding the potentially counterproductive effect of an uncomfortable placement, she responded firmly:

Comfortable? I don't want them to be comfortable. I want them out of their comfort zone. Otherwise (this area) is it for them! Broadening their horizons is so important.

(Head teacher, Essex)

A policy for widening horizons

What would a work experience policy designed to challenge students' existing social class-shaped conceptions, aspirations and emerging vocational identities look like? How could it widen horizons rather than limit and reproduce them?

1   Don't postpone work experience until after 16. The DfE has removed the statutory right to work-related learning for 14–16-year-olds. But employers disagree. The Confederation of British Industry (CBI), in its written evidence to the 2012 Education Select Committee's Inquiry into careers guidance for young people, insisted that, 'In order for schools to fulfil their new duty to full potential, [work experience] must sit within a framework for improving the school to work transition as a whole. This means retaining work experience for 14–16 year olds' (CBI 2012a: para. 5). See also CBI 2011.
2   Work experience must be high quality. The CBI report *Action for Jobs* says that 'many of the reports we heard in our consultation were of work experience that failed to sell the positive experience that work can be. A week

operating the photocopier does not inspire anyone' (CBI 2011: 10). In the more recent CBI report, 'The biggest concern among employers (voiced by 26 per cent) is that there is insufficient guidance and support on how to make work experience placements as worthwhile as they should be' (CBI 2012b: 29). Schools and local authorities must respond to this criticism.

3   Priority should be given, by both schools and employers, to students from low SES schools to have experiences of high status managerial and professional (as well as high skilled technical) workplaces. Policy would retain an element of student choice but situate it within an interventionist policy on the part of schools driven by educational and social justice objectives. Cooperating employers exhibiting corporate social responsibility could receive public recognition, perhaps in the form of a kite mark.

4   Begin in the primary school. Children's vocational identities – their aspirations, their conceptions of who they might become – begin to develop during primary school, much earlier than Year 10. By Year 10, vocational identities may have become quite firmly fixed. Young people may not have decided what their future careers are, but they may well have fixed ideas about what they aren't – many possible futures may simply not be part of their thinking. Therefore, the process of widening children's horizons needs to begin in the primary school, as has recently been recognised by the Office for Fair Access (OFFA), which has called on universities and colleges to step up the long-term work they do reaching out to schools and communities where few progress to higher education by engaging with children from as young as seven (OFFA 2013).

5   Work experience should be part of a range of experiences of and about the world of work, integrated with the school curriculum, primary as well as secondary, which would both develop the 'employability skills' that employers want and enable students to develop a critical understanding of the world of work and its place in society.

References

Confederation of British Industry and putting (CBI). (2011). *Action for Jobs*. London: CBI. Available from: www.cbi.org.uk/media/1138544/cbi_action_for_jobs_oct11. pdf [accessed 23 January 2013].

Confederation of British Industry and putting (CBI). (2012a). *Parliamentary business. Careers guidance for young people: written evidence submitted by CBI*. Available from: www.parliament.uk [accessed 23 January 2013].

Confederation of British Industry and putting (CBI). (2012b). *Learning to grow: what employers need for education and skills 2012*. London: CBI. Available from: www.cbi.org. uk/media/. . ./cbi_education_and_skills_survey_2012.pdf [accessed 23 January 2013].

Department for Education (DfE). (2011). *Wolf Review on vocational education: government response*. Available from: http://media.education.gov.uk/assets/files/pdf/w/wolf%20 review%20of%20vocational%20education%20%20%20government%20response.pdf [accessed 30 September 2011].

Department for Education and Skills (DfES). (2002a). *Work experience: a guide for secondary schools.* London: DfES.

Department for Education and Skills (DfES). (2002b). *Work experience: a guide for employers.* London: DfES.

Francis, B., Osgood, J., Dalgety, J. and Archer, L. (2005). *Gender equality in work experience placements for young people.* Working Paper Series No. 27, Institute for Policy Studies in Education, London Metropolitan University.

Hall, D. and Raffo, C. (2004). Re-engaging 14–16-year-olds with their schooling through work-related learning. *Journal of Vocational Education & Training*, 56 (1): 69–79.

Hamilton, S. (2003). *Equality in education: work experience placements. Spotlight 90.* Glasgow: The SCRE Centre, University of Glasgow.

Hatcher, R. and Le Gallais, T. A. (2008). *The work experience placements of secondary school pupils: widening horizons or reproducing social inequality?* Birmingham: Birmingham City University. Available from: www.educationandemployers.org/media/13203/the_work_experience_placements_of_secondary_school_students.pdf [accessed 23 January 2013].

Hillage, J., Kodz, J. and Pike, G. (2001). *Pre-16 work experience practice in England: an evaluation.* Department for Education and Employment (DfEE) Research Report RR263. London: DfEE.

Hodkinson, P. and Sparkes, A.C. (1997). Careership: a sociological theory of career decision-making. *British Journal of Sociology of Education*, 18 (1): 29–44.

Le Gallais, T. A. (2011). *What a person can be they must be – an exploration of the efforts of one school in the West Midlands, England to raise aspirations and widen horizons for their students through their work experience programme.* Paper presented at the Education & Employers' Conference, University of Warwick. Available from: www.educationandemployers.org/media/13922/tricia_le_gallais_conference_paper_2011.pdf [accessed 23 January 2013].

Lucey, H. and Reay, D. (2000). Identities in transition: anxiety and excitement in the move to secondary school. *Oxford Review of Education*, 26 (2): 191–205.

Office for Fair Access (OFFA). (2013). *OFFA asks universities and colleges to do more work with schools and communities to raise aspirations and attainment.* Press release. Available from: www.offa.org.uk/press-releases/offa-asks-universities-and-colleges-to-do-more-work-with-schools-and-communities-to-raise-aspirations-and-attainment/ [accessed 23 January 2013].

Rose, D. and Pevalin, D. J. (2001). *The National Statistics socio-economic classification: unifying official and sociological approaches to the conceptualisation and measurement of social class.* ISER Working Papers No. 2001-4. Colchester: University of Essex.

Semple, S., Paris. M., McCartney, P. and Twiddle, B. (2002). *Learning gains from education for work.* London: National Centre: Education for Work and Enterprise.

Part 4

Economic impact and employment outcomes

Chapter 13

School-mediated employer engagement and labour market outcomes for young adults

Wage premia, NEET outcomes and career confidence[1]

Christian Percy and Anthony Mann

Introduction: employer engagement as an untested policy imperative

For those in employment, there is a commonplace expectation that additional experience in work has the potential to improve performance at work and general employment prospects. It can seem an intuitive leap to argue that greater experience of the world of work, in its broadest sense, while studying in school should also confer benefits in accessing and successfully participating in employment later.

Such an ambition lay behind policies introduced in 2004 by education ministries in England, Scotland and Wales to introduce new expectations on secondary schools to better prepare young people for working lives through work-related learning and employer engagement, primarily via expanding the availability of pre-existing activities like work experience, careers advice, business mentoring and enterprise education (QCA 2003; Scottish Executive 2004; Welsh Assembly Government 2004, 2008; Huddleston and Stanley 2012). The policies were aimed at increasing opportunities for all pupils, regardless of attainment levels or vocational aspirations, and were delivered as co-curricular, typically stand-alone activities with the costs of school engagement with employers directly subsidised – in the English case, through £25 million annual funding of local Education Business Partnership Organisations (EBPO).[2] Schools had considerable freedom as to which activities to implement within constraints shaped in part by local EBPO provision and very rarely integrated them closely into defined programmes of study with discrete learning outcomes linked to qualifications.

Due to the many factors that influence success in the labour market and the typical time lag between secondary school and full-time employment, it has proved difficult to test the efficacy of such policies. In the UK context, studies have tended to touch on labour market outcomes only in terms of evidence of related increased attainment and/or perceived improved preparation for the workplace, rather than tracking and assessing actual progression (AIR UK 2008; Miller 1998; Green and Rogers 1997). This chapter takes a different approach to assessing the potential impact of school-mediated employer engagement. It exploits the results of a one-off survey, which asked young adults to recall the kinds of employer contact they had while at school, as well as providing details related to background and current economic circumstances.

Contact with employers is a key element of work-related learning. Over the period in question the evidence is strong that, despite the universal entitlement for work-related learning, pupils' contact with employers varied greatly (see Table 13.1, and also similar findings from Ipsos MORI 2009 and YouGov 2010). The aim of this chapter is to use survey data that exploits this variation, to examine the relationship between higher levels of exposure to school-mediated teenage employer contacts and young adults' NEET (Not in Employment, Education or Training) status, earnings and confidence in successful career progression.

Methodology

This chapter draws on the results of a survey of 985 adults aged 19–24 across England, Scotland and Wales conducted in February 2011 and undertaken by polling firm YouGov on behalf of the Education and Employers Taskforce.[3] All respondents were asked about the number of employer engagement activities they had undertaken while at school or college between the ages of 14 and 19.

> Some schools and colleges arrange for their students (aged between 14 and 19) to take part in activities which involve employers or local business people providing things like work experience, mentoring, enterprise competitions, careers advice, CV or interview workshops, workplace visits, taking part in classroom discussions. Did you take part in such activities between those ages? If so, on how many different occasions (more or less) did it happen?
>
> (For more details, see Mann and Percy 2013)

Table 13.1 indicates variations in employer engagement experienced by survey respondents, which can be exploited analytically to examine links with three other survey questions that, in different ways, provide indication of successful progression into the early labour market.

Table 13.1 School/college-mediated employer contacts (respondent count, unweighted)

No. of activities	#	%
Never	265	27%
Yes, just once	341	35%
Yes, twice	152	15%
Yes, three times	68	7%
Yes, four times or more	83	8%
Don't know	76	8%
Total	985	100%

First, individuals described whether or not they were in work, education or unemployment, enabling categorisation of individuals as NEET or non-NEET at the time of the survey.[4] Logistic regression analysis was used to relate levels of prior employer engagement to NEET status as given by this question. Second, those in full-time, salaried employment were asked to record their gross annual salary in £1,000 intervals, which lends itself to interval regression analysis. While these two questions investigated links between school-mediated employer contacts and evidence of more successful school-to-work transitions, a third question sought a personal perspective on the confidence in successful progression towards medium-term career goals: 'Thinking about the sort of job you'd like to be doing in 5 to 10 years' time, how useful do you think what you are doing now is as a way of achieving this?' This third question goes to the heart of the potential value of employer contacts while at school. By enabling better awareness of career choices and paths, extending relevant networks and providing experience of value to occupational ambitions, teenagers may feel better able to make next-step, near-term decisions and then be more confident that the path they are currently on will help them to achieve their career goals.

Respondents were also asked their age at the time of survey, gender, region, highest level of qualification and school types (independent, state selective or non-selective state school or college) attended between the ages of 14 and 19, allowing controls for background characteristics to be built into the analysis.

Each analysis drew on different subsets of the original sample of 985 respondents. For all analyses, 76 respondents were excluded who did not recall how much employer contact they had while at school. Similarly, when respondents failed to answer or chose not to answer key control variable questions, they were excluded from that analysis. The small number of individuals who had attended special schools was also excluded because the sample size was insufficient to enable targeted assessment of this group.

For the analysis on NEET status at the time of survey, this results in a sample size of 850 for the analysis, with 1 per cent attrition due to missing answers and 13 per cent attrition due to unspecified answers, such as 'don't know' or 'can't remember'. For the analysis on wage outcomes, only those reporting a full-time annual salary were included because individuals aged 19–24 who were working hourly or part-time were less likely to be working in their career of choice and to be in the midst of the transition from education to sustained employment. This approach results in a subsample of 169 respondents, with an attrition rate of 1 per cent due to missing answers and 15 per cent due to unusable answers. For more details on the underlying data as well as the interval regression analysis, see Mann and Percy 2013. Finally, for the analysis on confidence in medium-term career outcomes, all individuals with a full set of answers are included (835 respondents, with attrition rate of 1 per cent due to missing answers and 14 per cent due to unusable answers) because someone can comment on their future options without regard for current status or stage of life transition points.

Results

NEET status

Figure 13.1 demonstrates the overall, beneficial association between the number of times an individual reported contact with an employer while aged between 14 and 19 and their NEET status at the time of the survey.

The overall association provides an indication of strong advantage associated with employer engagement, but the significant differences across other characteristics between NEET and non-NEET cohorts suggests the possibility that this association may be coincidental, emerging from some other dominating relationship, rather than a result of underlying causal mechanisms. Possible confounding factors include level of education or social background – if more highly educated individuals from wealthier backgrounds or independent schools, for example, are found to be more likely to have higher levels of contacts with employers and to remain non-NEET, the association described earlier might be coincidental rather than causal, and hence misleading from a policy intervention perspective.

Logistic regression analysis provides a framework to control for such confounding factors, which are in the survey questions, and identify whether any remaining association is statistically significant, given the variation in the data and the sample size. We ran five models for employer contacts, which respectively included dummy variables to account for gender, highest level of qualification, school type attended, British region and ethnicity, running each model both with and without an age control to ensure that age at the time of the survey is not a dominating factor in our results.[5] In all cases, the odds ratio multiplier for two or more employer contacts was significant at the 90 per cent level or better (95 per cent level or better for all but one of the 10 model variants) and varied between 2.0 and 2.7. In the interests of space, three models are presented in the following tables, representing the control variables with the most interesting effects and

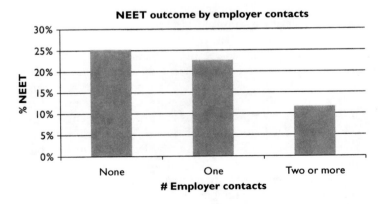

Figure 13.1 NEET outcome by employer contact. Weighted data (unweighted N = 850).

which are most likely confounding variables – highest level of qualification obtained (Table 13.2), social privilege indicator through attendance at independent schools (Table 13.3) and location across the British regions with their different average economic and employment characteristics (Table 13.4).

The most compelling model (Table 13.2) with respect to control variables is the control for high academic attainers versus low academic attainers. In this case, an individual with no employer contacts and attaining below level 3 has a 56 per cent chance of being non-NEET. Having attained a level 3 or above qualification, the average is a 79 per cent chance of being non-NEET. Adding in two or more employer contacts, the new probability becomes 89 per cent. For those without the level 3 or above qualification, the equivalent probabilities transition from 56 per cent to 74 per cent for those with two or more employer contacts. Including the age control variable and considering individuals at age 21, the equivalent probabilities of being non-NEET progress from 60 per cent to 81 per cent and finally to 90 per cent. Across the range of models for typical respondents, the benefit associated with two or more employer contacts versus none is about 5–20 percentage points improved probability of being non-NEET, with the largest effects associated with lower attainers based outside London.

In practice, this average effect is likely to vary both by individual circumstances and by the quality of the employer engagement experienced. Unpacking such effects statistically requires a different research design in order to enable the use of interaction terms. Nonetheless, it is compelling that a strong and statistically significant average relationship can be observed across such heterogeneous circumstances.

Table 13.2 NEET status – logistic regression output (model 2: highest level of qualification)[a,b]

Variable	Model 2		Model 2 with age control	
	Odds ratio factor	P-value of Z-stat	Odds ratio	P-value of Z-stat
(Intercept)	1.25	0.54	76.22	0.04
One employer contact	1.03	0.93	1.02	0.95
Two or more employer contacts	2.27	0.05	2.03	0.08
Highest qualification at level 3–5	2.98	0.00	2.84	0.01
Age	–	–	0.83	0.04

Notes
a P-value of Wald χ^2: 0.00 (14.8); age control: 0.00 (15.4); unweighted $N = 850$ (analysis weighted by current activity).
b Reference category: no employer contacts, individual attaining level 0–2 as their current highest level [age zero].

Table 13.3 NEET status – logistic regression output (model 3: school type attended)[a,b]

Variable	Model 3		Model 3 with age control	
	Odds ratio factor	P-value of Z-stat	Odds ratio	P-value of Z-stat
(Intercept)	3.62	0.00	232.92	0.01
One employer contact	1.18	0.61	1.17	0.62
Two or more employer contacts	2.67	0.02	2.37	0.03
Attended an independent school	0.82	0.68	0.89	0.80
Attended a state selective school	0.55	0.07	0.57	0.09
Attended other or mixed schools (excl. non-selective state school)	0.75	0.60	0.83	0.73
Age	–	–	0.83	0.03

Notes
a P-value of Wald χ^2: 0.10 (9.3); age control: 0.08 (11.4); unweighted N = 850 (analysis weighted by current activity).
b Reference category: no employer contacts, individual attending a non-selective state school aged 14–19 [age zero].

Table 13.4 NEET status – logistic regression output (model 4: region of residence)[a,b]

Variable	Model 4		Model 4 with age control	
	Odds ratio factor	P-value of Z-stat	Odds ratio	P-value of Z-stat
(Intercept)	4.29	0.00	410.23	0.01
One employer contact	1.17	0.64	1.14	0.69
Two or more employer contacts	2.55	0.02	2.23	0.05
Living in the Midlands/Wales	0.58	0.29	0.56	0.26
Living in the North	0.99	0.99	0.92	0.88
Living in the South	0.60	0.32	0.54	0.24
Age	–	–	0.82	0.03

Notes
a P-value of Wald χ^2: 0.09 (9.6); age control: 0.06 (12.0); unweighted N = 850 (analysis weighted by current activity).
b Reference category: no employer contacts, individual living in London [age zero].

It is important to note that this average benefit associated with two or more employer contacts would not be expected in an individual with only two contacts, except where those contacts are particularly high-impact, or the other factors to which they are correlated have high-impact effects in those circumstances. Instead, an individual would need to present the average of the 'two or more' cohort, which might be nearer to four employer contacts.

Annual salary

Having identified a positive association between employer contacts and labour market participation, the next step is to address the potential for improved wage outcomes among those 169 respondents in full-time, salaried employment providing full relevant data. Table 13.5 presents the results of the interval regression analysis,[7] indicating that each additional employer contact is associated with an extra £900 in annual salary on average (£909 is the point estimate given in Table 13.5), an analysis which is significant at the 5 per cent level or better. The p-value of 0.027 (rounded to 0.03 in Table 13.5) indicates only a 2.7 per cent chance that this data would be observed, and yet there is no relationship between earnings and school-age employer contacts.

Given that all such relationships are estimated with error, especially with such imprecise phenomena as wage return drivers, which vary widely by individual, this analysis is best interpreted as being 70 per cent confident that the average correlation between each additional employer contact and earnings is between £500 and £1,300.[8] With median earnings of £19,500 within the sample, this reflects a typical 2.5–6.7 per cent increase per additional employer contact.

Confidence in career progression

Table 13.6 identifies statistically significant relationships (at the 10 per cent level or better) between the volume of employer engagement undertaken in the past and confidence that activities currently undertaken represent a positive step towards ultimate career objectives. Whereas around one-third of respondents recalling zero activities (36 per cent) felt their current activity to be 'very useful', the proportion agreeing with the statement rises with the number of activities recalled to more than half (55 per cent) for those recalling four or more activities. The trend is also seen, if less starkly, in the answers of respondents who felt their current activity was 'not at all useful', with the proportion agreeing falling from 17 per cent of those who recalled no activities to 8 per cent of those who recalled four or more.

Tables 13.7, 13.8 and 13.9 present the results of an ordinal logistic regression, analysed on the same basis as NEET status, categorising the responses on a scale from 1–4 (where 4 is most useful) and including the same background variables as the logistic regression. As elsewhere, the number of employer contacts remains statistically significant (here at the 5 per cent level or better) in having a beneficial

Table 13.5 Results of interval regression[a,b,c]

Dependent variable: reported salary in intervals [annual wage in GBP, before deductions]

Variable	Estimate	Std error	P-value
(Intercept)	−5,603	10,047	0.58
**Age in years	914	398	0.02
White ethnicity	−964	2,149	0.65
Male	475	1,004	0.64
*Highest qualification at level 3	4,687	2,641	0.08
**Highest qualification at level 4	7,316	2,761	0.01
**Highest qualification at level 5	7,827	2,958	0.01
**Number of employer contacts	909	410	0.03
**Resident in the East of England	−1,576	1,375	0.25
Resident in the North East	−2,898	1,820	0.11
Resident in the North West	−117	2,633	0.96
Resident in the East Midlands	−2,880	2,677	0.28
**Resident in the West Midlands	−3,695	1,518	0.02
Resident in Wales	−4,012	2,575	0.12
**Resident in Yorkshire and Humber	−4,252	1,769	0.02
Resident in the South East	−1,288	1,560	0.41
Resident in the South West	−1,912	1,469	0.19
Resident in Scotland	−4,302	2,793	0.12
*Attended an independent school (14–16)	−2,656	1,465	0.07
Attended a selective state school (14–16)	208	1,731	0.90
Attended a non-independent, non-state school (14–16)	−1,749	2,811	0.53
**Left education at 16	6,326	2,913	0.03
**Attended an independent school (16–19)	4,287	2,108	0.04
Attended a selective state school (16–19)	749	2,129	0.73
Attended a different school type (16–19)	1,940	3,255	0.55
Attended a further education college (16–19)	971	1,563	0.54
Attended a sixth form college (16–19)	−277	1,294	0.83

Notes

a For readers unfamiliar with the table layout, the following explanation may be helpful. Each variable that was included in the original regression analysis is listed in the left-hand column. The 'Estimate' column indicates the average change in annual wage in GBP as a result of a unit change in that variable (e.g. a single year in age), holding the values of all the other variables constant. Given variation in the underlying data and the sample size, this change is estimated subject to uncertainty, which is quantified in GBP in the 'Std error' column. The P-value column combines this information to support a judgement on whether the variable has a statistically significant impact on annual wage, where a smaller value is preferred, indicating it is less likely that the observed correlation in the sample might have been observed by chance, despite there being no genuine underlying correlation.

b Wald statistic of 98.8 (p-value 0.00); * significant at the 90% level; ** significant at the 95% level; N = 169.

c Reference category: female, non-White, based in London, who went to a non-selective state school 14–19, attaining below level 3 with no school-mediated employer contacts.

Table 13.6 Relationship between teenage school-mediated employer engagement and confidence in career progression as young adults (unweighted *N* = 835; numbers may not sum to 100% due to rounding)[a]

		Number of school-mediated employer engagement activities experienced while at school, aged 14–19				
		0	1	2	3	4 or more
Thinking about the sort of job you'd like to be doing in 5 to 10 years' time, how useful do you think what you are doing now is as a way of achieving this?	Very useful	36%	39%	42%	45%	55%
	Useful	32%	32%	39%	25%	30%
	Not that useful	15%	14%	11%	13%	7%
	Not at all useful	17%	15%	8%	17%	8%
Respondent count (weighted)		249	328	137	56	65

Note
a Kendall's Tau B (unweighted) 0.07 (asymp. SE 0.03).

association with an individual's confidence that their current activity – and, by implication, previous choices of current activity – will support their future career goals.

Discussion

The survey paints a strikingly consistent story about the potential positive effects of school-mediated employer engagement on the school-to-work transitions of young adults. It appears that those who have greater levels of contact with employers through school or college are significantly less likely to be NEET, more likely to be confident that their current activity will support their medium-term occupational ambitions and more likely to be earning at a higher level if in full-time, salaried employment. This association is most tangible when comparing students who experienced no employer contact with those who experienced highest volume of episodes, with statistical controls in place for background characteristics. Those with higher levels of employer contacts are less likely to be sceptical that their current activity is useful for their future job ambitions, have 1.0–1.7× better odds of being in education, employment or training and, if in full-time employment, will be earning 10–25 per cent more on average. Due to the parameters of the survey, we do not know if the benefits extend beyond age 24 or whether the benefits of additional employer contact begin to diminish after four instances. Equally, it should be made clear that the findings

Table 13.7 Progression confidence − logistic regression output (model 2: highest level of qualification)[a,b]

Variable	Model 2 without age control		Model 2 with age control	
	Odds ratio	P-value of Z-stat	Odds ratio	P-value of Z-stat
One employer contact	1.08	0.71	1.07	0.72
Two or more employer contacts	1.52	0.04	1.47	0.05
Highest qualification at level 3–5	2.21	0.00	2.15	0.00
Age	–	–	0.93	0.10

Notes
a P-value of Wald χ^2: 0.00 (15.8); age control: 0.00 (16.9); unweighted $N = 835$ (analysis weighted by current activity).
b Reference category: no employer contacts, individual attaining level 0–2 as their current highest level [age zero].

Table 13.8 Progression confidence − logistic regression output (model 3: school type attended)[a,b]

Variable	Model 3 without age control		Model 3 with age control	
	Odds ratio	P-value of Z-stat	Odds ratio	P-value of Z-stat
One employer contact	1.14	0.53	1.13	0.54
Two or more employer contacts	1.59	0.02	1.53	0.04
Attended an independent school	1.06	0.80	1.10	0.68
Attended a state selective school	0.98	0.91	1.00	0.99
Attended other or mixed schools (excl. non-selective state school)	0.73	0.28	0.76	0.33
Age	–	–	0.92	0.07

Notes
a P-value of Wald χ^2: 0.13 (8.6); age control: 0.11 (10.5); unweighted $N = 835$ (analysis weighted by current activity).
b Reference category: no employer contacts, individual attending a non-selective state school aged 14–19 [age zero].

Table 13.9 Progression confidence – logistic regression output (model 4: region of residence)[a,b]

Variable	Model 4 without age control		Model 4 with age control	
	Odds ratio	P-value of Z-stat	Odds ratio	P-value of Z-stat
One employer contact	1.14	0.51	1.14	0.53
Two or more employer contacts	1.63	0.02	1.56	0.03
Living in the Midlands/Wales	0.93	0.77	0.93	0.76
Living in the North	1.16	0.53	1.12	0.61
Living in the South	0.97	0.89	0.93	0.77
Age	–	–	0.92	0.06

Notes
a P-value of Wald χ^2: 0.11 (8.9); age control: 0.10 (10.6); unweighted N = 835 (analysis weighted by current activity).
b Reference category: no employer contacts, individual living in London [age zero].

represent average results with significant variation across individual experiences. A deterministic line cannot be drawn between each individual instance of teenage employer contacts and predictable labour market outcomes. Nonetheless, it is clear that school-age employer engagement is closely linked to getting a good start in the labour market.

Critically, the results cannot be discounted as a mask for high achievement or simply a function of social advantage as reflected through different school types attended. It is not that students from independent schools or selective grammar schools, who would be expected to be from families of higher socio-economic status, or young people with higher levels of qualification participate in more employer engagement opportunities and have better labour market outcomes, without there being any direct link between those employer contacts and the labour market outcomes. The nature of the analysis is such that individuals who went to independent schools and had considerable employer contact are only compared against peers with less employer contact who also went to independent schools. Similarly, those with a highest qualification at level 3 or levels 3–5 are compared only against those with the same characteristics.

An alternative critique is that individuals with a proactive mindset or predisposition towards taking opportunities and working hard might both engage with employers and do well in the labour market, irrespective of any direct link between the two. Although the analysis does not enable statistical controls to be used to test for such a mindset, the nature of the UK educational system makes it unlikely that such character traits would be associated with high levels of employer contact. As Prue Huddleston, Emeritus Professor at the University of Warwick, states:

> In the British tradition of employer engagement in education, there is relatively little scope for pupil agency in determining whether or not they engage in many activities. Typically, over the last decade, schools have either required all young people in a year group or class to take part in activities such as work experience, one-day enterprise competitions and career fairs or chosen not to engage in them at all. Some pupils might show agency in choosing to take part in longer duration enterprise competitions or be selected themselves for business mentoring, but these commonly involve fewer than 10 per cent of pupils in any year group.
>
> (Interview by authors with Professor Huddleston,
> former Director of the Centre for Education and Industry,
> University of Warwick, December 2012)

As noted, academic literature exploring the labour market impacts of school-mediated employer engagement is sparse. However, a number of relevant studies have considered relationships between school-age exposure to the labour market and subsequent employment outcomes. A small number of US studies have looked for evidence of labour market benefits linked to participation in vocationally focused but primarily academic learning programmes rich in work-related learning and employer engagement. The results align with those presented in our study. Evaluations undertaken by Boston-based social enterprise Jobs for the Future (1998), the Applied Research Unit of Montgomery County Public Schools (2001), MacAullum et al. (2002) and Kemple and Willner (2008) all follow graduates of such programmes into early employment and find evidence of improved earnings outcomes at 6.5–25 per cent, against the control group. The most rigorous study is that of Kemple and Willner, who followed former students of the US Career Academies programme eight years after leaving high school and going into the labour market. Tested against a control group populated initially by randomised selection, at age 26 former students of the Career Academies programme were earning 11 per cent more than comparable peers.[9] From a different perspective, studies of adult labour market outcomes related to teenage part-time employment have also shown statistical significant positive relationships. Ruhm's (1997) analysis of US National Longitudinal Survey of Youth found that high school students who combined their full-time education with part-time employment generally enjoyed higher levels of economic attainment six to nine years after leaving school than those who did not. More recently, Crawford et al. (2012) have drawn on three British datasets (Longitudinal Study of Young People in England, Labour Force Survey and British Household Panel Survey) to interrogate the transitions of young people from final years of education into the early labour market. Comparing young people who, at 16–18, combined full-time education with part-time work with those who undertook full-study without any employment, the study finds the former group to have statistically significant lower probabilities of being NEET both one and five years later.

The current study provides further evidence, therefore, to suggest that early teenage exposure to the working world helps young people to better navigate transitions into the adult labour market. The conclusion prompts researchers to seek to understand causal factors behind such benefits. The question of causality is subject to limited attention in works cited earlier and a comparison of results and student experiences is likely to be of value. For example, while outcomes discovered by our research are comparable to evaluations of both evaluated US programmes and of teenage employment, clearly modes of employer engagement delivery considered in the current study are very different. In the US Career Academy environment, for instance, employer contacts are commonly embedded in a curriculum taught in a discrete project-focused learning environment combining theoretical and technical study over a period of many months or years. In Britain, by contrast, employer contacts are typically of short duration, episodic and unrelated to curriculum. And while a number of US commentators (Kemple and Willner 2008: 40; Jobs for the Future 1998: 2) have suggested that wage premia observed in early adulthood may be due to enhanced technical skills as well as improved insight into the labour market and contacts within it, the opportunity for technical skills development under the British delivery model is severely constrained. Within the British experience, employer contacts – activities like work experience, mentoring, enterprise competitions, careers advice, CV or interview workshops, workplace visits, taking part in classroom discussions – provide limited opportunities for skill accumulation and are rarely of lengthy duration. The most significant workplace exposure of the typical British learner would be a work experience placement of two weeks duration designed to be a taste of the workplace, rather than a programme including elements of work-based training, undertaken at age 14 or 15. Consideration of the British experience, therefore, suggests that beneficial impacts may be due to reasons other than technical skill development and that, to have some effect, workplace exposure need not necessarily be fully integrated into coherent learning programmes – although it remains possible that such integration might convey additional benefits. Further study might productively explore broader, potentially causal, factors such as social network extension, changing attitudes towards labour market progression and access to reliable, additional information about labour market opportunities.

Conclusion

This chapter presents findings from a rare study of the labour market relevance of school-mediated employer contacts. The results are striking and reflect findings from longitudinal studies of the impact of US work-related learning programmes and studies of the long-term economic benefits of teenage part-time employment. Further research, through both additional survey material and analysis of longitudinal datasets, should test findings with larger samples. It should explore the links between employer contacts and enhanced career navigation and skills acquisition, and test for the optimal timing of interventions. It should also dig into the character of the NEET population and the more specific nature of the associations observed. Larger surveys and a different research design could also introduce questions to unpack motivations, length of time NEET, ambitions and experiences in the labour market and underlying personality type, all of which would aid in isolating the potential benefit of employer contact in its own right. The question of where employer contacts take place and how they impact on the lived experiences of young people from different social backgrounds also demands further attention. For policymakers, the findings provide a validation of decisions to enhance the prospects of young people by extending their access to workplace contacts while still in education. The findings are supportive of the view that employer contacts to aid career exploration can be of high value to young people of all attainment levels and should, consequently, be integrated into mainstream schooling. It is noteworthy, moreover, that for two of the three analyses (NEETs and career confidence), experience of one employer contact has a directionally positive association but has too minor an effect to be statistically significant. Instead, the positive association is only identified for the cohort of respondents with two or more employer contacts. A lot of a little does appear to go a long way in helping young people successfully navigate the school-to-work transition.

Notes

1   A broader discussion of the issues discussed in this chapter can be found in Mann and Percy (2013). The authors are grateful to Michael Wagstaff (YouGov) and Ricardo Sabates (University of Sussex) for their support in production of this paper.
2   Direct funding of Education Business Partnership Organisations by the English Department for Education ceased in 2011, with the full costs of engagement being devolved to schools. The decision coincided with the announced repeal of the statutory requirement for work-related learning at key stage 4 in favour of enhanced workplace engagement at 16–19.
3   For full details of sampling methodology, see Mann and Percy (2013). In applicable analyses, weighting is applied to bring the survey respondents' profile of current activity (e.g. in school, in apprenticeship, in full-time work etc.) in line with the applicable Labour Force Survey profile for October–December 2010, of which the main effect is to give extra weight to NEET respondents.
4   The survey responses do not enable a more detailed analysis of NEET status (such as length of time NEET), motivation or planned fixed-period NEET status (such as gap years). Nonetheless, the snapshot of self-reported NEET status at the time of the survey enables some traction on the question. As with all self-reported survey data, no external verification is possible of the responses given by survey participants and misreporting cannot be discounted as a source of data error.
5   Due to sample size restrictions for logistic regression analysis and the need to meet minimum cell size frequency requirements, variables values are grouped into contiguous categories in most instances and the models are run with only a single background control variable. For more details, please contact the authors.
6   See the odds ratio multiplier factors of 2.0–2.7× in the range of point estimates from the earlier models.

7 Interval regression is an ML (maximum likelihood) linear regression technique in which the dependent variable falls into ranges (such as £1,000–£2,000) rather than point values (such as £1,501).

8 In exact figures, for easier comparison to the table, that is £909 per annum, give or take one estimated standard deviation of £410. The 70 per cent confidence interval is based on the 68.2 per cent value of one standard error (assuming an approximately normal distribution of the residuals in the analysis). Given a level of accuracy appropriate to the analysis, figures are rounded.

9 Orr *et al.* (2007) have used statistical analysis to demonstrate the significantly greater experience of employer contacts within Career Academies provision compared to the typical educational experiences of US higher school students.

References

AIR UK. (2008). *The involvement of business in education: a rapid evidence assessment of measurable impacts.* London: Department for Children, Schools and Families.

Applied Research Unit. (2001). *Post-secondary employment and college enrolment among Montgomery County Public School graduates: the role of career-focused programs.* Rockville, MD: Montgomery County Public Schools.

Crawford, C., Duckworth, K., Vignoles, A. and Whyness, G. (2012). *Young people's education and labour market choices aged 16/17 to 18/19.* London: Department for Education.

Green, J. and Rogers B. (1997). Roots and wings community mentoring: an evaluation from the Manchester pilot. *Mentoring & Tutoring: Partnership in Learning,* 5: 26–38.

Huddleston, P. and Stanley, J. (2012). *Work-related teaching and learning – a guide for teachers and practitioners.* London: Routledge.

Ipsos MORI. (2009). *Young people's omnibus 2009 – wave 15. A research study on work-related learning among 11–16 year olds on behalf of the Qualifications and Curriculum Authority.* Coventry: Qualifications and Curriculum Authority.

Jobs for the Future. (1998). *School-to-career initiative demonstrates significant impact on young people.* Boston, MA: Jobs for the Future.

Kemple, J. and Willner, C. J. (2008). *Career Academies – long-term impacts on labour market outcomes, educational attainment, and transitions to adulthood.* New York, NY: MDRC.

MacAullum, K., Yoder, K., Scott, K. and Bozick, R. (2002). *Moving forward – college and career transitions of LAMP graduates – from the LAMP longitudinal study.* Washington, DC: National Institute for Work and Learning.

Mann, A. and Percy C. (2013). Employer engagement in British secondary education: wage earning outcomes experienced by young adults. *Journal of Education and Work,* doi:10.1080/13639080.2013.769671.

Miller, A. (1998). *Business and community mentoring in schools.* London: Department for Education and Employment.

Orr, M. T., Bailey, T., Hughes K. L., Kienzl, G. S. and Karp, M. (2007). The National Academy Foundation's Career Academies: shaping secondary transitions. *In:* D. Neumark, ed. *Improving school-to-work transitions.* New York, NY: Russell Sage Foundation, 169–209.

Qualifications and Curriculum Authority (QCA). (2003). *Work-related learning for all at key stage four – guidance for implementing the statutory requirement from 2004.* Coventry: QCA.

Ruhm, C. (1997). Is high school employment consumption or investment? *Journal of Labour Economics*, 15 (4): 735–776.

Scottish Executive. (2004). *Determined to succeed – enterprise in education*. Edinburgh: Scottish Executive.

Welsh Assembly Government. (2004). *Learning pathways 14–19 guidance*. Cardiff: Welsh Assembly Government.

Welsh Assembly Government. (2008). *Careers and the world of work: a framework for 11 to 19 year olds in Wales*. Cardiff: Welsh Assembly Government.

YouGov. (2010). *EDGE annual programme of stakeholder surveys: report*. London: Edge Foundation.

Chapter 14

Exploring outcomes of youth apprenticeship in Canada

Alison Taylor, Milosh Raykov and Zane Hamm

Introduction

This chapter explores the pathways followed by former high school apprentices in Ontario and Alberta, Canada a few years after leaving school. The impetus for most provincial high school apprenticeship programmes is to address labour shortages in skilled trades; for example, an article in the *Edmonton Journal* suggests that Alberta employers could be short by as many as 70,000 tradespeople by 2020 (Halliday 2012). Educators also see apprenticeship as providing an alternative pathway for youth who may not have stayed in high school to earn a diploma which offers useful work skills that are in high demand.

However, there has been little follow-up of youth apprentices to evaluate the outcomes of such programmes. Our mixed methods research addresses this gap by examining former apprentices' training experiences and training and employment outcomes. Findings suggest that employers play an important role in providing training opportunities and in supporting apprentices' completion of training and advancement in the trade.

Employer engagement in training

International studies show that Canadian employers place less emphasis on training their workers than those in many other countries (Goldenberg 2006). For example, less than 30 per cent of adult workers in Canada participate in job-related education and training, compared to almost 35 per cent in the United Kingdom and nearly 45 per cent in the United States. American firms also spend about 50 per cent more (as a proportion of their payroll) on training than Canadian firms. In addition, worker training in Canada is highly concentrated among younger workers, those with higher education and skill levels and workers in larger firms (Conference Board of Canada 2005; Fortin and Parent 2008; Livingstone and Raykov 2009; Myers and Myles 2005; Rubenson 2007).

Concerns have also been raised about apprenticeship training completion rates, which are seen as related to economic factors, employer practices and to apprentices' backgrounds and behaviours. Completion rates were reported to be 39 per cent in 2002 (Sharpe and Gibson 2005). Some of the employer-related reasons for non-completion are:

- employer reluctance to pay for apprenticeship training because of the potential of poaching by other employers (Compas 2007);
- a lack of jobs and continuous work, especially in downturns and recessions, preventing apprentices from acquiring training credits (Sharpe and Gibson 2005);
- a lack of a training culture on the part of Canadian employers and misconceptions about the costs and benefits of apprenticeships (ITAC 2001); and
- a work environment that may be intimidating, discriminating and unwelcoming, especially for women, in many of the traditional male-dominated trades, as well as for visible minorities, immigrants, Aboriginal persons[1] and disabled persons (CAF 2005; Sweet 2003).

Of course, completion rates are also related to apprentices' backgrounds, attitudes and behaviours. For example, in one of the few Canadian reports about youth apprenticeship, Stone (2005) recommends that realistic expectations of skills and job prospects need to be provided to youth and parents earlier. She adds that some 'inner-city and Aboriginal youth' are dealing with social issues that make it difficult to continue apprenticeship training (Stone 2005: 56).

High school apprenticeship programmes in Alberta and Ontario

Youth transitions from secondary education to working life have become a focus for policymakers in most Organisation for Economic Co-operation and Development (OECD) countries in recent decades. A study of transition systems across 14 countries (OECD 2000) suggested that effective transition systems provide well-organised pathways that connect initial education with work and further study and widespread opportunities to combine workplace experience with education. In Canada, most provinces support a range of secondary school initiatives intended to facilitate youth transitions, particularly for non-college-bound youth, the 'forgotten half' according to a US report by the William T. Grant Foundation (1988). Provincial education departments have encouraged school authorities to make connections between curriculum and labour market destinations more transparent. One way to do this is through experiential learning opportunities, including cooperative education, work experience programmes, internships and high school apprenticeship programmes (Taylor 2007).

High school apprenticeship programmes allow students to work toward their high school diploma and apprenticeship certification at the same time. Attracting younger apprentices may improve apprenticeship completion rates, which have been lower than for other post-secondary options (Sharpe 2003). The Registered Apprenticeship Program (RAP) in Alberta allows students 16 years of age or older to earn credits toward their high school diploma while training in an apprenticeable occupation. The Ontario Youth Apprenticeship Program (OYAP) is similar except that students are not required to register as apprentices with the provincial Apprenticeship Board when they enter the programme.

In both provinces, high school coordinators help students find employers willing to provide on-the-job apprenticeship training, monitor youth in the worksite (e.g. ensuring safety standards are met) and ensure that youth complete both high school and apprenticeship training requirements. Youth usually complete the on-the-job hours required for the first year of their apprenticeship by the time they finish high school.

Our study

Data for this study were drawn from a survey and interviews with young people who participated in a high school-based apprenticeship programme before 2006 (see also Taylor *et al.* 2013). In Ontario, Apprenticeship and Industry Training, the government department responsible for monitoring apprenticeship, mailed an invitation to former youth apprentices to participate in our survey. In Alberta, a private–public foundation called CAREERS: the Next Generation helped us compile a database of former high school apprentices, and participants were also recruited through school district coordinators. In both provinces, an invitation to complete an online survey was sent to former high school apprentices, with an option to provide their contact information if they were willing to be contacted for an interview.

Our unpublished online survey (RAP/OYAP Survey 2010–2011) was completed by 125 former apprentices (68 OYAP, 57 RAP). Additional surveys were completed during the interview phase in Alberta, increasing the number of completed questionnaires to 173 (68 former OYAP and 105 former RAP). Questionnaires asked respondents about their family background, experiences in high school, and training and employment outcomes. We conducted interviews with 56 former apprentices in Alberta and 55 in Ontario. We tried to oversample 'non-traditional apprentices', for example females in male-dominated trades (i.e. trades other than hairstyling) and ethnic minority youth. Interviews, lasting an average of 60 minutes, were conducted in person or by telephone and were fully transcribed.

Findings

Opportunities for youth 'at risk'

The high school completion rate for our survey respondents was 96.4 per cent, which is higher than average. In Alberta (Table 14.1), the percentage of the population aged 20–24 years that was *not* a high school graduate and *not* attending school was 9.5 per cent in 2009/2010 (McMullen and Gilmore 2010), while the

Table 14.1 High school dropout rates (Canada, 20–24 years old)

	Alberta	Ontario	Canada
Provincial/national rates[a]	9.5	7.2	8.5
RAP/OYAP rates[b]	3.9	3	3.6

Sources: RAP/OYAP Survey 2010–2011; McMullen and Gilmore (2010).

Notes

a Percentage of the population (20–24 years old) not a high school graduate and not attending school.

b Not completed high school, average age = 22.4 years.

rate of high school non-completion for RAP apprentices was 3.9 per cent. Similarly, in Ontario the population aged 20–24 years not completing high school was 7.2 per cent while for OYAP apprentices it was only 3 per cent.

We interpret these findings in two ways. First, they are partly a reflection of selection criteria for youth apprenticeship programmes, which often require that students have passing grades, be 'on track' to graduate and have good attendance records. Further, school coordinators generally encourage motivated students who will be seen as good 'ambassadors' for their school to apply to apprenticeship programs (Taylor 2010). However, interviews with a minority of youth (all male) suggest that they may not have completed high school without the apprenticeship programme. For example, a young man who began his electrical apprenticeship in RAP comments:

> I was kind of a rebel in those days. At the end of grade 10, I had ten credits. You need 100 credits to graduate, so it wasn't looking very good for me. I got expelled from [high school] and went to [a different high school that had an apprenticeship program]. I buckled down and heard about the RAP program. I started doing the RAP program and at the end of grade 11, I had 55 credits . . . I had a lot of support from the teachers saying, 'keep up the good work. In two years you got half the amount of credits you need to graduate; you've got to buckle down big time.' So at the end of grade 12, I ended up graduating with 144 credits and two scholarships, one for most improved deserving student and one for my RAP scholarship. **That RAP program saved me**.
>
> (I-1, emphasis added)

Although most other youth in our study note that they would have completed high school with or without RAP, many acknowledged that they did not enjoy high school, partly because they did not feel that schools were open to their learning styles. Like the former high school apprentices in carpentry and auto trades interviewed in a related study (Taylor and Freeman 2011), a high proportion referred to themselves as 'hands on' learners who tolerated schooling but blossomed in a work environment.

A few also acknowledged having learning disabilities, which made high school very challenging. Our survey findings suggest that over half of the youth apprentices who did not complete high school had a learning disability.

For example, one youth, who is currently a third-year apprentice machinist, reflects:

> I went into RAP just because I had a noticeable and visible, very apparent learning disability and I figured that it was concerned with reading, so I probably should pick a career that involves less reading and less school. School is pretty much focused completely around reading skills . . .

> *How was high school for you?*

> High school was difficult because of being in 'learning strategies' [special programme]. I was never a popular kid but I always had lots of friends and did the best I could. High school was okay, it was okay.

> *What was your favourite subject?*

> My favourite subject was art class, obviously. I like to create things. That's another reason I wanted to get into the trades, because I knew I was really creative and I liked working hands on and I liked creating things. That's what tradesmen do, really . . .

> *How would you describe yourself as a learner?*

> I would say practically, on the field, I have to pick it up as I'm doing it. I'm an awesome learner. I'd say I pick things up quick and I remember things. I'm smart when it comes to learning new tasks and remembering new tasks, then progressively learning about them and improving on them. I would say I'm great in a hands-on environment. As far as a non-hands on environment goes, not very good.

> (I-49)

Our surveys of former youth apprentices also found that almost one-quarter was female, which is higher than the proportion of females in trades in Canada overall. In 2007, women made up 11 per cent of individuals who completed an apprenticeship training programme and most of these were in the 'food and services' trade group, which includes the female-dominated trade of hairstylist (McMullen *et al.* 2010). In other major trade groups, women made up only 1 per cent of completions (Skof 2010). In our survey sample, nine females (20 per cent) were in hairstyling trades and the others were in male-dominated trades.

This finding suggests that high school trades programmes are succeeding in attracting some non-traditional entrants who might not otherwise consider a trade.

Further, 43.4 per cent of former youth apprentices surveyed admitted that they had no contacts in the trades prior to entering the programme. Programmes therefore provide opportunities for some youth who lack social capital.

Initial outcomes for youth

In his longitudinal study of apprenticeship completion in Canada, Prasil (2005: 16) notes that the term 'completion' needs to be clarified because it may refer to those who complete 'on-the-job' training, 'in-class' training or both. Further, apprentices may complete both of these and not have written the certification exam, and individuals may write the certification exam without having been registered as apprentices.

According to our survey data, 42.8 per cent of youth respondents had attained a trade certificate or qualification. Overall, 44.7 per cent said they had completed apprenticeship training and 26.5 per cent were still apprenticing. While apprenticeship completion rates overall in Canada vary by trade, Sharpe and Gibson (2005) suggest that the overall rate in 2002 was 38.8 per cent,[2] which is lower than the certification and completion rates for our youth apprentices. Further, we can expect that the youth rate will continue to increase because we are considering completion at a very early stage, whereas large-scale studies indicate that most apprentices take longer than the expected training period to obtain certification. For example, a longitudinal study following a cohort of registered apprentices from 1992 until 2002 found that 11 years after registering, only about half of the apprentices had completed the trade they had started, between 5 and 12 per cent were still continuing and the remainder had dropped out (Prasil 2005).

Our interviews suggest that most youth who are still apprenticing are making good progress and are very likely to attain certification. Also, as Table 14.2 shows, a significant number of RAP/OYAP students attained a college certificate or diploma (28.2 per cent) or university degree (2.4 per cent).

There are factors working for and against higher completion rates among young apprentices. Factors encouraging higher rates include the fact that youth tend to find the 'in-class' apprenticeship training easier because their formal schooling is more recent, and they often complete their training before they have family responsibilities, which may make it more difficult for them to meet the

Table 14.2 Highest level of educational attainment

Educational attainment	%
Less than high school	1.2
High school	34.7
Trade certificate of qualification	33.5
College certificate or diploma	28.2
University degree	2.4

Source: RAP/OYAP Survey 2010–2011.

costs required to take the 'in-class' training. Many of the youth surveyed were at least partly supported by parents. But on the other hand, we might expect lower completion rates from youth apprentices who are less certain about career pathways, have less work experience in trades and are often in an exploratory phase with respect to career interests.

Analysis of our survey data also reveals workplace and labour market factors that are related to higher completion rates (see also Taylor *et al.* 2011). For example, youth who had more stable work (i.e. worked at one or two as opposed to over five companies) were more likely to complete their training. Related to this, youth who had lower earnings and hours of work were less likely to obtain certification.[3]

Furthermore, finding the best match for youth apprentices initially and ensuring that employers support training is very important. Our interviews suggest that a number of youth had experienced poor training practices and some took action to change their situation, as suggested in the following comments:

Why did you leave your last job?

It's partially because they were expecting more than what I could produce as an apprentice . . . everybody's just there to make money. They don't really want to help you.

(I-4 mechanic)

This fourth-year apprentice adds that his previous employer (a car dealership) paid piece-work rates, did not provide adequate supervision and did not provide opportunities for him to complete his 'in-class' training. When we asked another apprentice what was important in a job, he similarly responded:

Opportunity to learn, that's big. I quit a couple of places because there just was no opportunity.

(I-49 millwright)

Learning opportunities were related to having a willing and knowledgeable mentor on the job site, having opportunities to develop new knowledge and skills, and being supported in completing 'in-class' portions of the apprenticeship training.

Unfortunately, some youth left the trade when they did not experience the learning environment they sought and/or if the culture of the trade and workplace were not as expected. For example:

[Apprenticing as a chef] is not as glamorous as people think. You make no money . . . until you've worked in the industry for 10 or 20 years . . . There's a lot of drugs in that trade too, ridiculous amount of drugs . . . When I was 18, I drank enough and partied enough for the rest of my life . . . Every night we'd go out and then we'd wake up in two hours and go back to work. That was the lifestyle . . .

Do you think franchise restaurants are good places for students?

No, they're not. It's money, just a way to get money. If you want to learn, don't go to a franchise restaurant.

(I-31 youth not in trade)

Other youth discontinued their apprenticeship because they could not find stable work:

> I'm in the Bachelor of Commerce program [in college]. I worked several jobs after high school, not actually in the heavy equipment technician trade at all . . . the kinds of jobs I was getting weren't enough to pay the bills, so I needed to head in a different direction . . . that's why I'm at college.

(I-43)

Upward mobility?

The rate of high school non-completion (Table 14.3) for youth apprentices according to our survey data (3.6 per cent) is lower than for their mothers (7.0 per cent) and fathers (16.4 per cent). Therefore, many youth apprentices have already surpassed their parents' educational attainment. Although it is difficult to attribute this improvement to high school apprenticeship programmes, given the increase in high school completion rates generally over time, it does refute the idea of such vocational programmes as instruments of social reproduction (cf. Petherbridge 1997). However, further tracking of former apprentices would be needed to determine whether or not high school programmes offer an avenue of social mobility for youth (Crompton 1998; Wanner 2004).

Data from our interviews confirm that former youth apprentices are aware of the importance of a high school diploma and certification for future employability. For example, when asked how important trade certification was to him, this fourth-year welding apprentice replied:

> You can have a nice plaque hanging in your house so you know you're not just a high school dropout. I think you should finish high school – that's my view too. In this day and age you can't just drop out and expect to go anywhere fast. It's common knowledge that employers would rather hire a person with credentials over no credentials.

(I-50)

In fact, this youth was planning to pursue multiple trade tickets, moving from welding to pipefitting and then millwright. He comments, 'if an employer sees [multiple trade tickets] on your résumé it'll definitely give you a way better chance at a job, especially in a recession.' Some family occupations were also seen as unsustainable; for example, a number of youth from farm backgrounds (who

Table 14.3 High school dropout rate among RAP/OYAP
participants and their parents

	%
RAP/OYAP participants	3.6
Participants' mothers	7.0
Participants' fathers	16.4

Source: RAP/OYAP Survey 2010–2011.

made up almost 7 per cent of our RAP survey sample) indicated that although
they would like to farm in the future, other waged labour was also necessary.

Our survey data suggest that many former apprentices were planning further
education (see Table 14.4). While just over one-third (33.5 per cent) of former
youth apprentices aspired to trade certification as their highest level of education,
and almost one-quarter (23.4 per cent) are not sure about enrolling in further
education, one-fifth aspired to obtain college qualification (19.8 per cent) and
almost one-quarter (23.4 per cent) aspired to university certification.

Comparing respondents' aspirations to continue their education to parents' educational attainment (as reported by youth), we see that almost two-thirds of apprentices were aiming higher than their mothers' and fathers' attainment (Table 14.5).

In particular, young women who were former youth apprentices were likely to
aspire to attain other forms of post-secondary education. For example, two of the

Table 14.4 Aspirations of former apprentices

	%	% (excluding 'do not know')
Trade certificate	33.5	43.8
College	19.8	25.8
University degree	23.4	30.5
Do not know	23.4	

Source: AP/OYAP Survey 2010–2011.

Table 14.5 Educational aspirations compared to parents'
educational attainment

	Less (%)	Same (%)	More (%)
Educational aspirations compared to father's educational attainment	19.0	15.7	65.3
Educational aspirations compared to mother's educational attainment	26.4	9.1	64.5

Source: RAP/OYAP Survey 2010–2011.

young women we interviewed in non-traditional trades saw RAP as a 'back-up plan', to provide the financial security to pursue other goals. One comments:

> I wanted to go into nursing but I wanted that as my back-up plan, my trade. I know nursing or any course at university is really expensive, so I figured as long as I have a trade I can always work at it and have money.

> *So you would have to pay your own way through university?*

> Yeah, of course. I paid for my own way through trade school as well, with the exception of my second year. My employer paid for school the second year.
> (I-15 certified parts technician)

One reason young women in male-dominated trades do not see them as a long-term career is because they do not see the working conditions associated with trades work (e.g. long shifts, travel time to job sites, expected overtime) as conducive to future roles related to marriage and families. For example, a young woman working in the oil and gas sector muses, 'Hopefully by the time I plan on having children ... I will already have something else under my belt besides being a journeyman instrument tech' (I-13). She is already looking at 'what else can I do' in her workplace and is heartened by the fact that there are a few females in management positions in her company.

While the aspirations of males are not as high as those of females and tend to remain linked to trades, a number of interview participants aimed to move from trades into managerial positions or to own their own businesses – they did not see trades work as an endpoint, probably unlike their parents' generation. For example:

> *Where do you see yourself in five years?*

> Working as a journeyman. I'll still be working in the trade and maybe starting to go into the management process through [name of company].

> *Could you become a manager of a franchise?*

> Yes. There's something like 300 [franchises] across Canada.

> *Could you own a franchise?*

> It's not so much you own them, you just manage one and then you can work up to being provincial manager in western Canada. I'd probably go to something like an assistant manager. I could oversee the mechanical side of things.
> (I-4 fourth-year apprentice mechanic)

Because of the high growth economy in the oil and gas sector in Alberta, the youth were also entrepreneurial:

> I've got a couple of buddies whose dads started oilfield companies, that kind of stuff, self-made millionaires.

What are your goals for the next five years?

I'd like to start a business, for sure. I'm just firing up a little oilfield rental company right now, trying to rent out tanks and rig matting and that kind of stuff.

(I-20 second-year heavy-duty mechanic)

In sum, the interview data suggest that former youth apprentices in Alberta, like other Canadian youth, have high aspirations in terms of further education and careers, but also that gender plays a role in these aspirations.

Fostering positive outcomes for youth

The preceding discussion suggests that former youth apprentices are generally doing well – most completed a high school diploma and many are aiming higher than their parents in terms of education and careers. This is consistent with a survey of 15-year-olds and their parents in schools across Canada in 2000, which found that 61 per cent of youth expected to get at least one university degree (Krahn and Taylor 2005). However, our findings also suggest that if programmes actually want to foster social mobility for youth 'at risk' and for non-traditional apprentices (e.g. women in male-dominated trades), they need to actively recruit these youth and provide additional support. Youth who were at risk of dropping out of high school were under-represented in our study, which is not surprising given that most schools require youth to be on track to graduate in order to participate in apprenticeship. In fact, our interview data suggest that over half (excluding those who 'do not know') aspired to achieve more than apprenticeship certification (see Table 14.4).

Support for apprentices requires ensuring that youth know as much as possible about their chosen trade and career path, as suggested by Stone (2005), and building effective partnerships between schools, training centres and workplaces. However, apprentices tend to lack adequate career information prior to entering apprenticeship programmes, and most learned about their chosen trade after they began their placement. The former chef cited earlier is a good example of lack of awareness regarding working conditions, workplace culture and learning opportunities. Part of ensuring that youth are making informed decisions involves providing labour market information about employment rates, earnings, apprenticeship completion rates and opportunities for advancement in different trades, as well as information about the workplace culture of different trades.

While there tends to be a great deal of policy focus on preparing youth for the workplace, there is also arguably a need to prepare workplaces for young workers. A few youth spoke about poor training practices, including lack of mentorship, limited opportunities to develop knowledge and skills and a lack of opportunities to complete in-class apprenticeship training. Such feedback should inform school coordinators' practices, with the goal of ensuring that participating employers are committed to supporting and training youth and that there is a strong learning culture. Employer engagement in apprenticeship training is admittedly a problem and the challenges of school–business partnership are often underestimated (Taylor 2006). However, our survey data, suggesting a strong inverse relationship between the number of companies youth have worked at since high school and their completion of apprenticeship training, imply that trying to increase job tenure (e.g. by more careful initial matching of youth to training placements) would improve youth outcomes.

Finally, our interview data suggest that some youth left their apprenticeship and pursued other forms of post-secondary education because they did not see possibilities to keep learning and advancing in trades. For example, a young man who was a RAP electrician in high school but then decided to pursue an engineering degree at university admits that his knowledge of the trade has helped him in his work and that much of his current engineering knowledge has been learned on the job:

> University is more kind of a hoop, I guess, that you jump through. I don't need my current education for this job, but I wouldn't have this job if I didn't have that. Most companies figure if you can get through four years of university you can get through anything.
>
> (I-27)

However, this participant felt he had to choose between an electrical engineering degree and an electrical trade, largely because of the lack of articulation between these post-secondary programmes. Thus, if the goal is truly to increase social mobility, greater articulation between trades and 'professional' vocational pathways is also needed.

Conclusion

In sum, while our study suggests that outcomes for most youth apprentices have been positive, more could be done to attract and retain youth 'at risk' if we are to take seriously the goal of improving high school completion rates. Our data suggest that enrolling in apprenticeship programmes while in high school appears to improve training completion rates and many youth are surpassing the educational and occupational levels of their parents. For a small minority, enrolling in high school apprenticeships was important for them to graduate. In addition, programmes provide employment opportunities for many youth who lack contacts in trades.

However, some youth felt unsupported in their apprenticeship training and either changed jobs or left the trade. Supporting youth involves ensuring that the workplace is receptive to young learners and that youth are adequately informed about trades careers (including working conditions and workplace culture) so that their expectations are realistic. The initial matching of a youth to an apprenticeship placement requires deliberation and care because it greatly affects outcomes. In addition, youth need to be encouraged to engage in self-advocacy when they are not provided with the necessary opportunities to learn. Youth who take ownership of their training (as opposed to leaving it to employers) tend to have better outcomes. Finally, greater articulation between trades and other post-secondary education pathways would attract a wider range of youth to apprenticeship.

Acknowledgments

We gratefully acknowledge funding for this study provided by the Social Sciences and Humanities Research Council of Canada.

Notes

1 The category 'Aboriginal' includes First Nations, Metis and Inuit groups.
2 Sharpe and Gibson (2005) note the difficulty in measuring apprenticeship completion, noting that rates are constructed based on the aggregate data available in order to estimate the share of registered apprentices who receive their certification.
3 Recession has been found to influence employment of apprentices more than other occupations (Desjardins 2011).

References

Canadian Apprenticeship Forum (CAF). (2005). *Accessing and completing apprenticeship training in Canada: perceptions of barriers.* Ottowa, ON: CAF.

Compas. (2007). *What are the desirable characteristics of a well-functioning apprenticeship system?* Prepared by Compas for Human Resources and Skills Development Canada.

Conference Board of Canada. (2005). *Changing employers' behavior about training.* Issue statement. Ottawa, ON: Conference Board of Canada.

Crompton, R. (1998). *Class and stratification: an introduction to current debates.* 2nd ed. Cambridge, UK: Polity Press.

Desjardins, L. (2011). Apprenticeable occupations and the economic downturn in Canada. *Statistics Canada, The Daily.* Available from: www.statcan.gc.ca/daily-quotidien/110224/dq110224b-eng.htm [accessed 10 January 2013].

Fortin, N. and Parent, D. (2008). *Employee training in Canada.* CLSRN Working Paper No. 3. Vancouver, BC: Canadian Labour Market and Skills Researcher Network. Available from: www.clsrn.econ.ubc.ca/workingpapers.php [accessed 3 January 2013].

Goldenberg, M. (2006). *Employer investment in workplace learning in Canada.* Prepared for Canadian Council of Learning by Canadian Policy Research Networks (CPRN). Ottawa, ON: CPRN.

Halliday, D. (2012). Careers: the next generation promotes trades careers to youth in Alberta: non-profit organization tackles skilled labour shortage. *Edmonton Journal.* Available from: www2.canada.com/edmontonjournal/news/story.html?id=4f5170a5-eb70-473f-8076-39bcbce6b12c [accessed 30 January 2014].

Industry Training and Apprenticeship Commission of BC (ITAC). (2001). *Ensuring a skilled workforce for BC: a report to stimulate joint action on trades and technical skill shortages.* Burnaby, BC: ITAC.

Krahn, H. and Taylor, A. (2005). Resilient teenagers: explaining the high educational aspirations of visible minority immigrant youth in Canada. *Journal of International Migration and Integration*, 6 (3/4): 405–434.

Livingstone, D. W. and Raykov, M. (2009). Education and jobs survey profiles I: national trends in employment conditions, job requirements, workers' learning and matching, 1983–2004. *In:* D. W. Livingstone, ed. *Education and jobs: exploring the gaps.* Toronto: University of Toronto Press, 67–102.

McMullen, K. and Gilmore, J. (2010). A note on high school graduation and school attendance, by age and province. *Education Matters.* Statistics Canada Catalogue No. 81-004-X201000411360. Available from: www.statcan.gc.ca/pub/81-004-x/2010004/article/11360-eng.htm [accessed 23 July 2011].

McMullen, K., Gilmore, J. and Le Petit, C. (2010). Women in non-traditional occupations and fields of study. *Education Matters,* 7 (1). Statistics Canada Catalogue No. 81-004-X. Available from: www.statcan.gc.ca/pub/81-004-x/2010001/article/11151-eng.htm [accessed 9 October 2011].

Myers, K. and Myles, J. (2005). *Self-assessed returns to adult education: life-long learning and the educationally disadvantaged.* CPRN Research Report W|35. Ottawa, ON: CPRN.

Organisation for Economic Co-operation Development (OECD). (2000). *From initial education to working life: making transitions work.* Paris: OECD.

Petherbridge, J. (1997). Work experience: making an impression. *Educational Review,* 49 (1): 21–27.

Prasil, S. (2005). *Registered apprentices: the class of 1992, a decade later.* Research Paper. Statistics Canada Catalogue No. 81-595-MIE, No. 035. Available from: www5.statcan.gc.ca/bsolc/olc-cel/olc-cel?catno=81-595-MIE2005035&lang=eng [accessed 30 January 2014].

Rubenson, K. (2007). *Determinants of formal and informal Canadian adult learning: insights from the adult education and training surveys.* Gatineau, QC: Human Resources and Social Development Canada.

Sharpe, A. (2003). Apprenticeship in Canada: a training system under siege? *In:* H. Schuetze and R. Sweet, eds. *Integrating school and workplace learning in Canada.* Montreal, QC: McGill-Queens University Press, 243–259.

Sharpe, A. and Gibson, J. (2005). *The apprenticeship system in Canada: trends and issues.* Prepared by the Centre for the Study of Living Standards (CSLS) for the Micro-economic Policy Analysis Branch, Industry Canada. Ottawa, ON: CSLS.

Skof, K. (2010). Trends in the trades: registered apprenticeship registrations, completions and certification, 1991 to 2007. *Education Matters,* 6 (6), Statistics Canada Catalogue No. 81-004-X. Available from: www.statcan.gc.ca/pub/81-004-x/2009006/article/11127-eng.htm [accessed 9 October 2011].

Stone, J. (2005). *Seeking opportunity, respect, and good pay: school-to-apprenticeship programs in Canada.* Research Paper No. 36, prepared for Canadian Labour Congress. Ottawa, ON: Canadian Labour Congress.

Sweet, R. (2003). Women and apprenticeships: the role of personal agency in transition success. *In:* H. Schuetze and R. Sweet, eds. *Integrating school and workplace learning in Canada.* Montreal, QC: McGill-Queens University Press, 260–275.

Taylor, A. (2006). The challenges of partnership in school–work transition. *Journal of Vocational Education and Training,* 58 (3): 319–336.

Taylor, A. (2007). *Pathways for youth to the labour market: an overview of high school initiatives.* Prepared for Canadian Policy Research Networks. Ottawa, ON: CPRN.

Taylor, A. (2010). The contradictory location of high school apprenticeship. *Journal of Education Policy*, 25 (4): 503–517.

Taylor, A. and Freeman, S. (2011). Made in the trade: youth attitudes toward apprenticeship certification. *Journal of Vocational Education and Training*, 63 (3): 345–362.

Taylor, A., Lehmann, W. and Hamm, Z. (2011). *Tracking the experiences and outcomes of high school apprentices.* Paper presented at JVET conference, Oxford, UK.

Taylor, A., Lehmann, W., Raykov, M. and Hamm, Z. (2013). *High school apprenticeships: experiences and outcomes.* Research report for Government of Ontario and CAREERS. Edmonton, AB: Educational Policy Studies, Faculty of Education, University of Alberta.

Wanner, R. (2004). Social mobility in Canada: concepts, patterns and trends. *In:* J. Curtis, E. Grabb and N. Guppy, eds. *Social inequality in Canada: patterns, problems and policies.* 4th ed. Toronto, ON: Pearson, 131–147.

William T. Grant Foundation. (1988). *The forgotten half: non-college youth in America.* Washington, DC: William T. Grant Foundation Commission on Work, Family and Citizenship.

Chapter 15

Work experience

The economic case for employers

David Massey

Work experience is a vital part of the transition from education into work. Lack of experience is the number one concern of British employers who have recruited young people but found them poorly prepared and the main reason employers turn away young applicants. This chapter will explore the importance of work experience to the individual but also evidence of the value that employers derive from offering more work experience, and barriers to its provision.

The UK Commission for Employment and Skills (UKCES) is a publicly funded, industry-led organisation providing strategic leadership on skills and employment issues in the four home nations of the United Kingdom. As part of its role, the UKCES carries out large-scale research and analysis of the UK labour market and a consistent theme in this analysis is the considerable premium that employers place on experience when recruiting. Every other spring, the UKCES carries out the Employer Perspectives Survey[1] across 15,000 employers.[2] This survey is designed to be representative across all sizes of employers,[3] sectors (public and private) and nations and regions of the United Kingdom. In the 2010 spring survey, 29 per cent of recruiting employers said that experience is 'critical' and a further 45 per cent said that it is 'significant'. The importance of work experience is also consistently noted across a range of employer representative bodies in the United Kingdom, such as the Confederation of British Industry (CBI 2011).

The UK Commission's largest employer survey has a sample size of around 90,000 establishments UK-wide, making it one of the largest and most comprehensive of its kind in the world. This Employer Skills Survey (ESS) provides detailed information at a sectoral and spatial level on the nature of recruitment and skills. In particular, it provides insights into which employers are struggling with skills gaps for their current staff and which are finding it difficult to recruit because of a lack of skills and/or experience among job applicants. It also provides a wealth of information on employers' views of the young people they have recruited into their first job upon leaving education, whether from school, college or university.

The most recent results from an Employer Skills Survey are from spring 2011.[4] This survey found that while only a minority of British employers (24 per cent) had actually recruited a young person directly from education in the previous two to three years, the majority of those doing so found their new recruits well or very well prepared for work. Of those employers taking on graduates, 82 per cent found them well or very well prepared for work. This falls to 73 per cent for those taking on 17/18-year-old college leavers, 64 per cent of those taking on 17/18-year-old school leavers and 59 per cent of those employers taking on 16-year-old school leavers.

While the majority of employers are satisfied with their young recruits, a not insignificant minority are not. The Employer Skills Survey sheds light on why this is by asking employers why they find new recruits to be poorly prepared. The overwhelming factor is experience. Of all the employers who have taken on a 16-year-old school leaver, 23 per cent found them to lack experience, making this the single most common reason cited. By contrast, just 5 per cent cited literacy or numeracy as the issues (UKCES 2012). Similar results are found for people leaving college and university, although to a lesser extent.

There is a potential flaw in this analysis, however. The strength of the ESS is that it distinguishes between those employers who have recruited a young person and those who have not. This means that we can be more certain that employers' views reflect their own direct experience of recruiting young people as opposed to views based on negative media coverage, for example. These findings do, however, raise the question that, if so few employers recruit young people at all, might the reason be that many candidates simply aren't good enough?

This question was explored in the spring 2012 Employer Perspectives Survey by asking recruiting employers, i.e. those who had recruited someone in the previous 12 months, why they hadn't recruited a young person, if indeed they had not. The most common reason was that no young people applied for their vacancies; this reason was given by 40 per cent of those employers who had only taken on adults. However, for those who had young people apply, the main reason they were not successful was lack of experience. This was given by 29 per cent of those employers who had recruited adults only (UKCES 2013a).

Teenage part-time employment

These survey findings show that the importance of work experience to employers when recruiting cannot be understated and, as would be expected, the impact of experience of the workplace on the labour market outcomes of young people later on are clear. In December 2011, the Department for Education (DfE) published research (Crawford *et al.* 2011) that used the Labour Force Survey[5] and the Longitudinal Survey of Young People in England (LSYPE)[6] to look at how transitions into work varied for different groups of young people. This research found that young learners who combined work with their studies at age 16 and/or 17 were more likely to be in work later on and earn more than those who did not.[7]

The longitudinal data allowed the researchers to compare the status of learners at age 16/17 with their status when they were 18/19 and beyond. They compared a variety of different statuses, including full-time education, full-time education and work, part-time education and work, full- or part-time combined with and without training and NEET (Not in Education, Employment or Training). The group that had the lowest chance of being NEET at 18/19 was the group that combined work and learning at age 16/17 (7 per cent compared to 16 per cent for the sample as a whole). This result was also confirmed using multivariate regression analysis that controlled for a rich and varied range of factors. The research controlled for characteristics of the individual themselves, such as gender, ethnicity and attainment, alongside family characteristics, such as social class, parental level of education and income, and those of the local labour market, such as levels of deprivation and rurality.

However, recent trends in young people's working patterns suggest that when they do enter the labour market full-time, they do so increasingly with less experience. The share of full-time British teenage learners who combine work and learning has been declining for some time. The share of full-time learners at age 16/17 who combine work with their studies has fallen from 40 per cent in the late 1990s to around 20 per cent in the final quarter of 2012. The decline for 18–24-year-olds is less dramatic, falling from 40 per cent in 2006 to around 35 per cent in the final quarter of 2012. There is also a gender dimension to this trend, with young female learners much more likely to combine work and learning across both age groups. For 16- and 17-year-olds, 15 per cent of male full-time learners also work compared to 24 per cent of female full-time learners. For the 18–24-year-olds, the equivalent figures are 27 per cent and 37 per cent, respectively.[8]

This decline was widely reported in the British media as the 'Death of the Saturday job' and, given the importance that employers place on experience when recruiting, it cuts off a significant source of experience for young people making their transition into the labour market. This reduction in the combination of paid part-time work and learning is part of a broader and long-term structural change in the labour market (UKCES 2012). The UKCES Employer Perspectives Survey in 2012 asked employers who hadn't provided work experience placements to young people in education why they hadn't, and the largest single response, given by 37 per cent of this cohort, was that they 'had no suitable roles'. In her review of vocational education in England, Alison Wolf described the 'disappearing youth labour market', and there are indeed structural changes afoot, which mean that the actual occupations available are also changing. Many of the sorts of jobs that young people used to do are no longer required and the ones that are available are increasingly contested by older and more experienced workers. This in turn has an impact on the work experience provided to young people by their educational institutions as a means of enabling access to comparable workplace experiences (Fullarton 1999).

The new work experience

This reduction in combining work with education throws into sharp relief the importance of work experience undertaken while at school, college or university.

This in turn leads to the question of whether there are sufficient work experience opportunities available for young people to make a successful transition. Given the premium attached to work experience and persistent problems with youth employment, there is a need to improve access to work experience.

The level of work experience provided currently is significant; estimates by the Education and Employers Taskforce (EET) suggest that there were typically around half a million work experience placements per year over the last decade (Mann 2012). However, the focus of government policy on work experience in England has shifted recently. Between 2004 and 2010, the government had a policy of requiring 'work-related learning' for all 14–16-year-olds in England. The formal definition of work-related learning was 'Planned activity that uses the context of work to develop knowledge, skills and understanding useful in work, including learning through the experience of work, learning about work and working practices, and learning the skills for work' (DCSF 2009). This encapsulated a broad range of activities, including, but not limited to, work experience placements with an employer.

Reflecting the increase in the education participation age from 16 to 18 and concerns around the value of providing work experience to 14–16-year-olds, this requirement on schools to provide work-related learning to 14–16-year-olds has been removed (Wolf 2011). However, current government policy does continue to stress the importance of work experience, albeit with an emphasis on a different age cohort. From September 2013, the English Department for Education introduced new study programmes for 16–19-year-olds, and schools and colleges will be expected to deliver high-quality and meaningful work experience. The government's definition of meaningful work experience is as follows:[9]

- Purposeful, substantial, offers challenge and is relevant to the young persons' study programme and/or career aspirations.
- It is managed well under the direction of a supervisor in order to ensure that the student obtains a genuine learning experience suited to their needs.
- It ensures that time is well spent: the employer has prepared a structured plan for the duration of the work placement that provides tangible outcomes for the student and employer.
- It provides up-front clarity about the roles, responsibilities and the expectations of the student and employer.
- It is reviewed at the end: the employer provides some form of reference or feedback based on the young person's performance during their time on the work placement.

Both young people and teachers recognise the demand for more work experience opportunities. Research by YouGov carried out for the Edge Foundation in 2010 showed that half of those aged 14 and above would like more opportunities to gain work experience (YouGov 2010). In addition, the research showed that there is considerable demand for a much broader range of activities that includes full-time placements alongside workplace visits, careers advice from employers and mock interviews. This same research showed that half of all teachers believe that their students have insufficient opportunities to experience the workplace.

In summary, employers think that experience is vital when recruiting; young people and teachers alike want more opportunities; and it is a clear aim of government policy (in England). However, establishing more high-quality work experience opportunities is contingent on employers engaging with education and supplying the places. Consequently, the rest of this chapter looks at employers currently offering work experience placements, the benefits they derive and some of the barriers to getting more employers involved.

The supply of work experience placements

The spring 2012 UKCES Employer Perspectives Survey included a variety of questions on work experience placements, which allows consideration of the issue from the employer perspective. These data show which employers offer work experience and, for those who don't, the reasons why not.

In 2012, just over a quarter (27 per cent) of establishments said that they had offered some form of work experience placement in the previous 12 months. This equates to 465,000 establishments across the United Kingdom. The largest share of establishments offered work experience to those in schools (18 per cent), followed by college (9 per cent), university (7 per cent) and other schemes such as programmes for unemployed people.

The likelihood of offering work experience varies significantly by a range of employer characteristics. The major factors associated with offering work experience are size and sector. The larger the establishment, the more likely they are to offer work experience, to the point where the vast majority of the largest establishments offer it. In terms of sectors, there is a clear public, private and third-sector divide, with predominantly public sectors like education and health dominating. In the education sector, over 60 per cent of employers offer work experience; but in the construction sector, it falls to just 15 per cent (see Table 15.1).

Interestingly, there doesn't seem to be much relationship between employers offering work experience and recruiting young people more generally. In particular, the hotels and restaurants sector is far less likely to provide work experience while at the same time being the most youth-friendly recruiter.

To persuade more employers to get involved in work experience, it is useful to understand the reasons why employers do provide work experience and the value that can be derived from it. The UK Commission's Employer Perspectives Survey also provides the reasons that employers give for offering work experience. The overwhelming reason, given by just over half (53 per cent) of employers who offer it, is simply that it provides the experience young people need. This means that most employers who offer work experience do so because they recognise its intrinsic value: that it's a good thing and necessary for a successful transition into work.

Table 15.1 Proportion of employers offering work experience and recruiting young people by industry sector in 2012 (values in per cent)[a]

	(1) Share offering work experience placements	*(2) Share recruiting 16–18-year-olds*	*(3) Share recruiting 19–24-year-olds*	*(4) Share recruiting 16–24-year-olds*
Hotels and restaurants	17	45	73	84
Agriculture	21	34	51	79
Wholesale/retail	24	32	54	67
Community/social	39	29	51	65
Financial services	20	13	59	63
Health and social work	50	16	57	62
Transport/comms	25	18	50	58
Education	63	20	51	58
Construction	15	19	44	55
Manufacturing	19	21	47	55
Business services	28	13	48	54

Source: UKCES (2013a).

Note

a The base for column 1 is all employers; for columns, 2, 3 and 4 the base is all employers who have recruited in the previous 12 months.

Just under half (45 per cent) of employers who offer work experience are explicit about moral or Corporate Social Responsibility (CSR) reasons. These employers see work experience as a social good, benefitting their business and the young people involved, but also the community they work in. However, the business benefits of a CSR-driven approach should not be underestimated. Emerging research describes the existence of what might be described as savvy employers acutely aware of their customers' preferences. The ethos of such companies, the way they conduct their business and, in particular, their recruitment practices, are all viewed as increasingly important to business success. So if customers, especially young customers, see businesses offering work experience or indeed any kind of opportunity for young people to get into work, they will be more likely to 'approve' of and spend money on such businesses (Burston-Marsteller 2010).

A fifth (20 per cent) of employers who offer work experience do so because it helps them with recruitment. In fact, more employers have actually recruited young people from their work experience placement than the 20 per cent who said it helped them recruit: 22 per cent of employers take people on straight after the work experience placement, and a further 15 per cent recruit young people once they have finished their course. The likelihood of this happening increases with size, with the vast majority of the largest establishments (over 80 per cent) taking people on from work experience. Predominantly public sectors, such as education and health, are also particularly likely to recruit from work experience, with just over half of employers in these sectors doing so. This reflects the usefulness of work experience as a talent pipeline: taking young people on work experience builds employers a ready-made talent pool from which to recruit when the business need arises.

It is important to bear in mind the distinction between the reason an employer gets involved in work experience and the total benefits they derive. Many of the benefits are clearly evident to employers, for example helping recruitment, but others are more subtle, such as the effect on staff morale. A 2012 review of available evidence by the National Foundation for Educational Research (NFER) found the business case for employer engagement to range across six broad areas (Burge *et al.* 2012):

1   Recruitment opportunities

- Attract and retain employees by demonstrating corporate social responsibility
- Gains from larger pool of skilled employees
- Raising awareness of the industry
- Opportunity to interact with and attract potential employees
- An investment in future workforce

2   Improved skills base

- Employers can help education sector understand what candidates need to demonstrate
- Employers can recruit in areas of skill shortages
- Adding value to the growth of local industry

3   Philanthropic gains

- An awareness of challenges facing schools
- Providing input into education
- Supporting the development of a literate workforce
- Direct opportunity to give back to community by supporting young people

4   Staff development

- Employees benefit professionally through volunteer activity
- Encourages staff to rethink and challenge their existing practices, improving productivity

5   Staff morale

- Contributing to development of young people improves staff morale, motivation, self-esteem, job satisfaction and commitment to a company
- Personal satisfaction as apprentice/trainee learns and transitions to worker

6   Reputation benefits

- Improved community profile, promotional opportunities and being seen to be a socially responsible company.

In terms of recruitment imperatives, it is useful to distinguish between short-term requirements (as discussed earlier) and longer-term, strategic employer objectives. Some industries complain of long-term skills gaps and an ongoing struggle to attract new entrants to their industry. Establishing a long-term strategic relationship with educational establishments allows employers and, indeed, entire industries, to not just fill their current recruitment needs but establish an ongoing pipeline of talent for the future. An example of this kind of activity is that carried out by the UK organisation STEMNET, which creates opportunities to inspire young people in science, technology and maths, broadening awareness and encouraging educational choices of relevance to employers operating in the industry.

Beyond recruitment, there are clear benefits to employers in terms of developing their existing staff, which, although apparent, do not seem to be part of the reason employers give for providing work experience. There does, however, appear to be a strong basis for assuming that employer engagement with education generally does have tangible positive impacts on the staff development of volunteers. The 2010 Corporate Citizenship assessment of the development impact of volunteer participation in activities, such as literacy/numeracy support, enterprise workshops, business mentoring or acting as a school governor, explores the experiences of 546 employee volunteers and 31 line managers across 16 large private sector businesses. It found that

> ... for those companies seeking to develop core competencies – such as communication skills; influencing and negotiation skills; and planning and organisational skills – the cost of doing so through volunteering assignments is certainly no more expensive than traditional approaches to training and development, and might be considerably less.
>
> (Corporate Citizenship 2010: 85)

Barriers to supply

This evidence suggests that there are strong benefits to employers of offering work experience and engaging with education. If this is the case, what are the barriers to offering work experience? The chances of offering work experience are tied to overall economic conditions, particularly employer expectations of growth. The UKCES Employer Perspectives Survey shows that those employers who expect to grow significantly in the next year are far more likely to have had someone on work experience (28 per cent) compared to those who expect to contract (19 per cent) or possibly shut down (17 per cent). Similarly, those employers who have had a vacancy in the previous 12 months (34 per cent) are much more likely to have taken someone on work experience than those who have not recruited (21 per cent). This again suggests that work experience is far more important for recruiting than other evidence presented here might suggest.

However, it also suggests that until economic growth and recruitment activity improves significantly, there is likely to be limited scope for increasing the volume of work experience opportunities. According to the Office for National Statistics measure of vacancies across the UK economy, there were 495,000 vacancies in the final quarter (October to December) of 2012; however, at the pre-recession peak in the first quarter (January to March) of 2008, there were 694,000 vacancies. Current recruitment is therefore still 28 per cent below pre-recession levels.

The level of activity in the economy overall is only part of the story, however; the UKCES Employer Perspectives Survey for 2012 also asked employers who hadn't provided any work experience why this was. As noted earlier, the main reason, given by well over a third of employers (37 per cent) who didn't offer work experience, is the view that they have 'no suitable roles'. There is a range of potential reasons underlying this finding. As was noted previously in this chapter, the shape of the labour market, in terms of the actual occupations available, is changing and this may be behind employers' belief that they have no suitable roles. For example, the occupational balance of the labour market is shifting towards high skilled managerial and professional occupations (UKCES 2013a). The employers who specialise in these occupations and do not offer work experience are more likely to claim that they have no suitable roles (UKCES 2012). This may in turn reflect the traditional view of work experience among employers as being something for 14–16-year-olds and therefore not appropriate for the high skilled nature of their workplaces. However, because these roles have seen ongoing growth over the course of recession and recovery and are set to grow in the future, it is more important that young people have the opportunity to gain experience in them (UKCES 2012). Furthermore, these employers may need to be made aware of the shift in government policy to focus on an older cohort.

The fact that some employers say they have no suitable roles for work experience may also suggest that the traditional view of work experience as being two weeks full-time in a workplace at a certain time of the year (typically the summer in the British educational context) just does not work for many employers, particularly smaller employers. Instead, what is needed is a broader approach, including job shadowing, mentoring, challenges and competitions, site visits, mock interviews and talks in schools, alongside full-time placements. This is the approach adopted by a number of high-performing further education colleges in England (OFSTED 2012). Furthermore, the evidence from the Edge Foundation cited earlier suggested that this was exactly the range of activities that young people demand.

The second major reason for not offering work experience, given by a fifth of employers (20 per cent) in the UKCES Employer Perspectives Survey, is the lack of an approach from local schools, colleges or universities. This suggests that there is a ready pool of employers to tap into for offering work experience – they just need to be approached.

Finally, 16 per cent of employers who don't offer work experience say that they do not have the time or resources. There is less variation across sectors on this issue; the clearest pattern is by size. As would be expected, smaller establishments are more likely to see this as a barrier.

Conclusion

The importance of work experience, whether in paid part-time teenage employment or mediated through an educational institution to a successful transition into the labour market, cannot be understated. There is demand for more opportunities from young people and teachers and also more tangible benefits for the employers that get involved. However, there are a number of barriers that would need to be tackled for a significant expansion. Central to successful future policy will be the adoption of more strategic approaches to ensuring young people gain access to early relevant and meaningful experiences of the world of work during their teenage years.

Analysis in this chapter has shown that the extent of work experience opportunities varies by sector, suggesting the need for sector-led solutions. One of the key steps proposed by the current UK Government to engendering greater employer ownership of skills is establishing employer owned and run partnerships ('industrial partnerships') that will address some of the problems highlighted in this chapter. Such partnerships are designed to ensure an ongoing talent pipeline into employers' industries, addressing issues such as recruitment, work experience and apprenticeships as appropriate for the industry. Some of the functions industrial partnership could undertake may include setting standards, designing qualifications and developing career pathways. Industrial partnerships can have a role in making the case for work experience in their industry and coordinating work experience across their members (UKCES 2013b).

Notes

1 For full details, including findings, data tables, questionnaires and technical reports, please see www.ukces.org.uk/publications/er64-uk-employer-perspectives-survey-2012 [accessed April 2013].
2 This survey is 'establishment'-based and so, in the case of very large employers, the responses are individual workplace sites or workplaces within larger enterprises. This means, for example, that the responses would come from individual store managers at supermarkets as opposed to the director of Human Resources for the whole organisation or the CEO.
3 Only employers with at least one employee are included.
4 The 2013 survey went into the field in the spring of 2013, with first initial results scheduled to be available early in 2014. For the 2011 data, please see www.ukces.org.uk/publications/employer-skills-survey-2011 [accessed April 2013].

5 A large-scale nationally representative quarterly survey of 60,000 households.
6 The LSYPE is a large-scale panel study that began in February 2004, when the young people in the sample were aged between 13 and 14 and in Year 9 (mid-way through secondary school). It includes students attending both maintained and independent schools, as well as pupil referral units.
7 The results echo findings of US studies – see Ruhm 1997.
8 All figures in this paragraph are from the Labour Force Survey as reported in the Office for National Statistics monthly Labour Market Bulletin, Table A06.
9 DfE website, 'Post-16 work experience and enterprise education', www.education.gov.uk/schools/teachingandlearning/qualifications/b00223495/post-16-work-exp-enterprise-educ [accessed April 2013].

References

Burge, B., Wilson, R. and Smith-Crallan, K. (2012). *Employer involvement in schools: a rapid review of UK and international evidence*. Slough, UK: National Foundation for Educational Research.

Burson-Marsteller. (2010). *Corporate social responsibility perceptions survey*. Available from: www.burson-marsteller.com/bm-blog/the-2010-corporate-social-responsibility-perceptions-survey/ [accessed April 2013].

Confederation of British Industry (CBI). (2011). *Action for jobs*. London: CBI.

Corporate Citizenship. (2010). *Volunteering: the business case – the benefits of corporate volunteering programmes in education*. London: City of London Corporation.

Crawford, C., Duckworth, K., Vignoles, A. and Wyness, G. (2011). *Young people's education and labour market choices aged 16/17 and 18/19*. London: Department for Education.

Department for Children, Schools and Families (DCSF). (2009). *The work related learning guide*. 2nd ed. London: DCSF.

Fullarton, S. (1999). *Work experience and work placements in secondary school education*. Melbourne: Australian Council for Educational Research.

Mann, A. (2012). *Work experience: impact delivery – insights from the evidence*. London: Education and Employers Taskforce, UK Commission for Employment and Skills and Chartered Institute for Personnel and Development.

OFSTED. (2012). *Promoting enterprise in vocational courses for 16–19 year olds in colleges*. London: OFSTED.

Ruhm, C. (1997). Is high school employment consumption or investment? *Journal of Labour Economics*, 15 (4): 735–776.

UK Commission for Employment and Skills (UKCES). (2012). *The Youth Employment Challenge*. London: UKCES.

UK Commission for Employment and Skills (UKCES). (2013a). *Scaling the Youth Employment Challenge*. London: UKCES.

UK Commission for Employment and Skills (UKCES). (2013b). *Employer ownership of skills prospectus for round 2*. London: UKCES.

Wolf, A. (2011). *Review of vocational education: the Wolf Report*. London: Department for Education.

YouGov. (2010). *YouGov benchmarking surveys: attitudes to learning*. London: Edge Foundation.

Chapter 16

Conclusion

Julian Stanley, Anthony Mann and Louise Archer

The purpose of employer engagement

An interest in employer engagement in education and training is not a purely scientific concern. It arises from an impulse for educational reform, which is based upon a coalition of interests – a partnership between politicians, educators and employers to build cooperation between education and business sectors. In the United States, for example, the Pathways to Prosperity Network brings together stakeholders at state level, with the goal of ensuring that more young people complete high school and achieve a post-secondary credential with labour market currency. In England, for example, the Education and Employers Task-force operates at a national level. In both cases, research plays a significant role in the coalition – helping to raise questions about the status quo, to find solutions and to evaluate interventions.

Employer engagement has been proposed as a solution for a complex set of economic, social and political problems. Many of these problems have negative consequences for different social actors, for example high youth unemployment, skills shortages, unequal access to employment, unequal educational attainment and associated unequal life chances. Hoeckel (see Chapter 4) estimates that, even without a recession, about 30–40 per cent of school leavers in Organisation for Economic Co-operation and Development (OECD) countries are at risk of unemployment, either because they lack relevant education and qualifications or because they are poorly integrated into the labour market. At the same time, large numbers of employers report that they cannot find workers with the right skills to fill jobs (OECD 2012). It is because these issues constitute a societal problem (affecting individuals, communities, schools and employers) that the collaborative venture of employer engagement has been proposed as a useful and appropriate way forward – a joined-up response to a common problem.

It follows, however, that the character and volume of employer engagement will depend on the extent to which the interests of employers, educationalists, young people and the state really do coincide. If, as Holmes and Mayhew suggest in Chapter 6, employers in the United Kingdom currently face an excess supply of appropriately skilled potential recruits for their vacancies, then they will have little incentive to engage further with the education system. We know from Massey's work (Chapter 15) that recruitment interests are a significant factor for motivating employers to engage with schools. However, if employers fail to consider the full extent of social costs and public benefits, then employer engagement will not be sufficient – with an overall loss of welfare. In this case, it is the common or public interest that warrants public or third-sector interventions and funding for employer engagement as, for example, in the subsidy of apprenticeships or intermediary organisations in many countries.

As Hoeckel shows in Chapter 4, not only are youth always disadvantaged as new entrants to the labour market, but also the negative impact of the current global economic recession has fallen disproportionately upon them. The average youth unemployment across OECD countries rose 6 percentage points between 2007 and 2009, reaching a postwar high of 19 per cent in 2010 (Scarpetta et al. 2010). At a political level, the use of employer engagement to alleviate or prevent youth unemployment is framed as part of the responsibility of one generation for another; in other words, a form of intergenerational social justice. That said, many of the contributors to this collection make the point that employer engagement is not just a form of social intervention: it is also a normal feature of the way that many young people transition between education and employment. Huddleston et al. (Chapter 10), Stanley and Mann (Chapter 2) and Le Gallais and Hatcher (Chapter 12) show that the deployment of social capital to obtain or facilitate entry into employment is a commonplace and longstanding practice within particular groups of young people in the United Kingdom. It follows that advocates of employer engagement are not calling for more employer engagement *per se* but for a more extensive, fairer and/or more effective practice of employer engagement across social groups.

What is the scope of employer engagement?

In this collection, we are concerned with the way that employers participate in the education and training of young people who are either still in full-time education or who are in transition between full-time education and full-time employment. As discussed in this collection, employer engagement covers a variety of ways in which employers interact with education and training services, including:

- contributions to policy development, curriculum and qualification design and assessment;
- contributions through direct contact with teachers and students at school, for example, to provide careers guidance, teach projects or mentor individuals;
- contributions through the provision of work experience and work-based training for young people while still in formal education; and
- contributions through organisations that either jointly coordinate education/ training and employment or that broker such collaboration or promote collaboration.

This volume brings together research that focuses on the impact of employer engagement in its various forms, with chapters that focus upon context and upon changing policy and structures. It is our intention to improve the interchange between impact studies and contextual studies. In order to understand the impact of employer engagement, and the manner in which it interacts with other education and training activities, contributors to this volume have considered:

- systems of education and training (and transition) and how these relate to social and economic structures at national and local levels;
- the manner in which employer engagement is governed, brokered and funded;
- the manner in which educational and business organisations decide how the responsibilities and benefits from employer engagement will be allocated; and
- factors that encourage or discourage stakeholders (organisations and individuals) to participate in, or withdraw from, employer engagement activities.

The scope of research into employer engagement presented here might be understood as a matrix between the four ways that employers can seek to contribute to education and the four kinds of contextual factor that shape and constrain these contributions. Table 16.1 maps most of the 16 chapters in this volume against this matrix, revealing how they connect together and cluster around particular axes.

Many of the chapters in this collection explore how context affects the character of employer engagement. For example, Huddleston et al. (Chapter 10) have shown how the purpose and nature of work experience vary between the state-maintained and the independent school sectors in England. A number of chapters have drawn attention to how the political and economic context of employer intervention impacts upon its scale and intensity: the voluntaristic employer engagement in liberal market economies, such as the United Kingdom and the United States, is less pervasive than the statutory, corporatist employer engagement that we find in some European countries, such as Austria or Germany. Stanley and Mann (see Chapter 2) propose a framework that encourages more systematic consideration of the relationship between contextual factors and impact.

The gaps in the matrix suggest that some fields, in particular the way in which employer engagement might seek to shape educational and training systems and the manner in which employer–education partnerships function, are under-represented. It would be useful to explore, through literature and knowledge reviews, the state of research on these other fields. Future research could seek not only to fill in gaps but also to explore the connections between fields. For example, research could explore whether different forms of institutional partnership (e.g. chambers of commerce, tripartite social partnership organisations, public-sector agencies, private companies) shape the provision of employer engagement. In addition, researchers could investigate how different models of governance

Table 16.1 Mapping of chapters in relation to the research domain for employer engagement

Contextual factors	How employers contribute to education			
	Contributions to design of education and training	Contribution to implementation in schools	Contribution to work experience and work-based learning	Institutional partnership and collaboration
Educational, social and economic systems	Stone	Huddleston et al.; Norris and Francis; St Clair et al.	Huddleston et al.; Le Gallais and Hatcher; Norris and Francis; Holmes and Mayhew	
Governance and funding of employer engagement			Stanley and Mann	Huddleston et al.
Allocation of responsibilities and benefits	Stone	Huddleston et al.; Le Gallais and Hatcher; Mann and Kashefpakdel; Norris and Francis; Jones; Percy and Mann	Huddleston et al.; Le Gallais and Hatcher; Taylor et al.; Percy and Mann; Mann; Mann and Kashefpakdel; Norris and Francis; Jones Massey: Hoeckel; Holmes and Mayhew	
Factors that encourage or discourage participation of stakeholders		Archer; Huddleston et al.; Hoeckel; Holmes and Mayhew; Li and Devine		

and funding are associated with different distributions of the benefits and responsibilities of employer engagement.

In the name of employers?

Where the training and education system and the labour market are interacting to produce skills shortages and unemployment, analysts and policymakers have called for better alignment and better communication between the two systems (OECD 2010; European Union 2010). The advocates of employer engagement argue that better alignment and communication between the education and training system and the labour market can be achieved through the *direct* involvement of business and employers in education. As business people are the ultimate employers of young people, so the argument goes, they have a genuine interest and an incontrovertible credibility when it comes to signalling to the world of education what skills are wanted and what opportunities are available. However, when it comes to scaling up employer engagement, we often find that business works through intermediaries or through representative organisations that act for employers. In those countries where employer engagement is strongly institutionalised, such as the dual-system nations identified by Hoffman and Schwartz (see Preface) as providing a 'structure of opportunity', not only are there well-funded employer representative organisations (such as local chambers of craft and industry), but these organisations enjoy statutory powers in the education and training system.

Large-scale employer engagement is encouraged, depending on the country in question, by legislation, political leadership, subsidies, tax breaks, brokerage and social enterprise. However, there are issues about the extent to which employer engagement is funded and controlled by business and the extent to which it successfully represents the diversity of business interests. From the point of view of the hard-pressed work experience organiser in a local school, it might seem that any work placement is a good thing. However, if employer engagement is intended to communicate reliable information about careers opportunities, and if employers are also being given opportunities to shape the curriculum and to determine how public funding for training is deployed, then the 'representativeness' of those employers who engage becomes critical.

The chapters in this collection reveal that there is a variety of forms of employer engagement – producing a variety of social justice outcomes. Different forms of employer engagement are associated with different outcomes for young people and can entail different allocations of responsibility and cost or benefit. In a voluntaristic system, like that of the United Kingdom or the United States, where decisions about the supply and consumption of employer engagement are relatively decentralised, there is a need to provide employers and educational leaders with guidance about the differential impact of different kinds of learner experience; how different experiences can have cumulative effects; and how different models of brokerage and delivery impact upon the scale of participation, cost and the distribution of benefits.

In the United Kingdom, brokerage, whether at a national or local level, has always been critical to the generation of employer engagement and the matching of employer offers to educational consumers. With relatively modest state funding, local and national partnership organisations have mobilised educational philanthropy from hundreds of thousands of separate businesses. In England, by the 2000s, there was an expectation of virtually universal work experience for 14–16-year-olds, although it never became a formal requirement. This was supplemented with more selective take-up of employer engagement, by particular schools for particular groups of students, to support other parts of work-related learning, such as careers and enterprise education. The combination of an 'entitlement' model and low-cost, brokered provision led to a focus upon the provision of a two-week block of work experience for 14–16-year-olds, with an objective of improving young people's generic 'employability' rather than enhancing vocational learning or careers development. This became the dominant form of employer engagement, at least in state-maintained schools.

The practical and institutional forces that shaped the development of work experience in England constrained what objectives it could achieve. The scale, timing and management of work experience dictated that the purpose of work experience was 'generic', such that the character of the work placement and the needs of the individual learner were, in general, regarded as irrelevant (or as being of lesser importance). In other words, as is confirmed by several of the chapters in this volume, the outcomes of employer engagement do not always fully align with government policies: with regard to social and educational policy, employer engagement can be a rather 'blunt' instrument. The shift in policy brought about by the election of the Coalition Government in 2010 will provide an opportunity to study how, through legislation, exhortation and funding, policymakers seek to reshape the character of a service that the state does not fully fund or manage, and to consider whether their reforms render it more effective (or not) in relation to new policy objectives.

The impact of employer engagement

A number of chapters in this collection report positive consequences following employer engagement. Percy and Mann (Chapter 13) provide robust evidence that the experience of employer engagement contributes to positive labour market outcomes for participants, namely a reduced likelihood of youth unemployment and higher earnings. Massey (Chapter 15) also reports positive outcomes from employer engagement, for example 22 per cent of employers take on young people directly after their work experience placement and a further 15 per cent recruit once the person has completed their course.

Taylor et al. (Chapter 14) provide evidence that employer engagement, in the form of high school apprenticeships in Canada, improves high school completion rates and increases completion rates for apprenticeships. Huddleston et al. (Chapter 10), Jones (Chapter 11) and Mann and Kashefpakdel (Chapter 9) provide evidence that work experience is perceived by young people and teaching staff to be of assistance in accessing higher education – although it is yet to be seen whether such experiences do, in fact, improve access to higher education.

Taylor *et al.* and Mann and Kashefpakdel provide evidence that employer engagement can impact upon aspirations, but that it does so in conjunction with other factors, such as school, family and peer group. Indeed, Archer (Chapter 1) suggests that a narrow focus upon aspirations as a lever for social mobility would be misplaced. This is consistent with Percy and Mann's findings, which reveal that a package of employer engagement activities, that individually might be expected to bring different benefits to recipients, can have a cumulative impact in terms of generating positive employment outcomes. Mann and Kashefpadkel provide robust evidence that employer engagement is perceived by young people to impact upon careers decision-making. They also cite further evidence that suggests that the impact of employer engagement varies depending on the type and timing of the employer engagement activity in question. It may be that 'what works' is not so much upping the volume of employer engagement activities as providing a complementary diet of experiences which, taken together, support, *inter alia*, skill development, information needs, self-belief and aspirations.

Theory and methodology

Many of the chapters in this collection make use of the concepts of social, human and cultural capital to explain how individuals and groups are, or are not, able to operate within systems of education and employment to achieve their goals. What these contributors share is the view that different resources (economic, social and cultural) are accumulated, transmitted and deployed to advantage. This theoretical approach is both individualistic and structural: contributors acknowledge the agency of individuals (e.g. deploying resources and information to achieve their individual goals) and, at the same time, understand how individuals are also constrained by social structures. 'Habitus', as a structure of dispositions, is shaped by enduring social relationships and understandings that are generated by and through social axes such as social class, gender and ethnicity. Stanley and Mann have sought to show that a focus on both agency and structure is possible in the framework they set out in Chapter 2. However, the test of this approach lies in the success of particular research projects that seek to situate individual decision-making within social, economic and cultural contexts.

Theoretical differences and unresolved issues remain. In particular, the conceptualisation of, and boundaries between, cultural and social capital varies for the different authors. Should 'human capital' be regarded as part of economic capital because it has an economic value in the labour market? Or is it part of cultural capital because it is usually identified with the possession of credentials? Or is it perhaps a distinctive form of capital? Where social and cultural capital combine in a particular institution, such as the family or a school, should we construct a new concept, for example 'family capital'?

There is a persisting tension between 'rationalistic' accounts of human behaviour which typically conceptualise skills and social relationships as resources, or means, which can be deployed to achieve individual ends, and accounts that emphasise the influence of habit, ignorance or the exercise of power and social influence. A rationalistic approach would see individual students as doing work experience because it is a means to increase their labour market value or perhaps to signal to prospective employers, through social networks or credentials, that they are attractive employees. Likewise, employers engage with education because they see it as a way to recruit more productive employees. In practice, as advocates of behavioural economics argue, the explanations of how people behave may not be easily assimilated to some kind of rational model (Akerlof and Schiller 2009). Several chapters in this collection highlight a great deal of behaviour that is not obviously 'rational'. For instance, St Clair *et al.* (Chapter 7) demonstrate that adolescents enjoy high aspirations that bear little relation to the actual opportunities that exist either nationally or locally. They also recount how almost 50 per cent of 13-year-olds aspire to work in occupations classed as group 3 in the Standard Occupational Classification.[1] Holmes and Mayhew (Chapter 6) show that young people accumulate human capital, which is not, in fact, repaid by the labour market. Massey (Chapter 15) shows that the majority of employers who provide work experience placements believe that they do so to serve the interests of others rather than themselves.

The availability of both 'rationalistic' and 'behavioural' types of explanation makes for complexity. A 'rationalistic' approach would suggest that employer engagement helps to align education with the labour market because it provides individuals with reliable and timely information (Mann and Percy 2013). A 'behavioural' account would argue that employer engagement could improve social mobility by enabling young people to come into direct contact with those who have succeeded in order to raise and sustain their (otherwise relatively modest) aspirations. In contrast, a structural analysis highlights how imbalances of power and resources can produce different social outcomes. Elements of these different approaches can be seen across the contributions in this collection. For example, Norris and Francis (see Chapter 8), argue that reputational and cultural factors are part of the explanation as to why students in English further education colleges are less likely to progress to study medicine or law than students in sixth forms and they suggest that employer engagement is a resource that could help compensate for these effects. Jones (Chapter 11) quotes Waller *et al.* to a similar effect: 'more effort is needed to push academically-able working class young people towards placements that will increase motivation and widen horizons' (Waller *et al.* 2012: 1). Le Gallais and Hatcher (Chapter 12) describe the radical work experience policy pursued by one West Midlands school that ignores the nature of local job markets and discounts the preferences of its own parents and students, sending 15 per cent of its pupils onto legal and medical work placements. This collection suggests that we need to accommodate 'rationalistic' *and* 'behavioural' approaches to explain aspects of transition and to design successful social policy.

Some authors find it helpful to employ not only concepts of disposition (habitus) and capital (resources) but also the Bourdieusian concept of a social field (context). This has the advantage of highlighting how the value of capital is context-dependent. Moreover, individuals will feel and act differently in different social institutions or situations; for instance, the same individual may behave and feel differently at home, at school and on work placement. This implies that any one employer engagement activity will be differently received and experienced depending on the identity and background of the young person taking part. However, the nature of employer engagement is that it implies social interactions that extend between the social fields of work and education. It has been argued that the concept of 'boundary crossing', which conceptualises social interaction as an open-ended or 'expansive' learning process that bridges different social groups, is a useful tool for understanding employer engagement (QCA 2008; Felstead *et al.* 2011).

This raises the question of how employer engagement might lead to changes in educational institutions or educational practice, rather than merely providing supplementary or complementary services. Stone, in Chapter 3, calls for an integration of academic, technical and soft skills in a unified curriculum, whose delivery combines school and work-based provision. In many European countries, the engagement of employers in curriculum and qualification design has been a key educational policy, with the intention of improving the alignment of education and skills needs and enhancing the credibility of qualifications in the labour market (Cedefop 2012). More research into the role of employers in policy and system change would help us to understand alternative strategies for employer engagement.

Who is the audience for employer engagement?

Which young people should benefit from employer engagement and how should the benefits be distributed? Li and Devine (Chapter 5) show how improvements in social mobility in the United Kingdom between the 1940s and the 1970s can, in part, be explained by changes in the structure of employment, in particular by the growth in white-collar and 'middle-class' jobs. Since that period, social mobility has declined, although social scientists disagree on how best to measure what has happened. Nevertheless, there is general agreement that women have enjoyed increased social mobility since the 1970s, despite the absence of a benign change in the structure of employment. It is argued that increased female social mobility is due to improved educational and economic participation, providing encouragement that similar policies could improve social mobility for other disadvantaged groups. However, as Holmes and Mayhew point out in Chapter 6, the prospect of increased social mobility may lead to changes in behaviour. Wealthier parents may deploy their economic, social and cultural capital to access private education, work experience or internships, which will help them to combat the risk of downward social mobility that, faced with a 'level playing field', their children might suffer.

Le Gallais and Hatcher (Chapter 12) and Huddleston *et al.* (Chapter 10) provide evidence that the benefits of employer engagement are distributed in a manner that is likely to work against social mobility. Generalising, we can say that existing accumulations of social and economic capital influence access to employer engagement and its benefits. Taylor *et al.* (see Chapter 14) criticise a high school apprenticeship programme for failing to target more disadvantaged students (i.e. those who stand to benefit most from an alternative pathway). Stone, in Chapter 3, points out that the institutional separation of post-secondary, vocational and academic education in the United States means that, to a large extent, only part of the cohort can access a curriculum that incorporates employer engagement.

Given that employer engagement in many liberal capitalist countries is voluntaristic, it might be questioned whether it could be harnessed to serve the interests of social mobility. The high school apprenticeship scheme that Taylor *et al.* (Chapter 14) evaluate is designed not only to provide an additional pathway to students at risk of dropping out but also to meet the skills needs of employers. Does employer engagement imply some degree of trade-off between the interests of employers and the goal of social justice? And whose interests tend to predominate within such situations? Jones (Chapter 11) provides an analysis of the way in which the reporting of work experience, through personal statements accompanying applications to a competitive university, tends to advantage those students who have attended independent schools. Jones proposes a policy recommendation that this data should be excluded from consideration in the admissions process. An alternative recommendation is that all students have an entitlement to access work experience that is relevant to their aspirations for higher study – although measures would need to be put in place to ensure a fair and equitable distribution of types of work experience across different social groups. Holmes and Mayhew (Chapter 6) describe how recent changes in occupational structure have affected the labour market, in particular the decline of routine, skilled white- and blue-collar jobs. Their comparison of the experiences of two cohorts, aged 23 in 1981 and 1993, reveal that new entrants to the labour market in the second cohort, including university graduates, were more likely to seek first employment in lower-end, non-routine service and manual jobs and that both academic and vocational qualifications were of less value to new entrants as a means of gaining access to top occupations. In this situation, access to employer engagement, such as internships, may be sought as a source of competitive advantage. But how can we ensure that work experience does not simply play into the reproduction of existing social inequalities?

Furthermore, if employer engagement does facilitate transition into the labour market, what forms will that transition take when the labour market has the shape of an 'hourglass'? Under these circumstances, it might be expected that employer engagement would take on a 'selective' function, enabling employers to contribute to judgements that assign young people to tracks that will take them either to the top or to the bottom of the labour market. This prospect raises some difficult questions: how much voice should employers get in a tracking process that is likely to be critical to life chances, and at what point in their educational careers should young people be exposed to the judgements of employers?

Quantity or quality

According to Massey (Chapter 15), the main reason given by employers for providing work experience is that they believe it is an experience that young people need. The next most important reason given by employers is that they see the provision of work experience as part of their moral or corporate social responsibility. It would be difficult to deny that employers who provide such experiences support the transition and education of young people in a manner that goes beyond economic self-interest – although there are undoubtedly reputational and recruitment benefits that also accrue. In many ways, employer engagement in education can be framed as the practice of 'good capitalism' on a massive scale – with almost half a million individual workplace organisations involved in the United Kingdom in 2009/2010. Yet, Massey judges that the current supply of employer engagement in education is insufficient to meet the demand from young people and educationalists. The policy challenge is whether and how this supply might be increased: how can 'being good' be made more attractive, easier or more rewarding for employers? Or how can failure to be 'good' and unwillingness to contribute to a public good be made a less comfortable option? Policy options in the United Kingdom, and elsewhere, are complicated by reductions in public expenditure and reforms in the governance and funding of education and the credential system.

In addition to questions of quantity, there are still challenges to ensuring a high quality of provision. Many of the studies in this collection concern the quality and mode of delivery of employer engagement. The chapters identify the following factors as contributing to the success of activities: matching of student and activity; timing; levels of support; volume of activities; duration; matching of activity to the objectives it is intended to bring about; resource for managing employer activity; and preparation and the quality of input from employers. These factors are familiar from earlier research into work-related learning (for example, Huddleston and Stanley 2012; Mann 2012), and are consistent with the findings of large-scale surveys of work-based learning (Department for Business Innovation and Skills 2012).

The particular challenge for employer engagement in education is that not only is the quality of provision critical but that, by its nature, delivery implies some degree of partnership between educationalists and employers. There are different kinds of partnership and employers and educationalists can play different roles and fulfil different responsibilities in the provision of employer engagement. It would be valuable to investigate how different kinds of provision impact upon outcomes – and whether employers should always play the dominant role in employer engagement!

An interdisciplinary invitation

Research into employer engagement is interdisciplinary: it draws upon many research disciplines and upon the work of other research fields. The chapters in this collection suggest that there is mileage in exploring how these fields, and the problems that inhabit them, fit together. Not least because employer engagement straddles a number of disciplines, it suggests possibilities for resisting, or at the very least diverting, potential sociological and economic reductionism. Holmes and Mayhew (Chapter 6), for example, conceptualise employer engagement as a possible response for employers who are experiencing skills shortages. They argue that the supply of intermediate and higher skills among job applicants actually exceeds demand, which suggests that skills shortages could not explain a general readiness on the part of employers to provide work experience. Evidently, employer engagement is currently on offer in the United Kingdom on a substantial scale and it is not entirely a function of the demand for skills.

Turning to sociology, we have come to expect the concepts of social and cultural capital or 'habitus' to be used to explain how the decision-making and life chances of individuals are constrained or afforded by the social groups to which they belong. However, in Chapter 2, Stanley and Mann argue that we can understand employer engagement as a social investment – a generation and/or transfer of social, cultural and human capital between employers and young people. This raises an important question: why in a capitalist society should employers and employees, who own capital, share it with young people (to whom they are not related)? While Massey provides some answers to this question in Chapter 15, there is certainly room for further research. One way forward may be to investigate empirically what motivates employees and employers, with different life experiences, to engage with the education of younger generations at different stages in their careers.

Prospectus for future research

A recent spate of studies exploring teenage attitudes and career ambitions offer a potentially highly productive avenue for exploration. In the British context, Yates *et al.*'s (2010) study of data from the British Cohort Study found that at age 16, young people (born in 1970) who were uncertain about their career ambitions or whose occupational ambitions required higher levels of attainment than they themselves expected to achieved (the 'misaligned') were significantly more likely to experience six months or longer periods of being Not in Education Employment or Training (NEET) before the age of 19. Using the same database, Sabates *et al.* (2011) found considerable penalties linked to misaligned ambitions, identifying poorer employment records and wage differentials of 7–8 per cent at age 34. Using the US National Educational Longitudinal Study and adopting a similar methodology to assess misalignment, Morgan *et al.* (2013) have found significant variation in college entry linked to misalignment of occupational ambitions and educational expectations during sophomore year (aged 15–16). Staff *et al.*'s (2010) analysis of the US National Educational Longitudinal Study found, moreover, that teenagers (aged 16) who were uncertain about their career aspirations went on to earn less at age 26 than their peers.[2]

A striking finding from these studies is that high proportions of teenagers can be categorised as uncertain or misaligned (half of those in Yates *et al.*'s study), and it is young people from more disadvantaged social backgrounds who are more likely to lack realistic, formed ambitions at 16 (Schoon *et al.* 2012; Yates *et al.* 2010). Insights from longitudinal studies are especially valuable because researchers can apply controls for wide-ranging variables to test whether outcomes identified might mask other personal characteristics such as socio-economic status or attainment levels. The findings have led some researchers to suggest that schools should, as a policy response, provide students with better information about the labour market (Sabates *et al.* 2011: 17; Schoon *et al.* 2012: 72).

Looking more broadly at the extent of teenage engagement in the labour market, quantitative analyses in the United States (Ruhm 1997) and United Kingdom (Crawford *et al.* 2012) have shown teenage part-time employment, when combined with full-time study, to be significantly related to better employment outcomes for young adults. Research on social networks has, from a different perspective, also found significant relationships between teenage access to non-family members in employment and later positive labour market outcomes (McDonald *et al.* 2007; Jokisaari and Nurmi 2005). Researchers, moreover, investigating links between teenagers' access to economically important social networks and their later employment outcomes, have drawn upon social capital theory as a means to explain the phenomena observed. Exploring the connections between breadth of informal teenage networks and later economic outcomes (as revealed through an analysis of longitudinal databases), McDonald *et al.* (2007) draw on the work of American sociologist Mark Granovetter to argue:

> Relationships with adult mentors extend the social networks of young people and thereby help them bridge the gap between the adolescent world and the adult world. Therefore, it is important to consider the closeness of the mentoring relationship – i.e. the strength of the tie. Weak ties are well suited for this bridging function, as they provide greater access to non-redundant information about employment. In other words, connections with adults that operate outside the young person's close-knit social circle are more likely to provide new information about opportunities. Since weak ties are associated with the receipt of this non-redundant information, we expect that young people who maintain relatively weak relationships with their mentors will have the greatest access to labor market information and opportunities. This would, in turn, enhance their chances of being employed in young adulthood. Similarly, connections with non-kin mentors are also likely to provide superior access to labor market information by expanding opportunities beyond the family circle.
>
> (McDonald *et al.* 2007: 1332)

Ethnographic work describes how this process can apply to young people within the context of school-mediated employer engagement (Leonard 2005). Carlo Raffo and Michelle Reeves (2000) studied the experiences of disengaged teenagers taking part in extended (one day a week) periods of work experience, linked to a learning programme. They observed effective dialogues between young people and their working environments, which arguably have a clear relevance for facilitating future progression.

> What we have evidenced is that, based on the process of developing social capital through trustworthy reciprocal social relations within individualized networks, young people are provided with an opportunity to gain information, observe, ape and then confirm decisions and actions with significant others and peers. Thus, everyday implicit, informal and individual practical knowledge and understanding is created through interaction, dialogue, action and reflection on action within individualized and situated social contexts.
>
> (Raffo and Reeves 2000: 151)

This collection has brought together a number of different sorts of contribution: chapters that report on statistically significant relationships between interesting variables; chapters that offer theoretical accounts of different kinds of causality; and chapters that describe how decisions and experiences of employer engagement activities are perceived by participants. The complementarity of these approaches is demonstrated by the fact that the qualitative studies suggest processes that could explain the causal relationships that have been identified by more quantitative contributions. Percy and Mann (Chapter 13), like McDonald *et al.* (2007), draw upon social capital theory to explain the relationship between school-age participation in employer engagement activities and positive future employment outcomes. They suggest that school-age participation in employer engagement activities can generate social capital, which is subsequently converted into higher rates of employment and higher earnings.

However, this is a claim that invites further research. One challenge is to design research that can operationalise social capital in order to explore whether, in fact, employer engagement does lead to its accumulation and whether this accumulation is, in turn, linked to positive employment outcomes or to other benefits. Similarly, the claim that employer engagement leads to changes in the dispositions or aspirations of young people (cultural capital) or to the acquisition of new skills (human capital) could be tested in a robust manner through randomised controlled trials.

Another challenge is to better understand the ways in which different actors experience, understand, behave and make decisions regarding their educational and occupational experiences and futures. The evidence gives us some grounds to hypothesise that contact with employers can help young people to advance their career decision-making and even to align their own competences and potential to the opportunities that exist in the marketplace. However, we currently have a poor understanding of how young people execute this kind of decision-making and just how they employ different sources of support and information and different experiences to form their aspirations and make choices. Quantitative findings of the kind reported earlier should inform the design of qualitative research; for example, narrative biographical research might be used to follow young people through work experience in order to find out how their plans and behaviours were affected.

Further, if the improved employment outcomes for young people who have participated in employer engagement activities reflect employer judgement of their potential value as employees, there is value in exploring the consequences of school-age activity in terms of later incidence of skills matching, staff retention and engagement, and ultimately productivity within the workplace. Such an analysis might usefully build on the research set out by Massey (Chapter 15), testing whether reported views on recruitment behaviour relate to measurable economic gains.

A further means of testing the meaning of employer engagement relates to human capital theory. Analysts of US longitudinal studies, following the fortunes of young people moving into the early labour market after having undertaken learning programmes rich in workplace exposure, have hypothesised that the positive impacts observed may result from either improved 'career awareness' (linking to the social capital hypothesis) and/or enhanced 'career preparation' in a broad sense or, more specifically, from technical and/or employability skills development more relevant to the labour market than can be offered by non-participants (Kemple and Willner 2008: 40; MacAullum *et al.* 2002: 11, 13; Jobs for the Future 1998: 2). In England, many employer engagement activities have been explicitly designed to develop employability skills – but it has also been argued that the typically episodic, short duration and extra-curricular character of such provision actually works against achieving these outcomes (Mann and Percy 2013).

At this point in time we do not know whether, for example, the development of problem-solving or team-working skills through enterprise competitions has any measurable impact in the labour market. The concept of 'employability' is contestable (Simmons and Thompson 2011: 29–31) and research is required to test whether activities that are carried out in its name do deliver measurable outcomes. As English education policy moves towards a requirement for work experience between the ages of 16 and 19, with an emphasis on work experience forming part of the curriculum, the question of human capital development becomes even more pertinent. Can meaningful skills development be assured through work experience that is not integrated into the classroom curriculum?

Another area for research is to explore whether, and how, the relatively 'blunt' instrument of employer engagement activities can be sharpened, for example to support young people's transition into the labour market. Should work experience be focused more on career exploration or on the development of employability skills? Or should the two potential objectives be given equal weighting? Which activities are most cost-effective for different age groups – and which are best placed to meet different needs? And, importantly, can employer engagement be targeted to improve academic attainment as an outcome? These are areas where action research and evaluation studies will have much to contribute – and we look forward to the continued growth of this area of research.

Notes

1   Group 3 of the Standard Occupational Classification is defined as associate professional and technical occupations, which include uniformed services, nursing and midwifery, entertainment and sporting professions.
2   Some studies (Schoon *et al.* 2012; Gutman and Schoon 2012) suggest that teenage uncertainty does not necessarily lead to poorer adult outcomes. Observed penalties reduce considerably where parental educational expectations for children, own school motivation, perceptions of academic ability and access to careers advice deemed 'good' are taken into account, suggesting that for some young people it is a positive act to defer career decision-making.

References

Akerlof, G. A. and Schiller, R. (2009). *Animal spirits: how human psychology drives the economy, and why it matters for global capitalism.* Princeton, NJ: Princeton University Press.
Cedefop. (2012). *Curriculum reform in Europe.* Luxembourg.
Crawford, C., Duckworth, K., Vignoles, A. and Wyness, G. (2012). *Young people's education and labour market choices aged 16/17 to 18/19.* London: Department for Education.
Department for Business Innovation and Skills (BIS). (2012). *Evaluation of apprenticeships: learners.* London: BIS.
European Union. (2010). *The Bruges Communiqué on enhanced European Cooperation in Vocational Education and Training for the period 2011–2020.* Brussels: European Union.
Felstead, A., Fuller, A., Jewson, N. and Unwin, L. (2011). *Working to learn, learning to work.* Praxis No. 7. London: UKCES.
Gutman, L. S. and Schoon, I. (2012). Correlates and consequences of uncertainty in career aspirations: gender differences among adolescents in England. *Journal of Vocational Behavior,* 80: 608–618.
Huddleston, P. and Stanley, J. eds. (2012). *Work-related teaching and work-related learning.* Abingdon, UK: Routledge.
Jobs for the Future. (1998). *School-to-career initiative demonstrates significant impact on young people.* Boston, MA: Jobs for the Future.
Jokisaari, M. and Nurmi, J. E. (2005). Company matters: goal-related social capital in the transition to working life. *Journal of Vocational Behavior,* 67: 413–428.
Kemple, J. and Willner, C. J. (2008). *Career academies – long-term impacts on labor market outcomes, educational attainment, and transitions to adulthood.* New York, NY: MDRC.

Leonard, M. (2005). Children, childhood and social capital: exploring the links. *Sociology*, 39: 605–622.

MacAullum, K., Yoder, K., Scott, K. and Bozick, R. (2002). *Moving forward – college and career transitions of LAMP graduates – from the LAMP longitudinal study*. Washington, DC: National Institute for Work and Learning.

McDonald, S., Erickson, L. D., Johnson, M. K. and Elder, G. H. (2007). Informal mentoring and young adult employment. *Social Science Research*, 36: 1328–1347.

Mann, A. (2012). *Work experience: impact and delivery – insights from the evidence*. London: Education and Employers Taskforce.

Mann, A. and Percy C. (2013). Employer engagement in British secondary education: wage earning outcomes experienced by young adults. *Journal of Education and Work*, doi:10.1080/13639080.2013.769671.

Morgan S. L., Leenman T. S., Todd J. J. and Weeden K. A. (2013). Occupational plans, beliefs about educational requirements, and patterns of college entry. *Sociology of Education*, 86 (3): 197–217.

Organisation for Economic Co-operation and Development (OECD). (2010). *Learning for jobs*. Paris: OECD.

Organisation for Economic Co-operation and Development (OECD). (2012). *Better skills, better jobs, better lives – a strategic approach of skills policies*. Paris: OECD.

Qualifications and Curriculum Agency (QCA). (2008). *The Diploma and its pedagogy*. London: QCA.

Raffo, C. and Reeves, M. (2000). Youth transitions and social exclusion: developments in social capital theory. *Journal of Youth Studies*, 3: 147–166.

Ruhm, C. (1997). Is high school employment consumption or investment? *Journal of Labor Economics*, 15: 735–776.

Sabates, R., Harris, A. L. and Staff, J. (2011). Ambition gone awry: the long term socio-economic consequences of misaligned and uncertain ambitions in adolescence. *Social Science Quarterly*, 92: 1–19.

Scarpetta, S., Sonnet, A. and Manfredi, T. (2010). *Rising youth unemployment during the crisis*. Paris: OECD.

Schoon, I., Gutman, L. M. and Sabates, R. (2012). Is uncertainty bad for you? It depends . . . *New Directions for Youth Development*, 135: 65–75.

Simmons, R. and Thompson, R. (2011). *NEET young people and training for work – learning on the margins*. Stoke-on-Trent: Trentham Books.

Staff, J., Harris, A., Sabates, R. and Briddell, L. (2010). Uncertainty in early occupational aspirations: role exploration or aimlessness? *Social Forces*, 89: 1–25.

Waller, R., Harrison, N., Hatt, S. and Chudry, F. (2012). Undergraduates' memories of school-based work experience and the role of class and gender in placement choices. Journal of Education and Work, 1–27, doi:10.1080/13639080.2012.742183.

Yates, S., Harris, A., Sabates, R. and Staff, J. (2010). Early occupational aspirations and fractured transitions: a study of entry into 'NEET' status in the UK. *Journal of Social Policy*, 40: 513–534.

Index